Jack the Ripper FAQ

All That's Left to Know About the Infamous Serial Killer

Dave Thompson

APPLAUSE
THEATRE & CINEMA BOOKS
An Imprint of Hal Leonard LLC

Published in 2017 by Applause Theatre & Cinema books
An Imprint of Hal Leonard LLC
7777 West Bluemound Road
Milwaukee, WI 53213

Trade Book Division Editorial Offices
33 Plymouth St., Montclair, NJ 07042

The FAQ series was conceived by Robert Rodriguez and developed with Stuart Shea.
Printed in the United States of America

All photos are from the author's collection unless otherwise noted.

Book design by Snow Creative

Library of Congress Cataloging-in-Publication Data is available upon request.

www.applausebooks.com

To Colin Wilson (1931–2013), whose *Ritual in the Dark* launched a schoolboy into a life of Ripper reading

Contents

Acknowledgments

T hanks to everyone who threw something onto the chopping block, be it a hitherto unsuspected suspect, a muddleheaded movie "you just *have* to see" or the demand that I mention Judas Priest's "The Ripper." Which I now have.

But especial thanks to Amy Hanson, not only for sitting through several months' worth of television and straight-to-video documentaries—all of which promised to reveal the Ripper's true identity—but also for agreeing that we had even less idea now than we did before we began. And to J. R. Pepper, for her fabulous photographs.

Thanks, also, to all at FAQ Central Headquarters, but most especially John Cerullo, Marybeth Keating, and Josh Wimmer; to Alex Bell, to Jo-Ann Greene; Karen and Todd; Linda and Larry; Betsy, Steve and family; Jen; Chrissie Bentley; Tim Smith; Gaye Black; Oliver and Trevor; Mr. Mittens, King of the Deep; Barb East; Bateerz and family; the gremlins who live in the heat pump; and to John the Superstar, the demon of the dry well.

Author's Note

A word about currency which, in Victorian Britain, was reckoned in "pounds, shillings and pence"—that is, four farthings to a penny, twelve pennies to a shilling (or a "bob"), twenty shillings to a pound (or "quid") and twenty-one to a guinea. A "tanner" was six pennies, a "florin" was two shillings, and a "half crown" was two shillings and sixpence. And a "tuppenny upright" cost two pennies.

Decimal currency, introduced in 1971, swept away this colorfully confusing system. Today, a pound comprises 100 pence (or "pee"), and that's it. Almost every one of those other terms and denominations was consigned to the dustbin long ago, and none have arisen to replace them.

For readers looking to convert "old" money into "new," the Victorian penny equates to a little under half of a new penny (0.417); sixpence is equal to two and a half pence; the shilling is five pence, half a crown is twelve and a half pence; and so on.

Furthermore, one pound in 1888 was the equivalent to $4.87 in contemporary American money; in modern terms (August 2016), it equals around seventy-five pounds sterling, or approximately one hundred dollars.

Introduction
Questions, Answers . . .
. . . Answers, Questions

> There's something inherently seedy and salacious in continually picking the scabs off these crimes, peering at mutilated bodies, listing the undergarments, trekking over the tainted ground in quest of some long-delayed occult frisson. I abhor these hacks with their carrier bags of old cuttings.
>
> —Iain Sinclair, *White Chappell, Scarlet Tracings*

The naked statistics are appallingly straightforward. One killer, four months, five dead prostitutes. Between the end of August 1888 and the first week of November, the fiend known as Jack the Ripper held the poverty-stricken streets of Whitechapel, the decaying heart of London's East End, in a bowel-freezing vice of horror.

His victims, after all, were not simply murdered, although that would have been dreadful enough. They were viciously mutilated; in some cases, disemboweled; and in one instance, utterly eviscerated. Human life reduced to so much offal, human dignity shredded like hay through a thresher.

The slaughter took place everywhere—on a busy street, in a private back garden, in a darkened alleyway outside a lively club meeting. One killing even took place within the victim's own home. And the knifeman was neat. He left absolutely no trace of his own self. He departed as quietly as he arrived, and his work was undertaken in the same deathly silence.

He even, on occasion, had time to put on a show, the pitiful remnants of his victims carefully arranged, purposefully to shock. No Hollywood set designer could have been more fastidious; no artist could have created a more lasting effect.

Body parts were strewn according to some ghastly, deliberate pattern. Pieces were missing—a uterus, a womb, a heart. He taunted his pursuers with a stream of correspondence, and the claim that he'd devoured half a kidney for breakfast.

He has been described as the world's first serial killer; he is acclaimed as its best known, as well. And he never was caught.

This book is not about *that* Jack the Ripper.

It *is*, however, a book about the murderer who came to be known as Jack the Ripper, and it is also about his victims—the five who are "officially" attributed to him, and all the others who could be. For, even among those five, there is no certainty that they all fell prey to the same man. And no certainty that the others did not.

The media of the day certainly had no compunction whatsoever about linking slaying after slaying to one single, deranged individual; nor about expanding the killer's heyday from as early as December 1887 to as late as February 1891. So five becomes sixteen, and may even be twenty if other, similar crimes that took place during that same terrible span are included.

Two more could be added if one considers the mop seller in Southwark who was frightened to death by the lurid stories that she read in the newspapers; and the housewife on Hanbury Street, on the fringe of Whitechapel itself, who was so terrified of the monster in her midst that she killed herself before he could do it himself.

And that figure could climb even higher if we step into the unknown and suggest that not every person killed by every killer can always be neatly accounted for.

Ted Bundy, whose trail of terror was spread over at least half a dozen American states in the mid-to-late 1970s, confessed to thirty murders, but is a suspect in some twenty more, and admitted there were others that he would never confess to.

Dennis Nilsen, the so-called Muswell Hill Murderer of early-1980s London, killed at least twelve, but he, too, is believed to have murdered more. And that is in the modern age, with the police not only working with technologies that the law of 1888 never dreamed were possible, but also with the murderer himself behind bars.

How do you begin to reckon up all the victims of a serial killer who has never been caught?

As seen in the sidebar, there are both strong similarities and equally strong differences between every one of these murders.

All, at least among those women whose remains could be identified, involved prostitutes. All were characterized by brutal violence, and, with the exception of those in which other attackers were attested to (the gang

The Year(s) of the Ripper

December 8, 1888—Margaret Hayes (attacked, survived—suspected gang attack)

February 25, 1888—Annie Millwood (attacked, survived)

March 28, 1888—Ada Wilson (attacked, survived)

April 3, 1888—Emma Smith (beaten, raped, died of injuries sustained—suspected gang attack)

August 7, 1888—Martha Tabram (murdered—stabbed 39 times)

August 24, 1888 (estimated date)—unknown female dismembered, torso discovered October 3, Whitehall

August 31, 1888—Mary Ann Nichols (murdered, mutilated)

September 8, 1888—Annie Chapman (murdered, disemboweled)

September 11, 1888—unknown female's arm discovered in the Thames, estimated to have been in the water for two or three days

September 30, 1888—Elizabeth Stride (murdered, no mutilation)

September 30, 1888—Catherine Eddowes (murdered, disemboweled)

November 9, 1888—Mary Jane Kelly (murdered, eviscerated)

November 21, 1888—Annie Farmer (attacked, survived—probably injured while attempting to rob a client)

December 20, 1888—Rose Mylett (strangled, no mutilation)

June 1889—Elizabeth Jackson (dismembered body discovered in Thames—no known connection to Whitechapel)

July 17, 1889—Alice McKenzie (murdered, mutilated)

September 8, 1889 (estimated date)—unknown female dismembered, body discovered September 10, Whitechapel

February 13, 1891—Frances Coles (throat cut, no mutilation)

attacks on Margaret Hayes and Emma Smith), all could have been the work of a single assailant.

But was it the same assailant?

The case for there being just five victims—the so-called canonical quintet of Nichols, Chapman, Stride, Eddowes and Kelly—was most famously stated in 1894 by Sir Melville Leslie Macnaghten, a future chief constable of Scotland Yard, six years after the last of those killings.

But Chief Inspector Walter Dew, who was a part of the original investigative team, added Emma Smith to the toll, while discounting Elizabeth

Stride; and Dr. Thomas Bond, who examined many of the corpses, believed Alice McKenzie could also be numbered among the Ripper's prey.

Thomas Arnold, head of H Division, as the Whitechapel police were officially designated, credited the killer with just four murders, but named only three victims. (He omitted Eddowes and Kelly from the canonical quintet.) A contemporary private researcher and occasional suspect, Robert Donston Stephenson, insisted upon seven: Smith, Tabram, Nichols, Chapman, Stride, Eddowes and the unidentified Whitehall torso. And Chief Inspector Donald Swanson believed the same man accounted for nine women, and came close to making it ten (with Farmer).

If the investigators themselves could not make up their minds about how many deaths the Whitechapel murderer was responsible for, is there any wonder that so many disparate body counts have been thrown around by so many subsequent researchers?

Elizabeth Stride's omission from several of these lists is predicated on the fact that she suffered no mutilations, with the popular belief that her killer was disturbed being recognized for what it actually is—a convenient theory (albeit one that the timing of the body's discovery would appear to substantiate).

Similarly, Mary Kelly's killing is sometimes overlooked because, unlike its predecessors, it took place indoors. But so did the attack on Ada Wilson, at the outset of the rampage. Only the murderer's apparent clumsiness when slashing Wilson's throat allowed her the opportunity to cry out and alert her neighbors. Had she not been able to raise the alarm, there is no saying what might have befallen her.

Indeed, it is clear from any examination of, first, the attacks and then the killings, that they escalated in terms of both technique and brutality, suggesting (some say) that the killer was still learning the ropes, as it were. But, as fictional researcher Ed Buchan remarks in the 2009 British TV series *Whitechapel*, he was "a fast learner."

Likewise, while the suggested involvement of a gang of attackers in the Margaret Hayes and Emma Smith assaults definitely draws us away from the popular theory of a lone attacker, what are we to make of the testimony of Israel Schwartz, a possible witness to the killing of Elizabeth Stride, who was chased away from the murder scene by a *second* man, lurking in the doorway of a nearby pub?

On the one hand, it adds weight to the theory that Stride's killing was unrelated to the others. On the other, it lends credence to the possibility that the murderer had accomplices.

UNE RUE DE WHITECHAPEL. — Le Dernier Crime de Jack l'Éventreur.

A fanciful French view of the discovery of the third murder, Elizabeth Stride. *Alamy*

In the midst of all these theories, beliefs, body counts and butcher's lists, however, there is one thing that should never be forgotten, even if so many studies of the slaughter make it very easy to do just that:

These women—whether there were five, ten or even fifty of them—were not simply statistics to be glanced at in the latest lurid tabloid headline, and then shrugged aside with a weary "I see he got another one, then." History regards their names as some immutable catechism, or else an historical monument, a row of squat megaliths in some distant spittled field, windworn and bloodied, unmoving, unchanging, unseeing. In a mystery riven with uncertainties, they are the landmarks that everybody recognizes. It is difficult, reading some of the books, to remember they were ever even human.

But they were.

Once they were children; once they had dreams. They laughed, lived and loved, and did all the same little things that everybody does. Never in their wildest nightmares, not even once the killer started killing, could they ever have imagined that their last act on earth would be to pose in bloodied death for the series of photographs that single-handedly kick-started the modern fascination with gore-glittered *mortuaria*.

They were part of a community; many of them may even have been friends of one another—but *not* (as some authors suggest) connected as unwitting victims to some spider-webbed conspiracy that reached into the garish corridors of Buckingham Palace. They would have been friends because they knew one another; because they were fellow travelers through a world that history, again, has romanticized into one of gaslit cobbles and swirling fogs, men in capes with Gladstone bags, and worn, weather-beaten crones hissing seduction through toothless gums. But which was never so clear-cut as that.

In a neighborhood where the streets were dominated by fourpence-a-night common lodging houses, and a large proportion of the populace spent its nights drifting between them, it is impossible to say with any certainty where any given person stayed on any given night; whom they spent time with, whom they knew as a neighbor (even if only for a short time); or whom they considered a friend.

We do, however, know that Mary Ann Connelly (a witness at the Martha Tabram inquest), Annie Chapman and Elizabeth Stride (the third canonical victim) were all regular visitors to the lodging houses owned by John McCarthy and his friend William Crossingham on Dorset Street, while Mary Kelly was an actual tenant of McCarthy's, paying four shillings and sixpence for a single room in the adjoining Miller's Court.

We know that the victims' friends called them by pet names, nicknames and diminutives—Nichols was Polly, Stride was Long Liz, Eddowes was Kate. But we also know that when Eddowes was arrested, earlier on the night of her murder, she gave her name as Mary Ann Kelly, while one of the friends who was called in to identify the body said she knew her as Jane Kelly.

Both are common names, without a doubt (a woman named Ann Kelly was attacked with a knife in Shepherd's Bush in late September, prompting rumors that the killer was now operating in west London). But the names are intriguing in light of an earlier victim being *Mary Ann* Nichols, and the next being Mary *Jane Kelly*, particularly as psychologists tell us that many people, when giving a false name to the authorities, will deploy a variant on one with which they are already familiar, such as a friend or acquaintance's.

There are other links. Immediately following Police Constable Edward Watkins's discovery of Eddowes's body, he fetched a nearby night watchman he knew, a former cop named George Morris—whose younger brother Thomas, it has been suggested (albeit with nothing more than the coincidence of names to go by) *may* later have married Martha Tabram's former sister-in-law, Ann.

Again, all of this is supposition, circumstantial in some places, and wishful thinking in others. But so are the arguments *against* the women being acquaintances, such as we find aired eternally on internet message boards and forums.

These counterclaims are convincing, of course. According to contemporary police estimates, there were 1,200 women working as prostitutes on the streets of Whitechapel at the time, on either a full-time or occasional basis, and hundreds of lodging houses, many of them holding one hundred or more paying customers a night. Even looking for a familiar face in such a hubbub would have been akin to the proverbial needle in a haystack.

But we cannot say this definitively, and even if we could, if we expand each woman's circle of genuine friends to just a handful of other people, the odds against some kind of awareness of the others' existence become much shorter—even if that awareness did not blossom until another body was found.

If a friend of a friend, or even of a friend's friend, were found brutally mutilated a few streets from your home, you would soon hear about it.

McCarthy and Crossingham were just two of several major landlords in Whitechapel, small-time shopkeepers and businessmen who took advantage of the area's low prices and lowly lifestyle to snatch up property as it became available, and convert it into cheap lodgings for whoever could afford to pay fourpence for a bed.

A couple named Elizabeth Smith and Johnny Cooney owned many of the lodging houses on Flower and Dean Street, including number 55, which Catherine Eddowes occasionally called home.

Frederick Gehringer was the landlord of the City of Norwich Public House on Wentworth Street, but he also owned lodgings on George Yard, including number 18, where Emma Smith was living at the time of her death.

John Satchell's holdings included both number 19 George Yard, the house next door, where Martha Tabram spent her last night, and 32 Flower and Dean Street, a favorite haunt of Elizabeth Stride.

On that same street, James Smith owned number 48, known as the White House, which was one of Mary Ann Nichols's regular drop-ins; and Joseph Davies owned the house at 18 Thrawl Street (Wilmott's, named for a previous owner), where both Nichols and Frances Coles were familiar sights.

Each of these streets looms large in the story of the Whitechapel murders and, while one would not expect the landlords themselves to know every face that passed through the vermin-infested slums over which they held sway, the "housekeepers" they employed would have certainly known, or at least recognized, the more regular ones. If one of those regulars turned up dead, the housekeepers would soon have shared that acquaintanceship with their friends and other tenants. Publicans and store owners, too.

Links could, and have, been drawn from the women's attendance at the workhouse infirmary, the one place where the local poor could go for medical treatment—one hypothesis claims four of the five canonical victims were all treated by a single doctor, Welshman John Williams (and then deploys that supposed coincidence to suggest he was the murderer).

A Petticoat Lane street scene around the turn of the nineteenth century.

Other points of reference converge. Once the murders started, a number of women approached the police with details of possible suspects—the most famous of whom, "Leather Apron," was known to have regularly bullied and extorted money from local prostitutes. This, too, reminds us that these women did not, as cold print often suggests, exist in a vacuum.

They talked among themselves, passing on names and descriptions of the men they needed to beware of, exchanging life stories, recalling pleasant moments, bemoaning their current state—reminding us, if we still need to be reminded, that a community is not made up wholly of people who know one another intimately.

It can be any gathering of people, thrown together by geography and coincidence of circumstance, who come together in large numbers at a variety of common meeting points—lodging houses, pubs, shops, markets and so forth.

The possibility that the killer emerged from that same community remains one of the most pervasive of all the myriad theories that swirl around the mystery today.

There is another commonality, however, that must also be mentioned. Whitechapel was itself a world of stark divisions, principally between the established, and largely intermingled, communities of English natives and Irish immigrants, and a Jewish population whose numbers had recently been vastly increased by an influx of refugees from eastern Europe.

Both communities were poor, often grindingly so, and both resorted to whatever means were necessary to put food on the table, including widespread prostitution.

Again, we have no way of knowing for certain what social interactions occurred between these two groups, the so-called Irish Cockney prostitutes and their Jewish counterparts, but the general historical assumption is that there was very little. Contemporary studies of the area describe it as having been divided into virtual ghettos, with crime in particular very much staying within its own community. Jewish gangs terrorized Jewish storekeepers, Anglo-Irish gangs terrorized Anglo-Irish storekeepers; Jewish prostitutes walked the predominantly Jewish streets, Anglo-Irish prostitutes did likewise in their neighborhoods.

This was not a hard-and-fast rule—Leather Apron, when he was finally unmasked, was a Polish Jew. But a combination of fear, suspicion, prejudice and all the other negative emotions that we today band together beneath the single word "racism" nevertheless conspired to draw a cultural curtain between the two communities, and perhaps that is why all but one of the

Whitechapel murder victims were of either British or Irish descent, with that one exception (Elizabeth Stride) being Swedish.

Why was this? To some, it is "proof" that the killer was indeed Jewish, unwilling to sate his bloodlust on his own people. To others, it suggests he was most definitely not, and confined his activities to areas where his personal appearance would be least likely to attract attention.

To others still, it is the mark of some shadowy conspiracy to ferment racial unrest in the area—the East End at that time, and for several decades after, was a powder keg of plots and political causes, including anarchy and the then-highly suspect notions of socialism. Who knows what other dark dreams were fermenting in those streets?

And then, as if to puncture each of these theories, there was once (and there might still be) a belief that the murderer did, in fact, strike out at Jewish prostitutes, too—only for their community to hush it up, a tragic consequence of their own (very understandable) distrust of the authorities.

Over the course of the Whitechapel murders (again, as illustrated in the sidebar), at least three skillfully dismembered female corpses were discovered, respectively, in the River Thames, in a railway arch in Whitechapel and, most audaciously of all, on the site of what would become the Metropolitan Police's own headquarters in Whitehall.

All three were unidentifiable; all three were headless; and all three, insisted the police, were utterly irrelevant to the nightmare unfolding in Whitechapel. But that, according to this particular theory, is precisely what they were *supposed* to think.

Jewish prostitution was organized in a somewhat different way from its Irish Cockney counterpart. Within the latter group, while many of the women did have what modern parlance would describe as a "pimp," he was rarely some shadowy controller enjoying the high life from the proceeds of a network of willing whores.

While there undoubtedly were a few men who at least attempted to assume that role, for the most part women relied upon a boyfriend or live-in lover who had perhaps lost, or never found, a job, and understood that his woman's body was the only marketable item either of them possessed—one reason many of the local prostitutes were not necessarily working "full time." As soon as their man found a new job, they would be back off the streets, until the next time.

Or he might be a landlord, willing to overlook a tenant's overdue rent on the understanding that she would earn the money in whatever way she chose, who would then cream a little extra off the top both as payment for his generosity and as compensation for the legal risks he was running. (Living off the proceeds of "immoral earnings" was a crime then, just as it is now.) Indeed, Fiona Rule, author of *The Worst Street in England*, an enthralling social history of Dorset Street, levels this very charge at Mary Kelly's landlord, John McCarthy, even noting that his shop was perfectly placed for him to watch his tenants' comings and goings, and those of any men they might be accompanied by.

This casual setup extended even to the so-called brothels over which contemporary commentators shivered in such vicarious horror. Although there were undoubtedly exceptions to the rule, most were effectively no more than common lodging houses that allowed (or at least turned a duly compensated blind eye to) their guests taking their sexual partners to bed on the premises.

They were certainly a far cry from the famed bordellos of the West End, or even the vicious operations that scarred areas closer to the London docks, where prostitution was indeed organized with military-style zeal.

Prostitution in the Jewish neighborhoods was different again.

Among the thousands of immigrants escaping the anti-Semitic pogroms of Tsarist Russia in the early 1880s, many were young, single women and children, often bearing nothing more than an address or, at best, a letter of recommendation to distant family members or friends in London who would, it was assumed, take them in.

And so they did, but not all were happy to accept another mouth to feed, or even able to. Untold scores, even hundreds, of the new arrivals, then, were instead pressed into the only occupation available to them, within prostitution rings operated by pimps, or *shundicknicks*, who were far more organized than any their neighbors just a few streets away might have encountered.

This, perhaps, is another reason why the shadow of the Whitechapel killer seems never to have fallen over the Jewish areas—because those same *shundicknicks* kept an eye on their merchandise, either by protecting the women from harm, or by making sure that any they failed to save never came to the attention of the police.

Each of these factors (and many more besides) is essential to any understanding of the series of attacks and murders that benighted one of the most poverty-stricken corners of London in 1888, at the very zenith of Great Britain's claim to be the world's greatest and richest nation. And it all occurred just one year after that same city so vividly and excitedly celebrated the fiftieth year of the reign of its greatest-ever monarch, Queen Victoria.

Throughout 1887, on either side of the Golden Jubilee (June 20) itself, London partied. Special commemorative coins and stamps were issued, there were parades and marches, bonfires and fireworks, street parties and songs.

Rich and poor, young and old, all joined together in one voice, one spirit, to celebrate half a century of progress, invention and civilization; to glory in the newly penned words of the poet laureate, Alfred, Lord Tennyson, and obey them to the letter.

> *You then joyfully, all of you,*
> *Set the mountain aflame to-night,*
> *Shoot your stars to the firmament,*
> *Deck your houses, illuminate*
> *All your towns for a festival,*
> *And in each let a multitude*
> *Loyal, each, to the heart of it,*
> *One full voice of allegiance,*
> *Hail the fair Ceremonial*
> *Of this year of her Jubilee.*

The summer seemed warmer, the fall seemed more beautiful, Christmas seemed more Christmassy.

Of course, bad news didn't stop, just because it was Victoria's special year. Terrible fires killed hundreds at the Exeter Theatre in the English southwest, and across the channel at the Paris Opéra-Comique. There were riots in Ostend and a crisis in Bulgaria, an earthquake in Monaco and nihilists in Saint Petersburg.

It was the year in which police clashed with radicals in London's own Bloody Sunday; and the world mourned the death of Jenny Lind.

But it was also the year Paris began building the Eiffel Tower; Buffalo Bill brought his Wild West show to London; the Hermetic Order of the Golden Dawn was founded; and the painter Philip Richard Morris unveiled his masterpiece *Feeding the Swans*.

Beeton's Christmas Annual published the first-ever story of Sherlock Holmes, the intriguing *A Study in Scarlet*; Friedrich Engels's scathing *The Condition of the Working Class in England* was granted its first-ever English translation, forty-three years after it was written; and the American playwright Thomas Russell Sullivan produced the first theatrical adaptation of *Dr. Jekyll and Mr. Hyde,* Robert Louis Stevenson's spellbinding tale of a scientist whose discoveries unleash a horrifying alter ego.

And perhaps, if one wants to draw portents from the events of one year to inform those that would befall the next, those three books, very different though they are, are the place to start. A detective, the destitute and a devil in human disguise.

All three would have their parts to play in the ordeal that was to follow.

The Nemesis of Neglect

Welcome to Whitechapel

Dank roofs, dark entries, closely-clustered walls
Murder-inviting nooks, death-reeking gutters
A boding voice from your foul chaos calls
When will men heed the warning that it utters?
Red-handed, ruthless, furtive, unerect
Tis murderous crime—the Nemesis of neglect

—Punch *magazine, September 29, 1888*

Jacob Pavlovich Adler, the Yiddish actor who was born in Odessa in 1855, then moved to London in the early 1880s, put it best.

Driven from his Russian homeland by the pogroms, he was understandably drawn (or directed) to what was then the center of Jewish life in London, a region known as Whitechapel, a little to the east of the city's center, a few streets north of the river and the then-bustling dockyards.

It was a community founded upon what once had been open country, fields and farms, but which was now as black as they had once been green, as crowded as they had once been sparse, and as brutal as they had once been pastoral.

Little more than a stone's throw to the west lay the financial center of the British Empire, and its economic heartbeat as well, the banks, exchanges and countinghouses of the City. West of that, as its name implies, lay the West End—equally crowded, equally overbuilt, but brightly lit, too, a world of glitzy theaters and glittering stores, of high fashion and cultured entertainment. An hour's walk, but a million miles from the dark, dank depths of deprivation that characterized its East End equivalent.

"In the West End are those fortunate ones who are sent into the world with a kiss," wrote Adler. "In the East End are the others. Here live the poor, the shamed, those whom Fate, seeing how shrunken and bent they are as

THE NEMESIS OF NEGLECT.

"THERE FLOATS A PHANTOM ON THE SLUM'S FOUL AIR,
SHAPING, TO EYES WHICH HAVE THE GIFT OF SEEING,
INTO THE SPECTRE OF THAT LOATHLY LAIR,
FACE IT—FOR VAIN IS FLEEING!
RED-HANDED, RUTHLESS, FURTIVE, UNERECT,
'TIS MURDEROUS CRIME—THE NEMESIS OF NEGLECT!"

The true cause of the Ripper killings, the Nemesis of Neglect, as seen through the eyes of *Punch*.   *Wikimedia Commons*

they creep through the gates of life, spat in their face for good measure. In this East End, a corner has been set aside where, not content with the spittle, Fate sends the poor on their way with a blow, a kick, and their hats shoved over their eyes."

It was here, "in this spot, with the holy name of Whitechapel," that Adler realized he must "sink or swim, survive or go under, find bread or, if we could not, find death."

Most days were touch and go on every account.

Slums were not unique to the East End. On the very fringe of the West End, just a few blocks south of what is now New Oxford Street, the area around St. Giles Church was littered with mean dwellings, decaying tenements, wooden shacks and filth of every description—a rookery, in the parlance of the day, and one that nothing less than a vast, concerted and, most of all, merciless program of modernization could ever shift.

A little to the north, another rookery sprawled in the area that would later be devoured by the great railroad termini of Euston and Kings Cross. South of the river, beyond the warehouses that now lined the waterfront, there lurked more.

Charles Dickens visited one, Jacob's Island in Bermondsey, and recaptured it in his novel *Oliver Twist*. It was where Fagin, the greatest of all Dickens's criminal creations, had his hideout, but the description could apply to any of London's direst corners. This one just happened to be built across the Thames's stinking river mud.

> Crazy wooden galleries common to the backs of half a dozen houses, with holes from which to look upon the slime beneath; windows, broken and patched, with poles thrust out, on which to dry the

linen that is never there; rooms so small, so filthy, so confined, that the air would seem to be too tainted even for the dirt and squalor which they shelter; wooden chambers thrusting themselves out above the mud and threatening to fall into it—as some have done; dirt-besmeared walls and decaying foundations, every repulsive lineament of poverty, every loathsome indication of filth, rot, and garbage . . . .

Another such hellhole was visited by Thomas Beames, whose *The Rookeries of London* in 1850 followed Dickens in alerting the public at large of the sheer horror of these awful places. The rookery, Beames wrote,

was like an honeycomb, perforated by a number of courts and blind alleys, culs de sac, without any outlet other than the entrance. Here were the lowest lodging houses in London, inhabited by the various classes of thieves common to large cities.

Because all are taken in who can pay their footing, the thief and the prostitute are harboured among those whose only crime is poverty, and there is thus always a comparatively secure retreat for him who has outraged his country's laws.

Thieves and whores, it was said, were the prime residents of the rookeries, although there were more honest folk there as well, driven not merely to

A "typical" London rookery, as seen by the artist Thomas.

the very edge of desperation by their poverty, but beyond it, to what might well have been the end of the world.

There was only one place worse to live.

The East End.

Elsewhere across the metropolis, rookeries were little more than pockets of London's lowlife, contained within the trappings of finer residencies, wealthier people. They had boundaries, marked by the decaying alleyways that led into the heart of such places, and no right-thinking soul would ever dream of passing through the first grimy streets and into the stinking debris that lay beyond. Even the police gave such places a wide berth unless duty firmly demanded they enter.

The East End was a different proposition. The East End was itself a rookery, a vast, endless, squirming mass of the most corrupt human filth that opened at the gates of Bethnal Green, then sprawled to the outermost limits of the city. And the more people who were forced into its embrace—as the western rookeries were cleared and their populace pushed eastward, or the immigrant ships docked, and their passengers flowed outward—the filthier and more crowded the East End became.

Whitechapel lay at the heart of the this darkness.

Bordered on the west by Middlesex Street, to the south by Ratcliffe Highway, to the north by Fashion Street and to the east by Cambridge Heath Road, with its eponymous High Street a dart through its midsection, Whitechapel was a rookery within a rookery, a warren of narrow, dirty streets laid out not to the regimental order of a modern American city, or even the crazy-paving unpredictability of the West End, but as though a bowl of spaghetti had been upended on a garbage dump, and then topped by a garnish of unwashed humanity.

Romantic historians write of the rivers that once paid tribute to the Thames, but which were long ago buried beneath the growing city—Beverly Brook, the River Mole, the Silk Stream, Fleet, the Wandle and Yeading.

No such pleasantries here. Even before its reputation was sealed, Whitechapel was served by the Black Ditch, a forebodingly named waterway that fed the local ducking pond, and which had been rightfully blamed for more than one murderous outbreak of cholera. Of course it had. For many people it was the closest thing they had to a sewer. It was also the nearest thing they had to a water supply.

Even with a map, and a working knowledge of the principle thorough-fares, it was (and, as recently as the mid-1970s, remained) easy to find oneself getting lost in Whitechapel, to mistake one precipitous turn for another, to overlook a crucial alleyway as you searched for a certain street.

The only landmarks were factories, of which there were so many, and pubs, of which there were even more, and in an age before electric lighting; when even gas was considered an extravagance too far, once darkness fell, you entered an entirely different world.

It had not always been like this. Adler was correct when he referenced "the holy name of Whitechapel"—back in the fourteenth century, a small white chapel was dedicated to Saint Mary Matfelon, a welcome halt for travelers making their way along what had once been the road that linked the Roman cities of Londinium (London) and Camulodunum (Colchester), but was now better known as Whitechapel High Street.

No church stands there today. The original chapel was replaced in 1673 by a new parish church, which in turn was rebuilt in the 1870s—only to be destroyed by fire on August 26, 1880. Rebuilt again, it burned once more

The church of St. Mary in Whitechapel, rebuilt in 1880 but destroyed in the London Blitz.
above, Wikimedia Commons; below, Alamy

on the night of December 29, 1940, at the height of the London Blitz. Its ruins stood until 1952; today it is a public park.

Coaching inns, too, dotted the High Street of the Middle Ages, but slowly the expanding city of London began reaching into Whitechapel.

At first, it was a blessing, a vast weaving industry that took root around what is now Spitalfields Market and brought untold wealth to the region. But slowly the industry fell into despair and, by the early nineteenth century, the once proud and beautiful homes that housed the weavers had been converted into mean lodging houses as the nearby docks began to grow, and accommodation was demanded not only by their likewise swelling workforce, but also by all the people who moved to the area in search of work.

The modern reader catches a taste of the transition in historian Kate Williams' debut novel, *The Pleasures of Men*. There she depicts a once well-to-do patriarch, stubbornly remaining in his house filled with history, while the neighborhood descends into a cacophony filled by "the shouts of men, the cries of babies, howling dogs and an endless clanging and crashing of wood and metal . . . human sewage, rotting vegetables, dirty bodies and dogs."

The novel is set in 1840, during the terrifying reign of another (fictional) murderous madman, the Man of Crows, and Williams, paints his hunting grounds with stomach-churning precision. Forward forty years in time, and those would have felt like "the good old days." But even back then, there were difficulties.

A couple of miles south of Whitechapel High Street, the docks—in actual fact, part of a complex of ten different yards stretching more than twenty miles from Tower Hamlets to Tilbury, and each specializing in different commodities—were one of the finest jewels in the British Empire's glittering crown.

There, amid a vast network of waterways and warehouses into which flowed all the treasures of the world, you would find spices from the east, cotton from the west, iron from here, rubber from there, tobacco and alcohol from somewhere else. Meat and fruit, fabric and fur. Everything that the modern era transports by train, plane, truck or even internet, the Victorian age shifted by boat. Whatever commodity might be required by the United Kingdom, its first port of call was the London docks.

To an island nation, the docks were the heart and soul of civilization. It was the community that built up around them that would become the problem.

Ratcliffe Highway

The streets that lined the docks, and then marched up into those of Whitechapel, had earned a reputation for poverty and crime long before the Victorian age began with the ascension to the throne, in 1837, of the queen after whom that era is named.

Ratcliffe Highway was the worst of them all.

At least one version of the traditional ballad that is named for the highway includes an early hint as to its nature, when the song's narrator, a recently docked sailor, is cheated by a whore, or "doxy," as he refers to her—she asks if he has the money to buy some of her time, and he hands her a gold coin. Then, when he asks for change:

> This lady flew into a passion and placed both her hands on her hips
>
> Saying, "Sailor, you don't know our fashion, do you think you're on one of your ships?"

So he kills her.

> Then I put my old knife to her white throat and for my change, her life I did take
>
> And down the stairs I ran nimbly, saying, "Damn my old boots, I'm well paid."

He returns to his ship to hide out, but he will soon be ashore again, and taking further lives as well:

> [But] the Devil within me had opened a dark door way to hell
>
> For the spirit of killing was in me, and the others didn't live long to tell.

Murders of this type were common on the Highway, and were scarcely noted even by the authorities. There was no police force as such at the time, and those locals who were charged with maintaining law and order were scarcely going to expend much energy pursuing the unseen killer of an unknown whore.

In December 1811, however, Ratcliffe Highway's name took on a darker resonance when two entire families were slaughtered in their own homes, twelve days and just half a mile apart.

First, on December 7, the family of a linen draper named Timothy Marr—mother, father, infant and their apprentice—was slaughtered inside

THE FUNERAL OF THE MURDERD M.^r AND Mrs MARR AND INFANT SON

The Interment of this Murdered family was at St Georges in the East on Sunday Dec. 15 1811 the deceased were attended to the grave by Mr Marr's father Mother and brother and Mrs Marr's four Sisters and other relatives. their Shocking Murder was committed Decr 7 1811 Published Decr 21 1811 by G. Thompson N.º 43 Long Lane West Smithfield.

A contemporary depiction of the laying to rest of the Ratcliffe Highway murder victims.

their locked and bolted home, with no signs of how their killer either entered or exited the premises.

Then, just days before Christmas, the landlord of the King's Arms pub, his wife and their servant were murdered under similarly mysterious circumstances. Among the suspected murder weapons retrieved from the scene was what a police report described as a "ripping chisel."

An arrest was made, and a Scottish seaman named John Williams was charged, despite the evidence against him being sketchy to say the least. But Williams, who never ceased to proclaim his innocence, would not live to hear the verdict. He hanged himself in his cell on the fourth day of his trial, and the proceedings continued on without him. There was still no convincing evidence against him so far as the murders were concerned. His suicide was accepted as his admission of guilt.

Since that time, other crimes, other murders, other slaughters, had thrust the East End into the newspaper headlines, but it did not take much for them to be pushed out again. It was only the East End, after all. Close to the bright lights of the city it may have been, but it was no part of the city that the average respectable newspaper reader would ever care to visit. So its problems were casually swept beneath the carpet and there, for the most part, they remained.

Occasionally, the authorities would rise to the bait that a few decades' worth of Victorian reformers (Charles Dickens among them) dangled before them, and agree that something ought to be done.

Rarely, however, was that "something" at all meaningful, and even when it was, the nature of the area's own inhabitants ensured that its reality would swiftly be cruelly distorted.

In 1875, for instance, an Artisans' and Labourers' Dwellings Improvement Act came into force, under which private contractors were brought in to clear the worst of the slums and replace them with modern, so-called "model" homes.

The assumption (and though the modern reader may wonder at its naivety, the same imbecilic trust in philanthropy still underpins capitalism today) was that the people displaced from their old homes would simply be rehoused in the new ones.

But of course it didn't work like that. Though still "cheap" by standards elsewhere in the city, the rents demanded by these new landlords were far beyond the reach of the people the model homes were intended for. And so those people moved on, crammed in with friends and relatives in hovels that had already been overcrowded in the past, or thrown onto the conveyor belt of equally bulging boardinghouses, where a handful of coppers could buy a bed for a night and a fire to be warmed by, but little—if anything—else.

Suicide was common, sometimes in the most ghastly forms. In August 1887, a forty-nine-year-old inmate of the Whitechapel workhouse deliberately set herself on fire, burning herself to death in front of the two boys from whom she had just begged some lucifer matches.

Others chose the river for their final good-bye, leaping from bridges with their bodies weighted with stones; or the busy roadways, hurling themselves in front of carts and omnibuses. In 1876, Whitechapel underground railroad station opened for the first time, and the more sensationalist corners of the media were already reveling in this exciting new means of ending it all, stepping out into the path of an oncoming train. Whitechapel would have been no more immune to the fascination than any other station.

Disease was endemic—three major cholera epidemics swept the East End between 1848 and 1866, with no less than one-third of the beds at the London Hospital in Whitechapel given over to victims of the latter outbreak. Starvation was rife.

In 1857, over 400 East Enders were recorded as dying of hunger, but thirty years later, the philanthropist Charles Booth was still estimating that some 60,000 people living (if that was even the correct word for a state of abject subsistence) in the East End did so with no reasonable expectation of being able to put food on the table that day, or even that week. The 400,000 or so others who lived there could at least rely on a few scraps to eat.

One in four children born in the East End would die before they reached their fifth birthday—if starvation did not take them, then disease, neglect and violence were queued up behind it.

There was work to be found, of course. The docks were a major employer, even if many of the available vacancies were temporary, a day here, a day there—the equivalent of the zero-hour contracts that so many modern businesses have taken to offering.

Every morning, long before the dockyard gates opened, vast crowds of men would gather there, awaiting news of whether or not their services, manual labor for the most part, were required; some would even remain there all day, in the hope that an unexpected absence or injury might demand an extra body after all.

There were jobs to be had at the factories and warehouses that also dotted the streets, and if conditions at the docks were backbreaking, here they seemed determined to destroy the rest of the human body.

In an age before even the rudiments of health and safety awareness stepped into the workplace, employees were stuffed into cramped and crowded, airless rooms, there to work with some of the most noxious substances known to man—most of which you could smell from several blocks away.

As the rest of London grew and was gentrified, so those businesses whose output might offend the more delicate sensibilities—foundries, slaughterhouses, tanneries, waste incinerators, breweries, all of contemporary industry's most malodorous necessities—were shunted eastward, to resume their activities among the kind of people who (so polite society had convinced itself) might not even notice the stench, so accustomed to grime and filth were they.

Pay was as low as an employer could go; hours were as long as an employer dared. In July 1888, a government committee met to investigate reports that overcrowded workshops throughout the East End demanded anything up to a sixteen-hour day from their underpaid employees, knowing that for every person who balked at the hours, conditions or wages, there were dozens more who would kill for a job. The report was completed, but little was done.

And still the people poured into the area.

The Yiddish community into which Jacob Adler was welcomed upon his arrival in London was the largest of the immigrant populations in the East End, but it was by no means the only one.

The 1840s saw a vast influx of Irish families, fleeing that country's potato famine, while the sheer expanse of the British Empire, approaching its zenith as the century rolled on, encouraged other races, too, to come to the mother country—only to discover the only mother that awaited them was a disease-addled dissolute, soused on cheap gin, without even a pot to piss in.

Many arrived with nothing and were swiftly absorbed by the narrow, stinking streets. Others, who perhaps made the journey with a handful of possessions and maybe even some money, would find their first taste of English hospitality in the form of a smooth-talking con man who would trick them out of all that they owned and then send them on their way. That's what happened to the lucky ones, anyway. The unlucky ones would just be beaten up and robbed, and the *really* unlucky ones would be murdered. They had no one who would miss them, after all.

Unemployment, homelessness, crime, racial tensions and ruthless exploitation—all of these things were part and parcel of everyday life in Whitechapel.

Voices were occasionally raised in protest. In 1883, the Reverend Andrew Mearns published *The Bitter Cry of Outcast London: An Inquiry Into the Condition of the Abject Poor,* a book that warned "no respectable printer would print, and certainly no decent family would admit even the driest statement of the horrors and infamies discovered in one brief visitation from house to house in the East End," before glibly proceeding to do so.

> Few who will read these pages have any conception of what these pestilential human rookeries are, where tens of thousands are crowded together amidst horrors which call to mind what we have heard of the middle passage of the slave ship.

He described penetrating courtyards "reeking with poisonous and malodorous gases arising from accumulations of sewage and refuse scattered in all directions and often flowing beneath your feet; courts, many of . . . which the sun never penetrates, which are never visited by a breath of fresh air, and which rarely know the virtues of a drop of cleansing water."

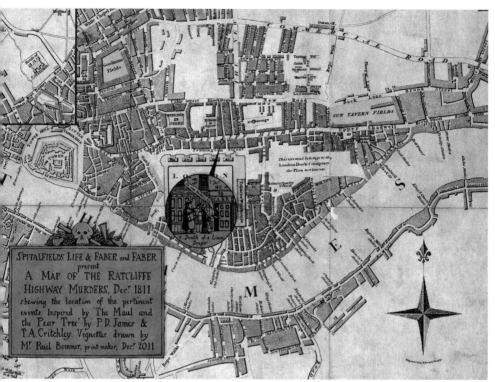

Another example of the period fascination with the Ratcliffe Highway killings—a map of Whitechapel and its environs.

> You have to ascend rotten staircases, which threaten to give way beneath every step, and which, in some places, have already broken down, leaving gaps that imperil the limbs and lives of the unwary. You have to grope your way along dark and filthy passages swarming with vermin. Then, if you are not driven back by the intolerable stench, you may gain admittance to the dens in which these thousands of beings . . . belong.

How the middle classes of Victorian England must have shuddered as the reverend related the nature of homes so vile that even "the poor creatures who sleep under railway arches, in carts or casks, or under any shelter which they can find in the open air . . . are to be envied in comparison with those whose lot it is to seek refuge here."

Matters were worsened by the knowledge that Whitechapel, farsighted compared to even the better-heeled neighborhoods to the west, had once been a pioneer in both street and personal sanitation.

The first public washhouse in the entire metropolis was opened in Glasshouse Yard by the grandly named Association for Promoting Cleanliness Among the Poor in 1845. By the mid-1870s, Whitechapel's local authority had snatched back responsibility for street cleaning, or "scavenging," from private (and often corrupt) private agencies, and was spending £7,000 a year on doing the job properly. That same decade, Whitechapel was among the first London authorities to purchase a monstrous "dust destructor," an incinerator capable of burning twenty-four tons of refuse a day and converting it to a mere four tons of clinker that could be used in road construction.

And still its streets were awash with mud, soot and manure; its alleyways littered with garbage; its malodorous inhabitants black with caked-in filth.

Household refuse was stored, often for weeks or even months at a time, in vast, immovable bunkers that overflowed long before they might be emptied; and though "night soil," as human waste was delicately termed, was for the most part emptied into the vast sewers that were the pride (and, in many ways, the savior) of Victorian London, the sewers themselves emptied out into the Thames just a few miles downstream, and washed back toward the city with every tide. On a warm or windy day, the stench was unimaginable.

And so the reverend described rooms barely eight feet square, their walls and ceilings black with filth, their windows long ago shattered and either inexpertly boarded up, or else stuffed with stinking rags, protection not only against the cold and rain, but also "the sickly air" which bears with it the stench of "the putrefying carcases of dead cats or birds, or viler abominations still."

> Here you are choked . . . by the air laden with particles of the super-fluous fur pulled from the skins of rabbits, rats, dogs and other animals in their preparation for the furrier. Here the smell of paste and of drying match-boxes, mingling with other sickly odours, overpowers you; or it may be the fragrance of stale fish or vegetables, not sold on the previous day.

And into each of these cell-like rooms was crammed one family, sometimes two. One family Mearns heard of comprised a father, mother, three children and four pigs, living together in a damp basement. Another, crammed into a single underground kitchen, included seven living people and one dead child—the parents were unable to afford a burial.

Furniture comprised of old packing cases and planks, beds were old boards draped with rags. And these were the homes of the more fortunate people—those who could actually afford a home. Far more were trapped into the endless wandering that was life among the boardinghouses, crammed one hundred or more at a time into dormitories the size of a wealthy family's parlor; and more still had plunged to even greater depths, unable even to "scrape together the two-pence required to secure them the privilege of herding in those sweltering common sleeping rooms, and so they huddle together upon the stairs and landings, where it is no uncommon thing to find six or eight in the early morning."

Then there was the last resort of all, the workhouse. Instituted during another of the government's fits of "something must be done—this is something, let's do it," the workhouses first cast their shadow on the land in the 1830s, as a means of combating the increasing problem of poverty.

Hitherto, the poor had been reliant upon charity and a system by which the lowest wages were topped up from local taxes. In the belief that this system served only to demoralize the laborers and keep wages low, it was now decreed that the able-bodied poor should instead apply to the newly instituted workhouses for relief.

Five "Unions," as they were called, existed in the East End, in St. George's, Stepney, Mile End, Bethnal Green and Whitechapel, and it has

A modern view of Whitechapel underground station—through which, it was said, the Ripper might often have passed.   *Sunil060902/Wikimedia Commons*

been estimated that one in ten East Enders had spent at least a night or two in one of them. In the census of 1860 alone, 5,000 people called one of these workhouses home, with as many as 10,000 more on what was called "outdoor relief."

Conditions, it was said, were a little better than jail, but only a little, and history, thanks to the commentaries of—among others—Charles Dickens, luridly paints the workhouse among the most inhumane social policies ever perpetrated upon a supposedly free people.

And so they were. Married couples would be separated; families shattered; any kind of social interaction forbidden. Set to work in exchange for food and accommodation, inmates found themselves doing the most menial tasks available—grinding bone for fertilizer, breaking rocks for construction, and so forth.

Indeed, it was Dickens, again, who first allied a reliance upon the workhouse with a living death; in 1856, in his essay "A Nightly Scene in London," he published an interview with five homeless women he discovered lying on the pavement outside the Whitechapel Workhouse on a wet and muddy night, and likened them to "five dead bodies taken out of graves, tied neck and heels, and covered with rags."

As the poet Thomas Crabbe was moved to muse:

> There children dwell who know no parents' care
> Parents who know no children's love dwell there
> Heartbroken matrons on their joyless bed
> Forsaken wives and mothers never wed
> Dejected widows with unheeded tears
> And crippled age with more than childhood's fears
> The lame, the blind and, far happier they?
> The moping idiot and the madman gay

The following year, in *Little Dorrit*, Dickens's titular heroine spends for the first time a night beyond the confines of the Marshalsea debtors' prison (where she lives with her father). She is happy to return to the jail; to be free from "the shame, desertion, wretchedness and exposure of the great capital." The message is simple—even prison is preferable to taking one's place among the degraded poor and homeless.

Small wonder indeed that more than one observer predicted that one day, these huddled masses would rise up and march westward upon the city, "cutting throats and hurling brickbats," as the reformer Margaret Harkness predicted, "until they are shot down by the military."

In 1888, that day seemed closer than ever. The anger was there, the discontent and the despair. More and more, the people believed they had nothing left to lose; that even death would be preferable to the hell to which circumstance, Fate, and an eternally uncaring government had consigned them.

All that was missing was the glue that would bind the disparate masses together—the common cause that would bring an end to the petty internecine squabbles that divided the community, and point them in the direction of the true enemy.

Across the last days of summer, and through the fall of 1888, they discovered that glue, they found that common cause.

But the enemy was not the government, the privileged or the rich.

The enemy, so many people believed, was the devil himself.

They called him Jack the Ripper.

2

Victorian England's Daughters of Joy

Prostitution in London's East End

> This life induced insanity, rheumatism, consumption and all forms
> of syphilis. Rheumatism and gout are the commonest of these evils.
> Some were quite crippled by both, young though they were.
>
> We have found girls at midnight who are continually prostrated
> by hemorrhage, yet have no other way of life open. In the hospitals,
> it is a known fact that these girls are not treated at all like other
> cases; they inspire disgust, and are most frequently discharged
> before being really cured. Scorned by their relations . . . there are
> girls lying in many a dark hole in this big city, positively rotting
> away . . . .
>
> —*William Booth*, In Darkest England and the Way Out, 1890

Of all the professions that thrived within the slums of Victorian
Whitechapel, prostitution was perhaps the most rife, because
for the unfortunates who chose that path, it was the only option
available to them.

Recoiling from reality, popular fiction has painted these ladies with
an utterly unbecoming glamor—the "whore with the heart of gold" who
first took literary wing in the pages of *Oliver Twist*, in the voluptuous form
of Nancy, was still going strong in 2001, in the Hughes brothers' movie
adaptation of Alan Moore's Ripper epic *From Hell*.

But we should never forget that behind Nancy's cheerful smile and
loving demeanor, and the ubiquitous greeting of "Hello, dearie," there
loomed the awful figure of her bullying lover Bill Sikes, a living personification of the fears that accompanied so many of the women who plied her
trade. Likewise, there is a bitter humor in the blandishments of the movie's
whores that utterly belies the erotic promise of their offerings.

Drink eased these deceptions even further. In 1857, the *East London Observer* asked "how many a modest woman has been forced into the roadway to avoid the half-dozen caricatures of her sex who, wildly drunk, are walking abreast occupying the whole of the footway, and singing, or rather screeching, snatches of obscene songs at the very top of their voices?"

Of course a whore wore a painted smile. If her clients had known how she really felt, they'd have run a mile to escape her.

Again, few of the women who chose that lifestyle, in that neighborhood, did so because they wanted to. Referring to whores as "Daughters of Joy," Victorian sensibilities liked to equate prostitution with nymphomania, camouflaging society's deeper doubts and misgivings behind the belief that only the most sex-crazed woman would even dream of prostituting herself.

For the vast majority of East End whores, however, their profession had absolutely nothing to do with sex, enjoyable or otherwise. It was simply a means of making the money that would enable them to survive another day and night.

Many, in fact, might even have recalled a time when they themselves would have recoiled from the nature of the lifestyle—a time when they lived well enough to know there would be a meal waiting at the end of the day, some spare coins to fritter on life's little luxuries, a roof above their head that they could call their own. Only for all of that to be snatched away, perhaps by an unfaithful husband, perhaps by sickness or death, perhaps by any of the myriad mishaps that can turn a life upside down, and leave a once respectable woman shivering on a street corner, learning to transform a passing stranger's glance into a much-needed handful of change.

We have no truly reliable figures to tell us how many women were working on those streets in the late 1880s, with even the most well-meaning estimate little more than an educated guesstimate, depending upon the motives of the author—soliciting sympathy for the fallen, or inviting opprobrium for the depraved.

The Metropolitan Police, who were in as good a place as any to calculate such numbers, suggested there were at least sixty-two brothels operating in the area at the time, and around 1,200 prostitutes "of very low class." Those numbers, however, most likely do not include women (and men) who took to the streets on an occasional basis, as a last-ditch supplement to any other form of income; nor do they recognize the women whose appearance and demeanor suggested that they were whores, yet who may well have been innocent of any such charge.

It was said that a red bandanna around the shoulders and a small cane in one hand marked out a woman as a prostitute, but that would be when business was good. As she aged, or drink and deprivation took their physical toll, those items would have long since been sold, lost or stolen, and now she was indistinguishable from the rest of the human refuse that lay around the streets, spent and drunk, and of interest only to men who had sunk to similar depths.

Which, if a woman confined her travails to Whitechapel alone, was likely a lot of them. Further afield, the docks could be regarded as a more lucrative hunting ground, with every tide disgorging another shipload of seamen, with jangling purses and hungry for women. But the competition was fiercer there, too, with every watering hole for streets around crowded with women from miles in every direction.

Closer to home, trade was largely restricted to the men who also called it home—young apprentices still gathering the courage to begin courting for real, but desperate for feminine company regardless; laborers and factory workers with their weekly wage burning a lustful hole in their pocket; lonely widowers, ancient sots and the occasional yahoo from further west, investigating Whitechapel as though it were darkest Africa, to see for himself whether it was as bad as it was painted.

They often discovered that it was.

The law's attitude toward prostitution at this time was reasonably lenient. Moves had been made to at least repress the trade; 1885, for example, saw the passage of the Criminal Law Amendment Act, designed "to make further provision for the Protection of Women and Girls, the suppression of brothels, and other purposes." The age of sexual consent was raised from thirteen to sixteen (where, in the UK, it still stands today), while homosexuality was criminalized, and would remain so until 1967.

But the police regarded the law as little more than a cosmetic remedy to a veritable plague of underlying problems, of which the vice trade was simply one simple symptom. Poverty was the real issue, and all the arrests on earth could not solve that. Indeed, no less an authority than Sir Charles Warren, commissioner of the Metropolitan Police, wrote off the new statute as a complete waste of police time, pointing out that time spent harassing prostitutes and watching brothels was time diverted from more pressing matters of law and order.

Even when a brothel was raided, it was unlikely that its owner would receive more than a caution; and when one was closed down, its owner, staff and clientele would simply move to another address—perhaps in a more respectable neighborhood.

Warren's policy was one of containment. If the police knew where the brothels were, and where the whores would congregate, then they could police that area accordingly.

"As long as there is a demand for prostitutes on the part of the public," Warren wrote, "there is no doubt they will exist . . . and the more they are driven out of their brothels [among the] slums, the worse it becomes for law and order and decency."

Sir Charles Warren, the Commissioner of the Metropolitan Police—the man ultimately expected to capture the Ripper, and every other felon in the city, too.   *Alamy*

Besides, prostitution itself was *not* a crime. It was the act of solicitation that was considered the offense, and that was damnably difficult to prove in court. A friendly "Move along, now" from a passing policeman was far more likely to have the desired effect than dragging a woman before the magistrate, there to learn she was merely asking a passing friend what time it was.

Indeed, that much was proven in June 1887 when one PC Endacott arrested a woman on Regent Street, in the heart of London's West End, on a charge of soliciting. It was nine in the evening and, although darkness had not yet fallen, he could imagine no other reason why a woman might be abroad at such an hour. (Indeed, until less than two centuries earlier, a curfew bell had rung out over London at that very hour, demanding that all citizens return to their homes for the night. To walk the streets after that was to invite immediate arrest as a nightwalker.)

The woman, a twenty-three-year-old milliner, Miss Elizabeth Cass, protested her innocence, insisting she had been on her way to purchase a pair of gloves. But, although the case against her was dismissed, she was nevertheless cautioned as to her future conduct; reminded indeed that "no respectable woman" would ever walk on Regent Street at that time of night; and, in the space reserved for "occupation" on the court record, the word "prostitute" was proclaimed loud and clear.

Miss Cass was, understandably, furious. She contacted the press, she wrote to her Member of Parliament. First there was a fuss, then a furor and, ultimately, the incident developed into a full-fledged scandal. The Home Secretary was censured, the police were humiliated, and another platform was torn from the Criminal Law Amendment Act, as Sir Charles issued an order *forbidding* his officers from arresting suspected prostitutes, unless they were acting upon a genuine complaint from a member of the public.

Of course, this led to its own problems. There were parts of London, Whitechapel included, where it was impossible for a man to walk even a handful of steps without being propositioned at least a few times.

Warren, however, remained unmoved, even when polite society begged him to reconsider the stance. Surely, he would ask them in a voice that dripped with sarcasm, it was better that a few men should be momentarily inconvenienced by a mumbled offer from a pathetic whore, than a respectable woman should have her dignity and reputation shattered by a wrongful arrest.

There really wasn't much of an answer to that.

If solicitation itself went unpunished, however, the law did maintain a loose grip on the situation. Most days would see a handful of streetwalkers brought before the magistrature on charges of drunkenness, theft or

GIN LANE.

William Hogarth's immortal depiction of "Beer Street and Gin Lane," drawn in 1751 but still a familiar scene over a century later.

assault—but again, any punishments that might be meted out tended to be little more than brief interruptions of a woman's daily routine.

The "problem" of prostitution was left, then, to the various charitable and philanthropic organizations that took themselves into the East End to try and redeem the profession's most hardened practitioners—well-meaning souls acting beneath such banners as the Society for the Suppression of Mendicity, the Parochial Mission Women's Fund, and the Stranger's Friend Society.

These and more besides would dispatch volunteers onto the streets to talk with the poor, tempt them to the society's headquarters with the promise of food and warmth, and then set about reforming them, usually with a healthy dose of religion.

The church, too, worked to purge the streets of sin. In 1858, the East London Association was formed (largely by clergymen) to combat "the class of public nuisances which consists of acts of Indecency, Profanity, Drunkenness and Profligacy," and it placed prostitution and its consequences firmly in its crosshairs—the "swarms of fallen women plying their trade, seamen beset and quarreled for by rival harpies, words and deeds obscene and disgusting, fights and often stabbings are the daily features."

At the time, it was popularly believed that the problem was largely confined to the Ratcliffe Highway as it passed by the dockyards (hence the reference to seamen).

But soon, the organizers prophesied, the disgrace of that one neighborhood would "become the shame of the Whitechapel Road and of every thoroughfare in the East."

And so it did. The Reverend Samuel Barnett, who presided over the parish of St. Jude's in Whitechapel, personally established a number of purely local societies aimed at either redeeming the fallen, or saving those who had not yet taken the final step—the Guild of Hope and Pity, the Evening Home, the Band of White and Good, St. Jude's Guild and more.

Barnett's wife sold some of her own jewelry to purchase three buildings that had hitherto been notorious brothels; on another occasion, she arranged for the child of a notorious whore to be kidnapped and sent to live with friends in the country.

The reforming zeal burned brightly in another local figure, too. Frederick Charrington was the heir to one of London's vastest brewery fortunes, but he had seen too much of the damage that cheap alcohol had wrought, and turned his attention, and his fortune, toward more philanthropic goals.

The brothels were a favorite target for his fervor, but when it became apparent that neither the police nor the court system seemed interested in closing them down, he took matters into his own hands—raiding the brothels in person, and then recording his impressions.

"In none of these houses," he wrote of one visit, "are there less than ten girls and women carrying on their nefarious trade, and in some of them there are as many as twenty. The scene on every night of the week at Lady Lake's Grove [a notorious street in nearby Mile End] is one of the most unqualified bestiality."

So great was Charrington's crusading rage, in fact, that even he has fallen under suspicion as the perpetrator of the Whitechapel murders! What better way, after all, to root out "unqualified bestiality" than to treat its practitioners as animals themselves?

His accuser, author M. J. Trow, admits he made his accusations with more than a hint of irony: "I . . . was showing how easy it was to put almost any contemporary [personage] in the frame."*

But other writers, less versed in the art of satire, have nevertheless taken Trow's researches and run with them, trumpeting Charrington not only for his life as the Ripper, but also for so cunningly camouflaging his deeds by being regarded as a radiant beacon of decency in an area that normally stifled even the merest spark. And that constitutes an irony that we will soon become depressingly familiar with.

Another of Charrington's favored targets was what was popularly known as the white slave trade, which he described as "an extensive system of procuration [whereby] the agents of Continental houses [find] their largest and cheapest supply of goods" in the East End.

He was especially mortified to learn how great a role the area's Jewish community played in this scandal. Chaim Bermant, author of *London's East End: Point of Arrival*, writes, "the number of Jews involved in white slavery, and the number of Jewesses trapped as white slaves was a deep cause of concern and heartache," particularly as

> Jewish prostitution was to an extent a byproduct of Jewish chastity. Among Jewish women . . . there was no middle class of the merely libidinous, and if a girl was no longer a virgin she was fit only for the streets.

---

* The same can hopefully also be said about those notions that suggest John Merrick, the Elephant Man, was the killer, on account of his time in Whitechapel— June 1886 until his death in April 1890—so neatly coinciding with the murders.

Another view of life in London's rookeries: a nest of crime, alcoholism and prostitution.

Furthermore, "in the upheaval of mass immigration, many young girls found themselves alone or among neglectful relatives; they were easy prey for seducers and, once seduced, they were quite easily led into prostitution."

Easily indeed.

We return to the docks. Another social reformer, Charles Booth, wrote of a visit he paid, to watch as a shipload of immigrants—many of them from eastern Europe, and unable to speak a word of English—landed for the first time. For a handful, friends and relatives might be waiting. But for the majority, Booth declared, a different fate awaited.

"[Among] the crowd gathered in and about the gin shops overlooking the narrow entrance of the landing stage are dock loungers of the lowest type and professional runners"—men whom Booth described as "among the most repulsive of the East London parasites."

> Boat after boat touches the landing stages. [The runners] push forward, seize hold of the bundles or baskets of the newcomers, offer bogus tickets to those who wish to travel forward to America; promise guidance and free lodging to those who hold in their hand addresses of acquaintances in Whitechapel or are friendless.

Within ten minutes, Booth estimated, eight out of ten of the newcomers would have been stripped of all they carried; but an even worse destiny awaited any girls or young women who fell into their clutches.

For them, the lodgings their new friend offered would likely be a brothel, and the job that was promised would be whoring.

What is interesting, however, is just how one-sided these commentaries are. Indeed, it is to history's eternal regret that the vast majority of contemporary writings on this subject were the work of, again, reformers, complainants and sensation-seeking newspapermen, particularly once the police effectively washed their hands of the issue.

A handful of erotic stories and novels from the era do paint a different picture, but of course they are equally unreliable witnesses, and while the void in between those two extremes has certainly been plugged with plethoric conjecture, the fact is, we know very little about the lives of what we might call "the average Whitechapel hooker."

Statistics attempt to fill the gap. We can read, for example, the average price she might have charged for her services; fourpence, the cost of a night in a boardinghouse, seems to be the accepted answer, although the once common slang phrase "tuppenny [two pennies] upright" is generally believed to date from the late nineteenth century.

Unfortunately, the data from which such figures are drawn is so limited as to be meaningless. It has, for example, often been noted that among the victims of the Whitechapel murderer, the average age was thirty-eight.

But is that common across the entire spectrum of local streetwalkers? Or does it simply suggest that the murderer purposefully sought out the most dissipated women, reasoning they would be less equipped to put up a fight than a younger, fitter girl, and perhaps less likely to be missed by a pimp?

We should also remember that the vast majority of women on the street, and the men with whom they consorted, would have been what modern sensibilities would term "uneducated"; that adult literacy was by no means universal, particularly as one descended into the realms of poverty; and even if it had been, would we really expect letters and journals to have been written, much less to have survived, answering the questions that modern researchers demand?

Again, the annals of Victorian erotica do delve into this world occasionally, but (understandably) in a manner designed to excite readers with a taste of corruption, as opposed to any attempt to actually document its reality.

Likewise, readers of Michel Faber's masterful 2002 novel *The Crimson Petal and the White* might well thrill to the journal penned by the book's narrator, Sugar, and her glorious descriptions of life in a brothel in the rookery at St. Giles. But in truth, they tell us no more than can be gleaned from any of the worthy documents published by the reformers of the age itself, even if Sugar does wield a far more readable pen, and seems to extract a certain satisfaction from her work as well:

> It's not as dirty as the factory, nor as dangerous, nor as dull. At the cost of her immortal soul, she has earned the right to lie in on a weekday morning and get up when she damn well pleases.

Yet those advantages are surely subjective. Dirt is in the eye of the beholder, and even the most exquisite occupation can be dulled by repetition. The ability to sleep late in the day can be seen as a refuge from the grind of a conventional job, but it can likewise be protection against the hunger, cold and violence that lurk beyond the door.

And as for danger, you should ask Fairy Fay for her opinion about that.

3

A London Particular

The Fog Fiend Cometh

Cities, like cats, will reveal themselves at night.

—*Rupert Brooke*

B ut wait! There is a third actor in this drama whom we have yet to meet, a third player who swirls through both fact and fiction, intrinsic not only to the atmosphere that today surrounds the murderous mayhem, but who might easily have facilitated it, just as it had facilitated so many other crimes, past and future.

The story of London is not, after all, a succession of historic events and remarkable personages. Or rather, it is, but there is a synchronicity among them that is surely more than coincidental.

For every Roman city growing on the site of a Celtic settlement, there was a Boudicca who burned the place to ashes.

For every Samuel Pepys, diarizing the day-to-day life of the city, there was a William Blake, mythologizing the nocturnes that stalk on the fringes of the daylight.

For every Christopher Wren, raising the city from the ashes of another great blaze, there was a Nicholas Hawksmoor, the "devil's architect" of so many recent fictions, within whose churches have been discerned the most infernal occult designs.

And for every bright summer's day, there was a darkness deeper than the blackest night, and fouler than the deepest sewer.

We have already established, though our focus has been confined to one district, that London in the final decades of the nineteenth century was a vastly different city from that of today. At the same time, however, it is even more recognizable than any modern vista.

The skyline is dominated not by vast glass and concrete phalli soaring vaingloriously into the heavens, but by churches and cathedrals. Their spires and towers, too, reach toward the clouds, but it is God whom they glorify, not the vanity of some trendy architect who should never have been handed that first box of Lego. (Or, more likely, who is compensating now for never having had one in the first place.)

The thoroughfares are as clogged by traffic as they are today, but it is not the choking fumes and angry roar of automobile, truck and taxicab that reddens the eyes and deafens the ears; it is the unhindered reek of heavy industry, the fruity stench of horse manure, the steady beat of several thousand hooves and the rusty rattle of metal-rimmed cart wheels, clattering across the cobbles.

There is no mind-melting music being piped into the stores, but the eternal hubbub of salesmen and hawkers, on and off the narrow sidewalks, has a raucous resonance of its own, the last living descendant of the picturesque cries of London that once entranced the city's inhabitants—watch the musical version of *Oliver Twist*, and the scene where the street sellers flock out to peddle their wares, and then multiply their numbers and their noise by every road in the city.

And there is no neon light or LED brashness, no eternal glare to translate the darkest night into a zombified day. But there is the fog, to perform the opposite feat. Because there had always been the fog. And, until

The fog swirls in this modern depiction of the lurking Ripper   *J. R. Pepper*

the deliberate passage of a Clean Air Act in the mid-1950s, there always would be.

J. J. Marric, author of a magnificent sequence of post–World War II police novels, all featuring the ubiquitous Inspector Gideon, caught the fog toward the end of its life span.

"Tall trees . . . seemed to be swallowed by the fog," we read early on in the aptly titled *Gideon's Fog.* "The trees close to the road were solid enough at the base, but even their higher, skeletal branches appeared to be fading away. Office workers . . . some holding torches, the beams pointing downward, were already wraithlike figures.

"It was going to be a foggy night, and [he] knew they could be either bad or very good for the police."

A classic London fog was like none you have ever witnessed, not even in the smog-choked capitals of the modern era. Pea-soup thick and pungent, it was so moist that every breath felt like you were drowning.

But not in water. You were choking on mud—a clinging, stinking miasma that shifted between noxious yellow, poisoned green and suffocating black, depending upon which pollutants were going about their business today.

Some days, it would be soot from the coal fires that blazed in every dwelling; others, it was the gases that flooded from every factory; and on others, it might be the sewers discharging soupy belches of filth, or the overcrowded graveyards disgorging putrefaction and decay. But usually, it was all of these things and more.

It was as though London were one vast chemistry laboratory, into which every conceivable combination of toxin was being constantly pumped. Usually, they dissipated on the breeze, but, when conditions were right and the river's mists congealed, they rose up and transformed the very air into what Londoners called, indeed, a pea-souper.

One, in 1952, clung so thick and cloying that, for five utterly windless days in December, more than 4,000 people died of respiratory disease, and up to 8,000 more were fatally sickened. And even after new laws cleaned up the city's act, the legacy of those fogs was apparent every place you looked, in the filthy brown patina that resurfaced every building and monument. It took years for the cleaners to blast them back to their original shades.

No matter. Prior to the Clean Air Act that finally rid the city of its deadliest houseguest, the London fog was as much a part of the capital as its churches, its traffic and its inhabitants. It was an integral part of the fabric of London and a part of the city's charm, as well.

Its cultural charm, anyway.

The first London fogs were recorded as far back as the 1200s, and even then, the correlation between the fog and air pollution was understood.

It was common practice then to burn a cheap bituminous rock known as sea coal, which itself produced a particularly noxious smoke, and the change-over to regular anthracite coal made little difference.

Into the 1600s, the foul London air was considered the leading culprit not only for respiratory diseases, but also for other illnesses that later times ascribed to bacteria and virus. And the modern meteorological phenomenon of "inversions," which bring the smog crashing down on our most populous cities, had already been discovered in the late 1810s, when the chemist Luke Howard described and popularized the phrase "heat islands"—that is, any urban conurbation where the generated heat was greater than that of surrounding rural areas.

A *New York Times* piece in 1880 explained the science behind the smog:

> Like every other mist, the fog which rises and is wafted along the valley of the Thames is composed of small particles of water, that ought properly to be dissipated by the action of the sun's heat. Only with difficult is the sun able to undertake the duty. The smoke poured out from hundreds of thousands of chimneys does not merely mix with the fog. It coats each watery particle with a tarry, oily film, giving it an unnatural character, and preserving it, so to speak, from immediate dispersion. A genuine London fog, therefore, is something more than a fog. It is a prodigiously large volume of mist, held in a kind of thraldom [sic] by oleaginous ingredients floated from the tops of chimneys.

This mist, the piece continued, would then blacken and thicken, until "the darkness even at noon is so great that dwellings and places of business have to be lit with gas as at night"—a gas, incidentally, that would then contribute to the sheer stink of the fog. "At times it is as difficult to get a breath of fresh air as it is to procure a good drink of palatable water."

The fog made its literary bow in 1834, in Theodore Edward Hook's *Maxwell: A Novel*. There, on "a wretched morning . . . there fell a mizzling rain through the peas-soup atmosphere of London, which chilled every living thing, while a sort of smoky misty, foggy vapour, hovering over the ground, made darkness only visible."

Other authors mentioned the fog in passing, but like Hook, usually only to establish a scene that the reader might find familiar. It was Charles Dickens who allowed it to scamper onto center stage, even if only for a moment.

We are three chapters inside *Bleak House*—published precisely a century before the Great Smog of 1952—when Esther arrives in London, convinced she has just missed the excitement of a great fire. "For the streets were so full of dense brown smoke that scarcely anything was to be seen."

"O dear no, miss," replies the young gentleman who meets her. "This is a London particular." And when it becomes apparent that Esther has never heard such a term, he hastens to explain: "A fog, miss."

Forty years later, Frances Hodgson Burnett's *A Little Princess* described an afternoon on which "the yellow fog hung so thick and heavy . . . that the lamps were lighted." T. S. Eliot mused on "the brown fog of a winter dawn" and, of course, the fictional industry that has grown up around the adventures of Sherlock Holmes still paints the nocturnal fog as his most natural ally, just as it was in the first Holmes story ever published, *A Study in Scarlet*.

There, "a dun-coloured veil hung over the house-tops." In *The Sign of Four*, the fog hangs "dense [and] drizzly . . . low upon the great city. Mud-colored clouds drooped sadly over the muddy streets. Down the Strand the lamps were but misty splotches of diffused light which threw a feeble circular glimmer upon the slimy pavement." And in the short story "The Adventure of the Bruce-Partington Plans," "a dense yellow fog" that has settled over London, will soon be transformed into "a greasy, heavy brown swirl . . . [that] condens[es] in oily drops on the windowpane."

For four days that week, Dr. Watson hazarded, "from the Monday to the Thursday I doubt whether it was ever possible from our windows in Baker Street to see the loom of the opposite houses."

The fog swirls through the world of Holmes, even on the occasions when it is not present. And likewise, it permeates the popular image of Jack the Ripper, regardless of whether or not it was actually present as the Whitechapel murderer went about his bloody business.

In fact, as we read through contemporary newspaper reports, all vying with one another to present the most obscure facts about the Ripper's reign of terror, not once do we hear of the killer either emerging out of or disappearing into the fog. And for very understandable reasons, as J. J. Marric explains, again in *Gideon's Fog*:

> If the fog [remained thin], it would be bad; the fog would be light enough to allow burglars and pick pockets, bag snatchers and smash-and-grab practitioners do their worst and escape in the misty gloom. But if the fog thickened, then thieves and honest men alike would stay at home . . . .

The Lodger was the movie that truly introduced the fog fiend to the Ripper legend.   *Photofest*

And if a traditional pea-souper was thick enough to keep the bag snatch-ers off work for an evening, imagine how it would have affected a surgeon as precise as Jack the Ripper proved to be. Hard enough even to find a victim when you can barely see your hand in front of your face, let alone transform a living human being into one half of a scarlet Rorschach test.

It was the great Alfred Hitchcock who confirmed the myth of the devil in the fog, when he subtitled his 1927 adaptation of Marie Belloc Lowndes's *The Lodger* as "a tale of the London fog."

Even in silent sepia (itself redolent of the stifling claustrophobia of a true London particular), the choking effluvium swirls among the horrified crowds who gather around the first corpse, a cast member in its own right, and clearly, the association between fiend and fog was one the popular imagination was unwilling to release.

And why should it? The fog hides the Ripper, but it also reveals him—not in a physical sense, but in a psychological one. The Ripper is in the fog, but he is also *of* the fog; one becomes a part of the other, two unnatural allies working together—one to force the victim to blunder into a perilous path, the other to hack her, in the words of Edward Gorey, "to collops."

The Ripper gives the fog an anthropomorphic life of its own, and it repays him by imbibing him with its own most unique characteristic—the ability to slip unseen and unheard through the tiniest opening, and then to expand to fill the space.

The fog choked the lungs as the Ripper slashed the throat; the fog blinded eyes as the Ripper extinguished life. And all was done in such thick, cloying silence that a person could be seated just a thin wall or window away from the death scene, and never hear a sound.

It is a wonderful image. But it is not true. The Ripper did not require the fog to muffle his footsteps or silence the screams. He did not need it to hide his approach or mask his getaway.

He was the Ripper. That was enough.

4

The Terror Begins

The Life and Death of Fairy Fay

London lies . . . under the spell of a great terror. A nameless repro-
bate—half beast, half man—is at large. The ghoul-like creature . . .
is simply drunk with blood, and he will have more.
—The Star, *September 8, 1888*

December 26, 1887 was cold, damp and overcast. Christmas still
hung in the air, and elsewhere in this grand metropolis, the
wealthier families were now celebrating Boxing Day, traditionally
the day when tradesmen and servants would receive their Christmas gift, a
box stuffed with goodies, from their customers and employers.

For Fairy Fay, though, and for thousands like her, the holiday had likely
been just another day, and had already been forgotten—either through lack
of interest in the entire affair, or else through the ministrations of hunger,
drink and apathy. It's hard to think of families merrily feasting when your
stomach has been rumbling for days on end, and harder still if you should
happen to think back to your own childhood, when Christmas was spent
with family and friends.

Far better to just sweep the whole thing from your mind, and press on
with the business of living.

Fay had certainly been drinking, probably down to her last coin, but
she was reasonably confident she could earn a few more before she finally
retired for the night.

From the last pub at which she'd halted, she could see the hollow that
was Mitre Square black against the darkness of the surrounding buildings.
Once, a priory had stood there, built by Queen Matilda around 1108, but
four centuries later it was dissolved and demolished, and merchants and
tradesmen began slowly to take over.

Another church tried to establish a foothold, but commerce swept
it out—St. James's was demolished in 1870, by which time its spire had

already been dwarfed to near insignificance by the warehouses that grew up around it.

Fay crossed the square and then out onto Aldgate High Street as it turned into Whitechapel High Street, at the junction of Middlesex Street. She hurried past busy Commercial Road as it doglegged a right angle to the other main streets, and then turned left into Osborn Street.

It was darker there, and dirtier, unlit even by the gas lamps that had started to spout on other thoroughfares. But she also knew it was within that darkness that she would most likely meet her next customer.

A few words, a swift transaction, and she would be on her way to earning the fourpence that would buy her a bed for what was left of the night.

Wentworth Street and Brick Lane lay ahead, and the towering bulk of the Taylor Brothers' Chocolate & Mustard Factory. If the wind was in the right direction, you could smell their products all the way back to Aldgate, one more odor among the myriad that made up Whitechapel's own unique perfume.

And there, in the shadows, the unmistakable figure of a man, his very presence in such an unforgiving corner suggesting he had only one thing on his mind.

Unfortunately, it was not the thing that Fairy Fay hoped.

According to a copy of *The Times* newspaper, dated almost two years later, her body was discovered at that same junction.

Journalist and historian Terence Robertson wrote, in 1950, "Two hours after [Fay] set out [from Mitre Square], a constable on beat shone his flickering oil lamp into a darkened doorway. At the inquest he said his lamp revealed a sight which sickened him."

Fifteen years later, another author, Tom Cullen, claimed Fairy Fay had been mutilated; yet another, Martin Fido, insisted in 1987 that a wooden stake had been thrust into her abdomen.

The police investigated, of course. But a dead prostitute on the streets of Whitechapel was scarcely headline news, and certainly lay far down on the law's list of priorities. According to Robertson, Inspector Edmund Reid allowed for little more than a cursory investigation before more pressing matters diverted whatever manpower he had devoted to the cause, and Fairy Fay was forgotten.

In fact, Fairy Fay did not actually exist to begin with. No woman of that name was murdered on Osborne Street that night; in fact, no woman was murdered in all of Whitechapel.

Wentworth Street—in sight of which Fairy Fay was murdered.

Wikimedia Commons

No matter that authorities as traditionally unimpeachable as *The Times* and author L. Forbes Winslow, in his (admittedly self-important) memoir *Recollections of Forty Years*, both insisted that what became known as the Whitechapel murders commenced in 1887, with the Christmas week discovery of "an unknown woman . . . found murdered near Osborne and Wentworth Streets, Whitechapel."

No matter that Winslow himself *would subsequently be interviewed by the police as the killings continued.*

The truth of the matter is, Fairy Fay's story and, indeed, her name were Terence Robertson's creation, coined for the October 29, 1950 edition of *Reynolds News*. Indeed, he admitted as much when he confessed he had christened her, "for want of a better name," by pulling a colorful slang term from a once popular American minstrel song, "Polly Wolly Doodle"—a young man's farewell to the whores he usually consorted with, before he leaves to meet his true love down South:

> *Oh I went down South for to see my Sal*
> *Play polly wolly doodle all the day*
> *My Sally is a spunky gal*
> *Play polly wolly doodle all the day*
> *Oh my Sal she is a maiden fair*
> *Play polly wolly doodle all the day*
> *With laughing eyes and curly hair*
> *Play polly wolly doodle all the day*
> *Fare thee well*
> *Fare thee well*
> *Fare thee well my fairy fey*
> *For I'm going to Louisiana*
> *For to see my Susyanna*
> *Play polly wolly doodle all the day*

However, although it may have been fictional, Fairy Fay's tragic story was not so unusual.

Just a few days before Fay's fabricated encounter, another prostitute, Margaret Hayes, had been attacked by a group of men who stopped her in the street and left her so badly injured that she spent the next two weeks in the infirmary. And less than four months later, on almost the same spot upon which Fairy Fay was said to have perished, at the junction of Wentworth Street and Brick Lane, one of Hayes's neighbors, Emma Smith, was likewise attacked with uncommon brutality.

It was Easter Monday, another holiday, but not one Smith could afford to observe. That day, the same as any other, she had spent the daylight hours in bed at her lodgings on nearby George Street, sleeping off the previous evening's noctivagant activities.

The five-foot-two brunette—around forty-five years old, but certainly looking older—was not considered a beauty. Any application of cosmetics was certainly ineffective when it came to masking the bruises, cuts, thick lips and black eyes she habitually sported. On top of that, Smith spent most of her time drunk, or on her way there.

She was a familiar face on the Whitechapel streets, though, as a former policeman named Walter Dew later recalled.

Dew was twenty when he joined the Metropolitan Police in 1882. He spent five years with X Division, based in Paddington Green, and then transferred to H Division, on Commercial Street in Whitechapel, in 1887, after being elevated to Detective Constable. Fifty years later, now a Detective Chief Inspector, Dew remembered Emma Smith as well as anybody else seemed to.

> Her past was a closed book even to her most intimate friends. All that she had ever told anyone about herself was that she was a widow who, more than ten years before, had left her husband [believed to have been a soldier, with whom she may have had two children] and broken away from all her early associations.

He did not disbelieve her story. His memoir continues: "there was something about Emma Smith which suggested that there had been a time when the comforts of life had not been denied her. There was a touch of culture in her speech [that was] unusual in her class."

This particular evening, then, Smith left the house around six, to begin her working day.

It would have been a dismal prospect, even for a woman hardened to the dirty streets. An early Easter caught London still in the grip of winter, icy rain and a bitter wind sending the night time temperatures plunging toward zero, and even tempting a few flurries of snow to fall.

But Smith had her lodgings to pay for, and food—and, perhaps more importantly, alcohol—to purchase. She walked the few miles that took her toward the River Thames and the dockyards there, confident that, among the newly-docked sailors, she would chance upon a client or two. And so she did. Shortly after midnight, her friend Margaret Hayes saw her at the corner of Burdett Road and Farrance Street in Limehouse, talking with a man dressed in dark clothing, topped with a white silk neckerchief.

Four hours later, she arrived back at her lodgings, beaten, raped ("outraged," in the media parlance of the time) and bleeding profusely.

It was around 1:30 in the morning, she said, when she saw a gang of youths hanging around outside Whitechapel Church. She crossed the road and turned into Osborn Street, but the gang were not shaken off. Rather, they increased speed, following her up the one street, and across Wentworth Street, before finally catching up with her in the shadow of the mustard factory.

A chilling view inside the over-crowded tenements of London's east end

There they knocked her to the ground, stole whatever money they could find, and then proceeded to beat her. As a parting gesture, what was later described as a blunt object was rammed violently into her vagina, with sufficient force that it ruptured her peritoneum.

With her shawl clutched between her legs to try and stanch the bleeding, it took Smith close to three hours to cover the 300 or so yards back to her own front door at 18 George Street. Nobody, it seems, saw her.

Her assailants, all who heard of the attack were convinced, were one of the so-called High Rip gangs that patrolled the East End streets, offering their own brand of "protection" to local prostitutes, in exchange for cash. Those who paid up would be left alone; those who didn't would most likely be added to the streets' already bloody toll.

There were dozens of these gangs, some whose names live on in writings today (the Monkey's Parade Gang, the Hooligans, the Regent's Park Gang); others whose identity might well be the product of some subsequent researcher's imagination. The original High Rip gang itself was actually a particularly infamous, but seemingly local, Liverpool concern; their existence elsewhere was assumed first from the coverage that their northern activities received from the media, and later from the pages of *The Whitechapel Murders, or the Mysteries of the East End*, a "penny dreadful" magazine that ran throughout late 1888 and was contemporaneous with many of the actual killings.

Whether or not she was attacked by a High Rip gang, however, is in many ways irrelevant. Either way, there was no mistaking that something terrible had happened to Emma.

Margaret Hayes was still awake at the time, talking with another of the house's occupants, Annie Lee, and the lodging house deputy, Mary Russell, as Smith stumbled through the door.

It was they who transported her to the London Hospital, about half a mile away on Whitechapel Road—itself a somewhat heroic undertaking, given the distrust and fear with which many people regarded hospitals at that time. Dr. Frederick Treves, head of the hospital's school of anatomy (and the physician who cared for the so-called Elephant Man, John Merrick, through the last years of Merrick's life), explained:

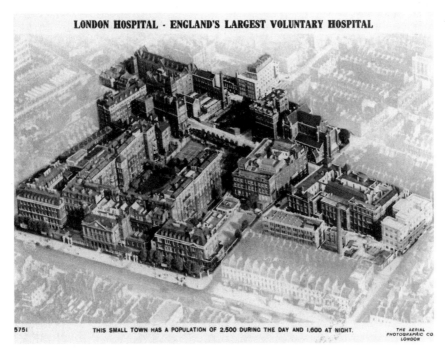

LONDON HOSPITAL · ENGLAND'S LARGEST VOLUNTARY HOSPITAL

5751   THIS SMALL TOWN HAS A POPULATION OF 2,500 DURING THE DAY AND 1,600 AT NIGHT.   THE AERIAL PHOTOGRAPHIC CO. LONDON

The London Hospital, a familiar place to so many of Whitechapel's unfortunates.

> The poor people hated [the hospital]. They dreaded it. They looked upon it primarily as a place where people died. It was a matter of difficulty to induce a patient to enter the wards.

On this occasion, Emma's fears were justified. Less than thirty-six hours after she was admitted to the hospital, she died of acute peritonitis. The coroner later declared that it was clear that the woman had been "barbarously murdered," and that he had never hitherto heard of "such a dastardly assault . . . it was impossible to imagine a more brutal case."

The jury had no alternative but to return a verdict of willful murder against some person unknown.

Among modern historians and scholars, Emma Smith is rarely considered to have been the victim of anything but gang violence. But Walter Dew was one of those who mused along other lines.

> The silence. the suddenness. the complete elimination of clues, the baffling disappearance [of her assailant] all go to support the view which I have always held, that Emma Smith was the first to meet her death at the hands of Jack the Ripper.

Neither was Dew alone in believing there was more to the attack than met the eye. According to police superintendent Arthur Butler, writing in *The Sun* newspaper in 1972, there might well have been an equally sinister twist to Smith's death.

Butler believed that Smith and her pimp, a street showman named "Fingers Freddy," were attempting to blackmail a local Brick Lane abortionist—who, though they could never have guessed—would later find a degree of speculative infamy as *Jill* the Ripper (see Chapter Seventeen). Emma was killed, Freddy . . . well, Freddy disappeared from the district and the historical record. Who knows what happened to him?

5

The Ones Who Got Away . . .

. . . and the Ones Who Didn't

> She stated that she had been attacked by a man who she did not
> know, and who stabbed her with a clasp knife which he took from
> his pocket. No one appears to have seen the attack, and as far as
> at present ascertained there is only the woman's statement to bear
> out the allegations of an attack, though that she had been stabbed
> cannot be denied.
>
> —Eastern Post, *February 26, 1888*

F our months passed between the attacks on Margaret Hayes and
Emma Smith. But there was no such respite from violence on the
streets of Whitechapel and its environs.

On the night of February 25, 1888, Annie Millwood, a thirty-eight-year-
old widow, was admitted into Whitechapel's Workhouse Infirmary, bleeding
from what the *Eastern Post* newspaper described as "numerous stabs in the
legs and lower part of the body."

Millwood made a full recovery, but clearly she was suffering from other
health issues too. On March 31, little more than four weeks after the attack,
she collapsed and died at the Whitechapel Union Workhouse.

A messenger named Richard Sage detailed her last moments. "I was
standing at the door conversing with the deceased, and my attention being
called in another direction I turned my back to her, and after a space of
three minutes I returned, to find her lying down with her face on the step.
I acquainted the porter, who had her carried into the corridor."

Thomas Badcock, the master of the workhouse, continued

> On Saturday the 31st . . . my attention was drawn to her as she was
> then laying down in the corridor, apparent[ly] in a fit. I immediately
> telephoned to the infirmary for medical aid, and finding the case to

be one of great urgency, I procured the services of Dr. Wheeler, of Mile End-road, who came at once and pronounced life to be extinct.

Dr. Arthur arrived shortly afterwards from the infirmary, and corroborated Dr. Wheeler, and I then placed her in a shell, and sent the body to the mortuary. She had never complained of feeling unwell, but on the other hand she seemed always in excellent spirits.

The coroner's report described the cause of death as a "sudden effusion into the pericardium from the rupture of the left pulmonary artery through ulceration"—in other words, natural causes. By which time, however, another woman had been attacked by a mystery knifeman.

On March 28, seamstress Ada Wilson answered a knock at the door of her home on Maidman Street, a small thoroughfare poised between the East India Dock and Bow Road, to be confronted by a man, a stranger, in his late twenties or early thirties, sunburned and mustached, in dark coat, light trousers and what was called a "wideawake hat," better known in the United States as a Quaker hat.

According to the *East London Advertiser* newspaper: "[He] demanded money from her, adding that if she did not at once produce the cash she had but a few moments to live. She refused to give the money, and the man drew from his pocket a clasp knife, with which he stabbed her twice in the throat, and immediately made off."

The newspaper continued, "[This] desperate attempt to murder a young dressmaker" was foiled by the sound of her screams. "A couple of young women rushed up to two police-constables, and said that a woman was being murdered."

> The two constables immediately ran to the house indicated, and there found a young woman, named Ada Wilson, lying in the passage, bleeding profusely from a fearful wound in the throat. A doctor was instantly sent for, who, after binding up the woman's wounds, sent her to the hospital, where it was ascertained that she was in a most dangerous condition. She, however, so far recovered that she was able to state what had occurred, and gave a description of the would-be murderer.

Some of Wilson's neighbors apparently pursued, and almost caught, her assailant. He escaped, however, and Wilson lived—to deliver, with mounting trepidation (and relief), the earliest published descriptions of the killer who would be stalking those same streets later in the year—a younger man with a mustache, a knife, and an unerring aim for the throat.

As for the murderer's other best-known characteristic, an apparent hatred of whores, "seamstress"—meaning a woman who supported herself by taking on various sewing and mending jobs for her friends and neighbors—was a career that many members of the oldest profession claimed as their own. Whether Ada Wilson herself was a prostitute is a matter of continued conjecture. For her would-be killer, however, the fact that she lived alone, with no visible regular means of support, might well have been all the evidence he required.

Or so sundry latter-day researchers have surmised. While several contemporary reporters included Annie Millwood within their lists of possible victims of the Whitechapel murderer, none considered Ada Wilson a likely candidate. It is only with the advent of behavioral profiling—that is, mapping out a criminal's likely motivation from the nature of his crimes—that the net was cast wider in the search of further victims, seeking not only for those who were actually killed in a manner that matches the profile, but also those who were merely attacked: dress rehearsals, if you will.

Few serial killers, it is widely believed, perfect their madness in dreams alone. The stereotype, at least, requires a lifetime of escalating cruelty, beginning with animals, perhaps progressing to younger siblings and playmates, before moving on to those people the killer believes to be inferior to him, and who he knows are the least likely to report him to the police.

A woman alone on the streets late at night, be she a streetwalker or a nightwalker (the two terms were not always indivisible), almost naturally fell into that category; even anecdotal evidence, as collected by the various charities and religious organizations that endeavored to "save" London's "fallen," can barely begin to tell the full story of the violence that was a daily hazard for the women who worked the city's darkest alleyways and passages.

But it does record the scars that many of them carried as souvenirs of the madmen they had encountered across their careers.

Few of these attacks were reported to the police, largely because there would have been no point. It would have been the girl's own fault for following the lifestyle she had chosen. Although Victorian England was beginning, at last, to comprehend that poverty was not necessarily the consequence only of an individual's stubborn refusal to make something of themselves, still there was the prevailing belief that the Daughters of Joy chose their career solely to satisfy their unnatural lust.

Joy, however, was the last thing on many of their minds. Mere survival was far more pressing.

Many people believed the sheer weight of poverty and crime in Whitechapel made the district impossible to police thoroughly.

The Next Victim

Months passed and, if the newspapers of the day are to be trusted, a sense of relative peace descended again upon the streets, at least inasmuch as no further murderous attacks were reported. Of course, the day-to-day violence continued, some incidents leading to hospitalization, others not.

Hindsight, however, might also point out that there had been no more public holidays since Easter; and that the next one was not scheduled until early August, when the annual summer bank holiday fell on Monday, August 6.

Today, bank holidays in Britain are synonymous with the mighty traffic jams that stretch from the major cities to the nearest coastal town, as vast swaths of the population head hungrily for a day or two at the seaside—bank holidays are traditionally placed on a Monday, to allow for a long weekend.

In earlier times, the holidays would be celebrated locally. London's parks would blossom with fairs and attractions; streets would be decorated, or at least become more rowdy as people celebrated a day away from the grind of work in whatever fashions they chose. And so it was in Whitechapel in 1888. The pubs did a roaring trade, and so, it might be assumed, did the women who worked the streets.

Women like Martha Tabram.

Martha was born in Southwark, on the other side of the River Thames, on May 10, 1849. Her father, Charles White, was a warehouseman, and he and his wife, Elizabeth, already had four children when Martha came along. She was twenty when she married the man whose name she would bear into the annals of the Whitechapel murders—Henry Tabram was thirteen years her senior, a foreman in a furniture warehouse in Deptford, and the marriage seemed well starred at its outset.

Martha, however, had a weakness for drink, and by 1875, it appears Henry had had enough of it. He left her, paying for this desertion when Martha took him to court to force him to support her with a weekly payment of twelve shillings.

The court agreed, but as Martha's drinking increased, so did her demands both for more money and for revenge. Convinced that Henry's sister, Ann, had encouraged him to break up the marriage, Martha began systematically harassing the woman, a campaign that ended only when she was sentenced to seven days' hard labor for smashing all of Ann's windows during a particularly bitter drunken rage.

Henry, too, was under constant attack, as Martha took to lying in wait for him as he went about his business, demanding he give her more cash.

Henry refused; in fact, he began reducing the amount he was already committed to pay her, sending Martha back to the court to force him to at least abide by the terms of the original judgement. But then Martha took up with another man, breaching her side of the arrangement, which bound Henry to support her only while she lived alone. The payments ceased immediately.

Martha's latest paramour was William Turner, a street trader who made what living he could from selling cheap trinkets. Martha, by this time, had also found a trade—prostitution—and her years with Turner were a tumult of drunken binges, bitter arguments and regular separations.

In fact, their most recent breakup occurred shortly before the bank holiday, which itself was the sort of occasion upon which Turner could rely on making a fair amount of profit. The last time he saw Martha, on the preceding Saturday, he even gave her a handful of coppers to enable her to purchase some odds and ends she could sell to the crowds.

She probably drank it. As her ex-husband later remarked, whenever Martha had money, she "generally spent it on drink. In fact, it was *always* drink."

Martha was living in Whitechapel now; in fact, her address—a lodging house at 19 George Street—was right next door to Emma Smith and Margaret Hayes's home. There, Martha and another of the lodgers, Mary Ann Connelly, or "Pearly Poll" as she introduced herself, took to teaming up when they went out, not only for security but also because prospective clients frequently came in pairs.

And so they did that bank holiday Monday, a pair of soldiers—a private and a corporal—who happily took the two women out drinking. Or so Pearly Poll said. But Ann Morris, Martha's former sister-in-law, insisted she saw her former nemesis quite alone that night, going into the White Swan pub on Whitechapel High Street around 10:00 p.m.

Pearly Poll's story fit the known facts, however. The drinking at an end, it was time for the rest of the evening's business to be conducted. The two women, with their sozzled soldier-boy companions, meandered a short way up the High Street, and then separated—Pearly Poll took her man into Angel Alley, while Martha led hers through a covered archway between John Telfer's pawnbroker shop, and another pub, the White Hart, into George Yard.

The next time anyone saw her, she was dead, thoroughly perforated by close to forty vicious knife wounds.

George Yard was not a secluded spot, but it was dark. The local newspaper, the *East London Advertiser*, shuddered, "George-yard is a narrow turning out of the High-street, and it leads into a number of courts and alleys in which some of the poorest of the poor, together with thieves and roughs and prostitutes, find protection and shelter in the miserable hovels bearing the name of houses."

Great brick buildings soared up on every side of it, including the newly (as of 1886) built St. George's Residences, which offered "board and lodging for respectable girls." The George Yard Ragged School backed onto the alleyway, alongside a varnishing factory called St. George's Works, while the air was thick with the fumes from the Whitechapel Board of Works' garbage incinerator.

Those aforementioned "miserable hovels" pocked the yard, too, including George Yard Buildings, a three-story, forty-seven-room block built and operated by a local philanthropist known as Mr. Crowther. Here, rooms were let to deserving poor families, among them a delivery driver named Joseph Mahoney, and his wife, Elizabeth, who worked at a match factory in Stratford.

They had been out celebrating the bank holiday until late—according to Joseph, they didn't arrive home until 1:40, at which point Elizabeth went out again to buy a late supper. (Many stores stayed open late into the night, catering to those people whose own workday could stretch fourteen or more hours at a time.) She was gone only five minutes and saw nothing.

But another of their neighbors, John Saunders Reeves, described hearing so loud a "disturbance" from the yard around that same time that he and his wife, Louise, had actually gone out onto their balcony to investigate; while a police constable named Thomas Barrett was passing by and not only saw, but also spoke to, a soldier in the uniform of a Grenadier Guardsman standing by the entrance to George Yard.

Barrett asked the man what he was doing, but was satisfied by his explanation—that he was waiting for his friend, who had gone into the alley with a girl. Barrett continued on his beat, and the guardsman disappeared from history.

It was close to two hours later, at 3:30 a.m., that a young cabdriver named Alfred Crow returned to his own home in George Yard Buildings, and noticed a woman lying on the landing at the top of the first flight of stairs. (In English usage, this would be the first floor, with that at street level known as the ground floor.)

The old narrow Whitechapel alleyways and streets can still be traced by the modern city walker.   *Shutterstock*

It was not an uncommon sight—for all Mr. Crowther's good intentions, the public areas of George Yard Buildings were frequently used as a temporary resting place by nonresidents. But when the aforementioned John Reeves set out in search of work at 4:45 a.m., the woman was still lying there, and the state of her body made it clear she was not simply asleep.

PC Barrett was still on his beat as Reeves rushed out onto the street in search of help; the constable inspected the corpse, then sent Reeves to fetch a local doctor, Timothy Killeen. By 5:30, the doctor had arrived and was able to estimate the time of death—around 2:30.

Killeen detailed the injuries he found at the inquest, held in the Alexandra Room library and lecture hall of the Whitechapel Working Lads' Institute on High Street.

> The left lung was penetrated in five places, and the right lung was penetrated in two places. The heart, which was rather fatty, was penetrated in one place, and that would be sufficient to cause death. The liver was healthy, but was penetrated in five places, the spleen was penetrated in two places, and the' stomach, which was perfectly healthy, was penetrated in six places.

He did not believe the injuries were all caused by the same weapon, Most were clearly the work of a penknife, but the one that actually passed through the woman's breastbone could have been caused only by a dagger or, perhaps, a military-style sword bayonet.

The victim's identity was not immediately apparent—it would be several days before Martha was formally identified. But with Pearly Poll's description of the soldiers to hand, the investigation swung into action, with the newspapers not far behind.

Emma Smith's murder, brutally shocking though it was, had scarcely caused a drop of ink to be spilled in any but the most local newsrooms. Martha Tabram's slaying, however, reached papers across the country—indeed, by the time the local paper, the *East London Advertiser*, hit the streets with its weekly edition on August 11, the story was almost in danger of feeling old.

But whereas elsewhere, in the further-flung regions of the country, Martha's murder was simply a terrible thing that had happened in London, the *Advertiser*'s local knowledge was to layer an extra veneer of horror over the slaughter.

Whitechapel High Street, walked by Martha and her soldier boy attacker.
Wikimedia Commons

In George-yard, Whitechapel, there was perpetrated on Tuesday morning last a mysterious murder, which has not been equalled in shameful brutality for many years past . . . . The body was that of a woman apparently about 35 years of age, she was about 5ft. 3in. in height, complexion and hair dark. Her dress, which was totally disarranged and torn, was a dark green skirt, a brown petticoat, a long black jacket and a black bonnet.

The circumstances of this awful tragedy are not only surrounded with the deepest mystery, but there is also a feeling of insecurity to think that in a great city like London, the streets of which are continually patrolled by police, a woman could be foully and horribly killed almost next to the citizens peacefully sleeping in their beds, without a trace or clue being left of the villain who did the deed. There appears to be not the slightest trace of the murderer, and no clue has at present been found. Inspector Edison has placed the case in the hands of Inspector Reid, of the Criminal Investigation Department, and no pains are being spared to bring the criminal to justice.

Although a military angle to the murder was the best lead the police had to go on, Inspector Reid was quickly able to discount the use of a bayonet as a crucial clue. Military in origin it might have been, but bayonets, and many other weapons too, littered the trader's carts, pawnshops and junk shops of the area, and there was a great many of all three.

Old soldiers selling off mementos of past wars, bereaved relatives disposing of a dead man's possessions. As late as the 1970s—that is, almost a century after Martha Tabram's death—rusted and battered militaria dating back at least a century further could still be had for little more than its scrap value on the street markets of the East End. For the investigation to base any firm theories around the use of a bayonet would be akin to poking its own eyes out.

The eyewitness statements of Mary Ann Connelly and PC Barrett, too, felt shaky, although the modern reader might discern more snobbery than detection in Walter Dew's reasoning:

Lest such a statement should malign soldiers as a class, I hasten to add that it was not a practice of the Tower soldiers to frequent the East End and associate with women of Martha Turner's type. The majority of them had too much decency and too much common sense to penetrate at night into the haunts of Whitechapel. But there were always a few, generally among the younger ones, who were not so mindful as they should have been of their own reputations or of the dignity of their uniform.

In any case, these avenues were quickly closed. An identity parade was staged at the Tower of London, the headquarters of the Grenadier Guards, but Barrett proved hopelessly inadequate, picking out *two* men as the man he saw, both of whom had cast-iron alibis.

Connelly, on the other hand, didn't even turn up for the parade, opting instead to visit a friend in Drury Lane, deep in the heart of London's West End. Then, when she was finally brought in, she simply marched up and down the line of men, more like she was inspecting troops than seeking out a madman, before declaring loudly, "He ain't here."

She also coldly contradicted PC Barrett's evidence with her description of the men with whom she and Martha had gone off—not Grenadier Guards at all, but Coldstream Guards, easily identified by the white bands around their caps.

A second identity parade was arranged, this time at the Coldstream's base at the Wellington Barracks, in the shadow of Buckingham Palace. And this time, she seemingly had no hesitation whatsoever. Two men were singled out, both privates (contrary to her assertion that one was a corporal), named George and Skipper. But both quickly detailed their own alibis, and that was more or less it.

The police did continue their inquiries, not only into the movements of soldiers that might fit the now all-but discredited descriptions provided by Barrett and Connelly, but also among the regulars of the pubs Connelly claimed she and Martha had visited on that fateful night.

Another line of inquiry looked into the activities of the gangs that then haunted the area—it was not unknown for its members to act alone, if they chanced upon a likely target, after all.

Another clue would be delivered, ironically, during the inquest into the next Whitechapel murder victim, Mary Ann Nichols. Thomas Ede, a signalman with the East London Railway Company, claimed to have seen a man of the most "peculiar appearance" standing outside the Forester's Arms pub. According to *The Times*, reporting on the aforementioned inquest, this man

appeared to have a wooden arm, as it was hanging at his side. Witness watched him until he got level with the Foresters' Arms. He then put his hand down, and witness saw about 4 in. of the blade of a long knife sticking out of his trousers pocket. Three other men were also looking at him and witness spoke to them. Witness followed him, and as soon as he saw he was followed he quickened his pace. Witness lost sight of him under some railway arches. He was about 5ft. 8 in. high, about 35 years of age, with dark moustache and whiskers. He wore a double peak cap, dark brown jacket, and a pair of overalls over a pair of dark trousers. He walked as though he had a stiff knee, and he had a fearful look about the eyes.

Inquiries swiftly revealed this peculiar man to have been one Henry James, "a well-known harmless lunatic" who, furthermore, did not have a wooden arm. The investigation had run head-first into another dead end.

6

Murder by Numbers

Mapping Out the Murder Mile

Many girls get into mischief merely because they have in them an element of the "black kitten," which must frolic and play, but has no desire to get into danger. Do you not think it a little hard that men should have dug by the side of her foolish dancing feet a bottomless pit?

—*[Ms.] Ellice Hopkins, the London Female Mission to the Fallen, 1858*

It didn't seem to matter where the police looked. Everywhere, they constantly ran up against the same obstacle, clue after clue dissipating into nothing. And at the same time, they added further weight to their own workload by deciding, very early into the investigation, to keep the newspapers at what Detective Constable Dew described as "arm's length."

The modern media's ghastly tendency to not only "investigate" but also "solve" modern criminal cases, and sit in judgment of those it deems "guilty," is not, in fact, a modern development at all. For as long as the printed page has sought readers, journalism has shadowed the law not only with straight reportage, but with rampant speculation as well.

Whenever a high-profile trial is forced to move to another jurisdiction, often miles from where the crime took place, it is invariably adverse media coverage that forced the shift.

Whenever potential jurors are dismissed on account of having already made up their minds over a person's guilt, it is usually media coverage that led them to draw those conclusions.

And whenever a police investigation is compromised by its quarry being tipped off, it is very often the media that did the tipping.

So the police kept quiet, refusing to discuss whatever progress they might have been making, refusing to say whether they had any leads, and effectively blacking out any official detail whatsoever. As what would become known as the autumn of blood continued, that blackout would lead to a great deal of ill will—a process which had, in fact, already begun, as the *East End Observer* newspaper tartly remarked:

> A considerable amount of mystery surrounds the whole affair, which the police have entirely failed to unravel, and the evidence they have been able to obtain has been very meagre indeed. No arrest has been made, and it would seem that as usual the "clever" detective officers have been relying upon some of the same miserable class of the wretched victim to "give them a clue."

In other words, even this early on, Walter Dew's later remarks regarding the unlikelihood of the average proud military man ever stooping so low as to carve up a whore were being prophesied by journalists who believed class played as great a role in the investigation as any other factor.

The law's willingness to conduct identity parades at the Tower and Wellington Barracks was undermined by the suspicion that only the lowest-ranking soldiers were called upon to stand in line—that officers (in an era when that rank automatically equated to "gentlemen") were not even to be considered likely suspects.

Similarly, while it was common knowledge that detectives had visited the streets and pubs around the murder site, and even ventured down to the docks to question newly arrived seamen, not once did they appear to have considered the possibility that the killer might have ventured into the East End from a better-heeled neighborhood.

Yet almost any local resident could have told of the gangs of aristocratic youth who would descend upon the area in search of what we might call diversion—namely, cheap whores they could knock about without fear of retribution.

In fact, one such character committed his memory of such excursions to print, in the form of what is regarded as the most voluminous erotic memoir ever published. And which has more recently been portrayed as the longest confession any killer has ever set to paper.

"Walter" was the pseudonym adopted by an author whose true identity remains as open to conjecture as Jack the Ripper's; and *My Secret Life* was his life's work, an eleven-volume manuscript comprising close to a million words, in which he detailed, in extraordinarily pungent detail, every sexual encounter he had ever had throughout a life well lived in Victorian London and elsewhere, besides.

There were a lot of them, too—conquests that conveyed him from the heights of society to the depths of the gutter, and back and forth thereafter.

A view of the London docks, thick with smoke and pollution.   *Library of Congress*

No woman appears to have been safe from his lusts, be she the youngest child or the oldest hag, a lady of quality or the humblest whore. In fact, he had an especial fascination with whores, one that even led him, as a teen, into the East End with a friend by the name of Henry, where they would secrete themselves behind walls or in basements, and watch the prostitutes as they went about their business.

Growing older, he took to taunting the women, springing out on them in darkened corners and accusing them of having robbed him, then laughing as they fled at his threat to call a policeman. Or he would visit brothels in the guise of a doctor, and offer to perform examinations on the younger women who lived there.

He admitted he was a rapist, and that he paid older whores to procure victims for him—the younger the better, and best of all, virgins. Sometimes he dressed as a sailor and amused himself by consorting in the kinds of places which they might frequent, "in an atmosphere thick and foul with tobacco smoke, sweat and gas."

And yet, despicable though Walter might have been, depraved and deviant, too, the suggestion that he was the Whitechapel murderer, first raised in 2010 (in the book *Jack the Ripper's Secret Confession* by David Monaghan and Nigel Cawthorne), simply doesn't hold water in any respect.

Beyond the mutilation of his victim's genitals, and whatever sexual connotations can be derived from that act, the Whitechapel killer left no hint whatsoever that he was pursuing instant sexual gratification—and sexual gratification, for page after page, chapter after chapter, volume after volume of *My Secret Life*, is *all* Walter is searching for.

He mentions his penis, and its manifold talents, at every available opportunity; describes his orgasms with the passion of a true connoisseur; and, though he is certainly not averse to inflicting pain, or fear or embarrassment, the only occasion on which he wields a knife is when he is cutting holes in the wall to spy on women.

The authors certainly do a fastidious job in matching some of Walter's more perverse observations (a youthful obsession with women's bonnets, for example) to elements of Ripper lore (several of the victims were wearing one at the time), but their efforts prove little, if anything.

There is the coincidence of him describing an assignation with a prostitute named Mary Davis, in an area that could be construed as Whitechapel (Davis is believed by some to have been Mary Kelly's married name); there is Walter's vague (and it *is* vague) conjecture that he might once have spent time with one of the victims of the Thames Torso murders, based on the fact that both women appeared to have a similar scar. And perhaps we can construe confessions of more sinister content from those swaths of the book that Walter confesses to have destroyed prior to its publication.

But without knowing precisely what they were, who can say? If they were truly more shocking than what he did make available for public consumption, it is true that they must have been fairly base. But one must pass through an awful lot of other unmentioned sexual practices before one arrives at serial mutilation.

The Silence Before the Storm

> Only two or three years ago I saw a book of police reminiscences (not by a Metropolitan officer), in which the author stated that he knew more of the "Ripper murders" than any man living, and then went on to say that during the whole of August 1888 he was on the tiptoe of expectation. That writer had indeed a prophetic soul, looking to the fact that the first murder of the Whitechapel miscreant was on 31st August of that year of grace.
>
> —Sir Melville Macnaghten, *Days of My Years*, 1914

Among those doughty souls who have devoted their lives to unraveling the mystery of Jack the Ripper, the dozen or so killings that constitute the Whitechapel murders fall into two categories.

The first, the so-called canonical victims, allows for just five women unequivocally believed to have fallen prey to the Ripper himself. The remainder are grouped together, according to the researcher's sympathies, as either "forgotten" victims, or another killer's responsibility altogether.

Martha Tabram falls into that latter category.

No matter that the savagery of her murder filled every observer with unprecedented horror; no matter that personages as lofty as Walter Dew, Sir Robert Anderson (head of Scotland Yard's Criminal Investigation Department—the CID) and Inspector Frederick Abberline, who would soon be leading the search for the killer, all believed that Martha was slaughtered by the same man who would later strike down Mary Ann Nichols, Annie Chapman, Elizabeth Stride, Catherine Eddowes and Mary Jane Kelly.

Other sources, including the chief constable of Scotland Yard, Sir Melville Macnaghten, credited their man with just five killings. But they do not necessarily do so on evidential grounds alone.

A "typical" Whitechapel alleyway, albeit seen from a century or more's distance. *Alamy*

Today, it is a source . . . not of pride, but of at least a certain satisfaction, that the Whitechapel murderer was never caught. For if he had been, where would the mystery be?

For over a century and a quarter, some of the keenest minds in criminology, professional and otherwise, have wrestled with the known facts, the accepted guesses and some frankly abominable theorizing, in their bid to solve the case.

For them, no matter how seriously they take their endeavors, it is a fascination, but it is also a hobby—a part of the vast industry that has grown up around the murderer's story, and which reached its most garish crescendo in 2015, with the opening of a Ripper Museum on Cable Street, in nearby Shadwell, wherein family-friendly fun activities include posing for photographs with actors playing both Jack and his victims.

From that perspective, letting "Jack the Ripper" escape was one of the most farsighted things Scotland Yard ever did.

For the men actually charged with capturing the killer at the time, however, their failure to apprehend him was a crucifying disgrace, a black mark on their careers that no future glory could ever erase.

Walter Dew, for example, would go on to win the admiration of all via his dogged pursuit of the murderous Dr. Crippen, literally chasing him across the Atlantic to arrest him as Crippen docked in New York. By the time of his retirement, Dew could proudly claim to have solved every murder he ever investigated. All apart from one—Whitechapel.

Again, Dew believed that the same man killed more than five times. But his superiors shook their heads. Five killings was quite enough for one unknown assailant to be credited with.

It didn't solve the mystery surrounding all the other deaths that fell beneath the banner of the Whitechapel murders, but it allowed them to be pushed into the shadows, so that today, many of the people who know "the Ripper's" story are completely unaware that there were any other deaths, a conspiracy of ignorance that not only affects "official" studies of the case, and nonfictional accounts of events, but which has transmitted itself to entertainment as well.

The local press was equally reticent to link the deaths and attacks that had so far taken place, at least until circumstance demolished any belief that the murder of Martha Tabram was an isolated occurrence. In an editorial published in its August 25 edition, the *East London Advertiser* proclaimed:

> It has been our unpleasant duty, these last few weeks, to chronicle
> an exceptional amount of crime which has been committed in the

East End. We readily admit that it is to the sensitive mind unpalatable reading, but the obligation is laid upon a newspaper to reveal in its social diagnosis the worst as well as the best features of human action.

This week the record of crime has been increased by another tragic murder, together with three cases of supposed infanticide. So quickly has one tragedy followed another that it would almost seem as if there was a reason for crime as well as a reason for everything else.

But after all, reducible as most things are now to a spiritual or natural law, all these unhappy circumstances may only be a chain of singular coincidences, having not the remotest connection with each other.

Already, however, there was a belief that the East End was suddenly being viewed as London's own Murder Mile in the eyes of the rest of the metropolis.

In January 1888, a woman known locally as Mad Florrie was charged with killing her newborn daughter. In July, a dead baby boy was found wrapped in brown paper in an alleyway in Limehouse. In August, the decomposing remains of a newborn girl were discovered on an underground train heading toward the East End.

It did not seem to matter that similar cases were also reported from as far west as Battersea and Kensington, as far north as Stoke Newington and Edmonton, and as high up the social chain as Mayfair. Angrily, the newspaper continued:

Now a murder in Whitechapel or Bethnal Green is regarded by the public altogether differently from a similar occurrence in Belgravia or Mayfair. "Crime clothed in greatness" . . . is always treated very tenderly by Mrs. Grundy [a popular term for the upper-class busybodies who were prone to pontificate on matters of class and breeding], who has ever much sympathy for those "rich in this world's goods". But let a poor man sin in East London—that dreadful vile place to her way of thinking—then "virtue rears a high seat, and justice stern must fill it."

Perhaps she even goes so far as to suggest a moral top-boots and blanket society for the poor savages in the howling wilderness of the East End. Indeed, some fearful-minded persons think the inhabitants of particular parts of our district are all ruffians and viragoes, who acquired a taste for thieving and violence in their mother's arms. The finger of scorn is only too frequently held up to us by those whose sense of justice and even common honesty should tell them how undeserved is this wholesale condemnation. Such opinions and sentiments are so ridiculous that were it not for the harm they do, it would not be worth while to notice them.

According to the newspaper's own understanding of "the facts," statistics proved that the East End was no more a hotbed of crime than any other part of the city, or even the country.

Taking into consideration its area, which is extensive, and its population, which is most varied, there is but an ordinary average of public offense, although the customary sensational headline, "Another East-End Tragedy", is frequently to be met with.

Notwithstanding the unusual amount of recent crime in our district—crimes in which the worst human passions have been shown in all their fiendish ignominy—there is no cause for despair over the state of the people.

Indeed, those same statistics, spread over two generations of East End life, suggested that there had actually been "a happy improvement in our condition."

The defensive tone of the editorial was not misplaced, even then. The events of the following Friday, August 31, however, would perhaps go some way to offering some succor to the paper's intended targets.

7

Firing the Canon

The Murder of Mary Ann Nichols

Another most horrible murder was perpetrated in Whitechapel yesterday morning. At an early hour, as a police-constable was on his beat in an obscure thoroughfare, he came upon the body of a woman, with her throat cut from ear to ear.

On the arrival of a doctor she was removed to the mortuary, where an examination revealed the fact that there were many other shocking wounds upon her person. Though lifeless she was not quite cold, showing that the crime had not been long committed. Late in the day she was identified as a woman named Nichols, who had led a loose and miserable life, and had at one time been an inmate of the Lambeth Workhouse. So far the police have no clue to the murderer.

—Daily Telegraph, *September 1, 1888*

There is one other significant reason why some of the Whitechapel murders are attributed to a single killer, and others have been pushed to one side, and that is the nature of the killings themselves. For they, too, fell into two distinct categories.

Extravagant violence was common to all, together with merciless savagery. But some, once beyond those extremes, were nevertheless relatively straightforward, inasmuch as the victim was killed, or at least left for dead. Others, however, could be said to have continued on after the murder itself, an entire new sheen of horror and premeditation to be spread across the initial act of brutality.

The argument for all (or most) of the murders to be blamed on one killer begins with the assumption that the attacker had not yet refined his methods—that he was still finding his way into the labyrinth; or, perhaps, that he had a greater fear of disturbance or discovery than he would later evince.

Against that is the belief that he simply knew what he wanted to do, and didn't need any practice. Both are fine theories; both have their merits.

And both converged in the early hours of August 31, 1888, in a mean little street called Buck's Row.

Like so many of the neighboring streets, the two-up, two-down cottages that opened onto the sidewalks of Buck's Row were overshadowed by industry. Brown and Eagle's wool warehouses lined the north side of the street; Essex Wharf, a railroad terminus linked to a coal depot loomed at one end of the street. There was a pub, the Roebuck, on the junction with Brady Street; Brown's stable yard; and, overseeing them all, the magnificent Victorian edifice of the Buck's Row Board School.

It was twenty of four in the morning of August 31 and one Charles Cross was passing the stable yard gates when he spotted what looked like a bundle of tarpaulin lying there. Crossing over the road to investigate, he realized that the bundle was, in fact, a woman. Her skirts were drawn up toward her waist, her bonnet lay on the ground close by.

He was not alone on the street; another man was walking a few yards behind him. Cross hailed him—"Come and look over here." The stranger, Robert Paul, joined him, and Cross knelt to touch the woman's hands, lying unmoving at her sides. He thought she was dead; Paul, however, placed a hand on her chest and was certain he felt a faint heartbeat. Her face, too, still felt warm.

Knowing there was nothing they could do, the pair rearranged the woman's skirts, and then set out to find a policeman—not realizing that there was one whose beat had just taken him onto Buck's Row, a few yards behind them.

PC John Neil was not based at Whitechapel—his headquarters were in Bethnal Green—but the two division's territory overlapped in a number of places, and this was one of them.

Now he, too, was confronted by a corpse.

It is Cross's discovery of the body that caught Swedish journalist Christer Holmgren's attention in the late 1980s. Apparent inconsistencies within Cross's tale of the discovery, and in particular the amount of time that elapsed between that moment and Robert Paul's arrival, made Holmgren wonder how much else about his story was perhaps unreliable.

For the inconsistencies did not end, even after the two men did locate a policeman, PC Jonas Mizen. According to the PC's testimony, Cross told him that a woman was lying on the ground in Buck's Row, although they weren't sure whether she was dead or drunk, and then claimed there was already a policeman at the scene, and that they were effectively delivering a message from him. This was the lie, said Holmgren, that instantly grabbed his attention.

However, Cross was quizzed on that very same point at the inquest, and denied ever having said such a thing, "because I did not see a policeman in Buck's-row." And besides, by the time Mizen reached the site, there *was* a PC inspecting the body.

Neil had already passed down Buck's Row once, around 3:15, and noticed nothing. Now, at 5:15, he too spotted the bundle and went over to investigate. Then, holding up his police-issue lantern, he saw something that the two men had missed in their more cursory, shocked examination. The woman's throat had been cut, and blood was still oozing from the wound.

He heard the familiar tread of another policeman on Brady Street, and he flashed his lantern to signal for aid. PC John Thain, a friend of Neil's, ran toward him, then doubled back to fetch a doctor whose surgery was barely 300 yards away.

A crowd was beginning to gather. Charles Bretton, Henry Tomkins and James Mumford worked at a slaughterhouse on nearby Winthrop Street, and had been drawn to the scene by PC Thain's excited cries of murder.

Patrick Mulshaw, a night watchman at the sewage works, followed them—he had been tipped off, he said, by a passerby whose manner of speech certainly marked him out as a cut above the Whitechapel norm: "Watchman, old man," this stranger called out. "I believe somebody is murdered down the street."

PC Mizen was next to arrive, only to rush off to call an ambulance, by which time Sergeant Henry Kirby had arrived on the scene. Together, he and PC Neil began their investigations, awakening the residents of the nearest cottages to ask whether they had heard any sounds in the night.

They had not, and that despite the women of both households claiming to have been either awake, or sleeping lightly, throughout the early hours of the morning.

By now, Dr. Llewellyn had arrived, and once he had pronounced the woman dead, the body was lifted onto the handcart that doubled as an ambulance and pushed to the workhouse mortuary in Eagle Place—leaving the men who had lifted the body onto the cart to marvel at the amount of blood they had got on their hands.

There was more blood on the sidewalk, but a bucket of water thrown by one of the occupants of New Cottage, closest to the murder scene, washed it away, around the same time as, at the mortuary, two of the Whitechapel Workhouse's pauper inmates were busying themselves washing the woman's corpse. And discovering, to their horror, the true source of all that blood, details that duly appeared in the *East London Advertiser* the following day.

> It was found that, besides the wound in the throat, the lower part of the abdomen was completely ripped open, with the bowels protruding. The wound extends nearly to her breast, and must have been effected with a large knife.
>
> As the corpse lies in the mortuary, it presents a ghastly sight. The victim seems to be between 35 and 40 years of age, and measures five feet two inches in height. The hands are bruised, and bear evidence of having engaged in a severe struggle. There is the impression of a ring having been worn on one of the deceased's fingers, but there is nothing to show that it had been wrenched from her in a struggle. Some of the front teeth have also been knocked out, and the face is bruised on both cheeks and very much discoloured.
>
> [The] deceased wore a rough brown ulster, with large buttons in front. Her clothes are torn and cut up in several places, bearing evidence of the ferocity with which the murder was committed.

Omitted from the piece was Dr. Llewellyn's belief that not only would it have taken the killer some five minutes to complete his handiwork, but also that all the signs pointed toward a killer with at least a rudimentary knowledge of anatomy.

Meanwhile, inquiries were still taking place on Buck's Row. It seemed, again according to the *East London Advertiser*, that "an affray" of some kind had been heard on Buck's Row "shortly after midnight"—that is, some three hours before PC Neil's first visit to the street. "But no screams were heard, nor anything beyond what might have been considered evidence of an ordinary brawl."

Of one thing, however, the paper was prophetically certain: "the police unfortunately will have great difficulty in bringing to justice the murderer or murderers."

Meanwhile, the fears of that earlier newspaper editorial, regarding the outside media's own attitudes toward Whitechapel and the East End, were borne out by the rest of the morning's headlines.

From *The Times*: "Another murder of the foulest kind was committed in the neighbourhood of Whitechapel in the early hours of yesterday morning."

From the *Evening Standard*: "A woman of the class known as 'unfortunate' was murdered under circumstances of a most revolting character in Buck's row, Whitechapel road, yesterday morning; and as this is the second murder of the same kind which has taken place within three weeks, the whole district is in a great state of excitement."

And from *The Star*, the closest thing to a modern tabloid that the era had to offer:

> Have we a murderous maniac loose in East London? It looks as if we had. Nothing so appalling, so devilish, so inhuman—or, rather non-human—as the three Whitechapel crimes has ever happened outside the pages of Poe or De Quincey. The unravelled mystery of "The Whitechapel Murders" would make a page of detective romance as ghastly as "The Murders in the Rue Morgue." The hellish violence and malignity of the crime which we described yesterday resemble in almost every particular the two other deeds of darkness which preceded it. Rational motive there appears to be none. The murderer must be a Man Monster . . . .

It was some hours before the body was finally identified, as police followed up a marking on one of the woman's petticoats that could be traced to the Lambeth Workhouse on Princess Road.

Immediately, the establishment's matron was called in, and while she failed to identify the body, another of the workhouse's occasional inmates, Mary Ann Monk, was able not only to name the dead woman, but also to recall that they had indeed met at Lambeth Workhouse, some six years earlier. More recently, they had been drinking together just a few weeks earlier. The body was formally identified the following day by both the dead woman's ex-husband and her eldest son.

Mary Ann Nichols had just marked her forty-third birthday, on August 26, when she was murdered. A tiny woman, just five-foot-two with delicate features, high cheekbones and a youthful flare that belied what was then considered her advancing age, she nevertheless bore the scars of a rough life—graying hair, missing teeth and what friends described as a melancholic spirit.

Little was known about her life before she took to the streets, just the same snatches of conversation or asides that many of the women in her profession uttered. Further details, however, were filled in by her father, a blacksmith named Edward Walker.

She had been married once, to a printer named William Nichols, and they'd had five children before the marriage ended—apparently when William embarked upon an affair with another woman. That was in early 1880, and by September, Mary Ann was living at Lambeth Workhouse.

In 1883, she moved in for a time with her father, but she was already drinking heavily and soon moved away again. She also took up with a young man she had dated prior to her marriage, one Thomas Stuart Drew, but the relationship was short-lived. By the end of 1887, Mary Ann was sleeping rough on the streets around Trafalgar Square, and returned to the workhouse.

Early in the new year, 1888, Mary Ann's life seemed to turn around. Through the workhouse, she was offered a job as a domestic servant with a family in Wandsworth, Samuel and Sarah Cowdry. The last letter she ever wrote to her father overflowed with her excitement at being presented with such a fresh start in life.

> I just write to say you will be glad to know that I am settled in my new place. and going all right up to now. My people went out yesterday and have not returned, so I am left in charge. It is a grand place inside, with trees and gardens back and front. All has been newly done up.

HE SAW A BODY ON THE PAVEMENT.

Finding the corpse of Mary Ann Nichols, from a period magazine.   *Alamy*

They are teetotallers and religious so I ought to get on. They are very nice people. and I have not too much to do. I hope you are all right and the boy has work. So good bye for the present.

She signed the letter "Polly," a childhood nickname that she still used in adulthood. (At least one of the women who were called to identify her body knew her, indeed, by that name alone.)

Her new lifestyle did not last long, however. One day her employers discovered that a small amount of clothing had gone missing—stolen and presumably sold by their servant.

Mary Ann was dismissed and by the time summer rolled around, she was sharing a room with three other women at Wilmott's boardinghouse at 18 Thrawl Street. Even more humiliatingly, she could not always even guarantee having the four pennies she needed to pay for a bed.

On at least one night during the last week of her life, she wound up at the White House—which, despite its grand name, was effectively a doss house on Flower and Dean Street, where the inmates were shelved two per bed, with no separation of the sexes. Small wonder, then, that many people regarded it as little more than a brothel.

The last day of Mary Ann's life saw her back on Thrawl Street, probably spending her day in the pubs, but perhaps wandering further afield as well. Earlier that evening, a fire had broken out down at the docks, in a vast warehouse packed with alcohol. The ensuing conflagration could be seen for miles around, and attracted crowds to match, as countless barrels of brandy exploded, while the fire ships clustered helplessly on the river around it, pumping the Thames into the flames.

Now a boat moored alongside the warehouse caught alight; and then a neighboring warehouse filled with coal. It was one of the largest conflagrations the docks had seen in years, and of course, the crowds could not get enough of it, cheering every explosion, willing the flames to spread and increase the spectacle. Only as it became clear that the firemen were finally gaining the upper hand did the crowds begin to disperse, and maybe Mary Ann had spent some time there. Crowds were always a fine place to meet customers.

By half past midnight, however, she was back in Whitechapel, as she was seen leaving the Frying Pan, a pub on the corner of Thrawl Street and Brick Lane, by a passing police officer, Detective Inspector Helson. Fifty minutes after that, she was back at Wilmott's, sitting by the fire in the communal kitchen area when the lodging house deputy asked her for her nightly fourpence.

She didn't have it, but she seemed confident she would be back soon enough with the necessary coin. "I'll soon get my doss money," she said as she scooped up the black hat that sat beside her. "See what a jolly bonnet I've got now."

A little over an hour later, another of Mary Ann's friends, Emily Holland, was making her own way back to Wilmott's, having spent most of the evening watching the warehouses burn. Turning into Osborn Street, she saw Mary Ann coming toward her; they paused and, while a clearly drunken Mary Ann slumped against a wall, talked for a while.

Mary Ann explained what had happened back at Wilmott's, and Emily tried to convince her to come back with her, adamant that together, they'd persuade the deputy to let Mary Ann stay the night. Her entreaties, however, were in vain. Still confident she could raise the money with ease, Mary Ann continued on her way, turning onto Whitechapel Road.

So far as the historical record is concerned, she would be seen by just one more person that night. Her killer.

Once again, the police were faced with a murder and no trace of the murderer; once again, they conducted their investigations with as little public fuss as possible; and once again, the public itself construed their silence to denote inactivity.

But what could the police do? They lived, after all, in an age when even the vaguest rudiments of forensic science were still in their infancy. Fingerprinting had only been suggested as an effective method of detection in 1880, and Scotland Yard was still two decades away from adopting it. Blood and semen typing had yet to be discovered. Indeed, even those methods that were in use, the detection of poisoning, for example, were still viewed with the utmost disdain, a consequence still of the scandalous trial, thirty years before, of the English Dr. Thomas Smethurst.

Charged with poisoning a woman to whom he was bigamously married, Smethurst was condemned by one of the leading toxicologists of the day, Dr. Alfred Taylor, only for the learned man to then admit, in front of a crowded courtroom, that he had made a mistake and there were no traces of poison whatsoever to be found in the woman's body.

That, coupled with the presiding judge's insistence on Smethurst being convicted regardless and the bemused jury's eventual verdict of "guilty," did much to besmirch both justice and the methods used to determine it in the eyes of public and police alike. Science, it was sagely agreed, was no substitute for good, honest police work.

Which is not to say the police turned their backs completely on technology and its potential. For example, there was a widespread belief, or at least a popular theory, that photographing the eyes of a murder victim could offer up a clue, based on the notion that the very last image the eyes registered would be imprinted upon the retina. According to contemporary gossip, the police did try that.

It didn't work.

In general, then, detective work was reliant upon the most physical of clues—bloody footprints leading away from the crime scene; gore-soaked clothing being spotted by a passerby; the careless boasting of a drunkard and so forth. And, as Chief Constable Fred Wensley pointed out in his *40 Years of Scotland Yard* autobiography, there was no substitute whatsoever for simply pounding the beat and keeping your eyes peeled.

Wensley joined the Metropolitan Police's uniformed branch in January 1888, and his early years in the service, many of which were spent in Whitechapel, speak of the rigors that a policeman faced in that neighborhood, at that time.

On several occasions, he suffered a beating at the hands of the mobs that rose up to protect one of their number from arrest, and following one such attack, he spent as long on the sick list as his assailants did in prison, a total of four months. "There were no ethical rules in the . . . code for a rough-and-tumble with a policeman," he wrote. "I thought every rib in my body was broken."

A gifted detective even during his years on the beat, Wensley got a unique and lingering glimpse inside the reality of the life he had chosen, from his berth in Whitechapel, once he'd transferred to the CID: "Men and women ripe for any crime from murder to pilfering were to be found in its crowded slums and innumerable common lodging houses," he wrote.

Many of these were foreign: "the off-scourings of the criminal population of Europe—Russians, Poles, Germans, Austrians and Frenchmen—found a refuge there," he continued. But violence knew no racial boundaries. "British as well as foreign carried knives and guns which they did not hesitate to use.

"Organized gangs of desperate men and lads, armed with lethal weapons, infested the streets, terrorizing whole areas, blackmailing tradesmen, holding up wayfarers and carrying out more or less open robbery."

They all needed to be caught.

"Brain and body were constantly on the alert," he wrote. But while Wensley admitted there were "tricks in every trade," and detection was no exception, he also acknowledged that public expectations were streaking far ahead of the police's own capabilities.

Barely had the Whitechapel murders commenced than a little-known author named Arthur Conan Doyle was publishing his first Sherlock Holmes stories, relating the adventures of the world's most brilliantly analytical detective, and convincing his readership that *this* was how police work should be conducted.

Wensley knew otherwise. He could not, he readily confessed, "miraculously deduce the author of a crime from a piece of burnt matchstick." What he could do was say, "often with reasonable certainty, who was the probable author of a crime by the circumstances in which it was carried out."

Of course he was not perfect, but who (apart from Holmes) can be said to be? Sometimes he blundered, sometimes he missed the mark altogether. And on one instance that he recounts in his autobiography, a piece of deduction that *would* have made Sherlock proud was undone by a criminal who had obviously read the same books!

A series of burglaries was under way, and all seemed to be the work of one man. A man who, according to a single specimen discovered at one of the crime scenes, had a fancy for elaborate, foreign-made buttons.

A modern memorial marking the site of Mary Ann's murder.   *Alamy*

A few days later, Wensley was certain he had his man, a known criminal who was walking up Whitechapel Road wearing a waistcoat adorned with the exact same buttons, *from which one was missing.*

Inquiries were made. The button had been lost on the night of the break-in. The man was arrested, charged and was soon up in court, before the magistrate. At which point he broke the stoic silence that had enveloped him since his arrest, by speaking up in the most public arena possible. The button that the police had in evidence still had its shank attached. But had they inspected his waistcoat (which, in those days before items were routinely taken into police care to be used as evidence, he was still wearing), they would have seen that the shank from his missing button was still in place. Meaning, unless the court believed that a button had been made with two shanks, it could not be the one he had lost.

No matter that it was obvious he had simply had somebody provide him with a shank, which he had then attached to the waistcoat. No matter that he was as guilty as the day is long. The court had no alternative but to acquit the man, and Wensley had no choice but to stand silently by as the freed man wallowed in triumph. "Thought yourself clever, didn't you?" he taunted Wensley. "I was too clever for you that time."

Mary Ann Nichols's killer, like the man or men who slaughtered Emma Smith and Martha Tabram, left no buttons behind. No footprints. If they were seen in the aftermath of their dreadful handiwork, no bloodstains screamed "Murder!" to any observant passerby; no laundry ladies came forward to speak of strange stains on a customer's clothing; no neighbors reported curious comings and goings from a particular house. Or, if they did, the police investigations that followed the tip-off turned up nothing more than an innocent, reasonable, explanation for everything.

Charles Cross was among the men who gave evidence to the inquest, and his story was accepted at face value. It would be over a century later before Christer Holmgren questioned it, and then set out to discover whether Cross could have been involved in the later killings, too.

Admittedly deploying more than a little overeducated guesswork (which included even trying to recreate the route Cross would have taken to get to work), Holmgren finally determined that yes, Cross could have been responsible. His occupation—delivering meat for a company based at Broad Street railroad station—his home address and numerous other tiny incidents all seemed to point to Charles Cross as a likely suspect. And the police had, in fact, questioned him one hundred years before.

Hanbury Street, the scene of the first of the "canonical" killings.

Wikipedia

Unfortunately, Cross was just one of the countless hundreds that the investigating officers had to slowly, painstakingly sift through, a process which, again, translated into a public belief that they simply weren't doing enough to catch the killer.

Because while the police were hunting for the killers of three women, the butcher had now claimed a fourth. On September 8, the body of Annie Chapman was discovered on Hanbury Street.

8

The Vigilante and the Vivisectionist

The Slaying of Annie Chapman

> Something like a panic will be occasioned in London to-day by the announcement that another horrible murder has taken place in densely populated Whitechapel. This makes the fourth murder of the same kind, the perpetrator of which has succeeded in escaping the vigilance of the police . . . . Four poor women, miserable and wretched, have been murdered in the heart of a densely-populated quarter, and not only murdered but mutilated in a peculiarly brutal fashion, and so far the police do not seem to have discovered a single clue to the perpetrator of the crimes.
>
> —Pall Mall Gazette, *September 8, 1888*

Throughout the first weeks of September, several so-called "citizens' committees" were formed, or at least mooted, among the concerned citizens of Whitechapel, all of them proclaiming much the same aims: that they augment the police's own policy of methodically walking the nighttime streets; that they encourage the public in general, and prostitutes in particular, to increase their own vigilance and awareness of their surroundings; and that no suspicious activity whatsoever should be allowed to pass unchallenged.

Circulars were printed, setting out these aims for all to read, and were painstakingly delivered door-to-door around Whitechapel; and, perhaps more importantly (or, at least, temptingly), plans were in motion to raise the money to pay a substantial reward to anybody whose information led to the apprehension of the murderer.

The *Illustrated Police News* tabloid reported upon one such meeting on September 15, at the Crown Tavern on Mile End Road:

> In the absence of Mr. Lusk, the chairman, Mr. Aarons, the proprietor of the tavern, was voted to the chair, and in opening the

Bloody Sunday ranks among the most ignominious actions in the history of the nineteenth century London police force.   *Alamy*

proceedings, said that he had great pleasure in announcing that
Mr. Spencer Charrington, of the brewery adjacent, had, with his
usual liberality, responded to the appeal made to him on behalf of
his fellow creatures. He had sent a cheque for £5, and he would not
have done that unless he had been convinced the amount was for
a much-needed object.

Both Mr. Lusk and Mr. Aarons also contributed five pounds apiece (a
tidy sum in those days), while other donors were named and thanked. It was
even agreed that should the reward not be paid out, the money subscribed
would be donated to the London Hospital.

One cloud, however, hung over the proceedings that no amount of
public generosity could dispel.

Reward money had once been a commonplace incentive; indeed, long
before even the first semblance of a regular police force had been formed,
in 1629, the government of the day instituted a series of rewards designed
to encourage the public to surrender criminals to the authorities. The
earliest act promised a princely forty pounds to anyone handing in a highwayman, with similar sums soon placed on the heads of forgers, burglars
and murderers.

It was a noble gesture, but of course it led to abuse. Men who themselves
were no better than common criminals took to styling themselves "thief-
takers," and not only ratted on their friends, but would also frame others
for crimes of which they, the thief-takers themselves, were guilty.

Legendary among this especially loathsome new breed of criminals, one
Jonathan Wild (1682–1725) was subsequently immortalized in novel form
by both author Henry Fielding (*Jonathan Wild the Great*) and playwright
John Gay—Peachum, the despicable thief-taker in *The Beggar's Opera*, was
unmistakably based on the recently executed Wild.

The policy of offering rewards for pertinent information was officially
discontinued in 1884, but the system continued to be abused. There
were also doubts as to whether it even worked—more often than not, the
announcement of a reward would lead to nothing more than extra work for
the police, as hundreds of spurious tips came in, desperate guesswork from
people hoping to somehow snatch the cash.

The need to bring a swift resolution to the Whitechapel murders must
surely have tempted the authorities to reverse that decision, but nevertheless
they resisted—and, in so doing, aroused even greater public resentment
against the law's apparent lack of concern over the killings. As the *Illustrated
Police News* report continued,

> With one exception, every donor [to the fund] had expressed an opinion that it was the duty of the Government to offer a substantial reward in such cases . . . . Many persons who were ready to lay down £100 towards any charitable object . . . flatly refused to subscribe to this fund on the ground that it was the imperative duty of the Scotland-yard authorities and of the Home Office to offer a pecuniary inducement to persons (not the actual murderer) to come forward and give information.

In the world of fiction, it is one of these vigilante groups that recruits Sherlock Holmes to the cause, a blurring of hard fact and absolute fantasy that comes together in one of the Whitechapel saga's most enjoyable movies, 1979's *Murder by Decree*.

It was not Holmes's first encounter with the murderer; neither would it be the last. Arthur Conan Doyle, although he personally refrained from introducing the two in his own writings, nevertheless took the time to apply his own mind to the riddle, and gifted the world (albeit unintentionally) with the Jill the Ripper theory.

Subsequent writers were less recalcitrant, however; chronologically, Holmes and the Ripper are a perfect fit, after all, and in 1965's *A Study In Terror*, a veritable who's who of British acting talent was conscripted to either solve, or fall prey to, the Whitechapel murders. John Neville played Holmes, Donald Houston was Watson, and around them, Frank Finlay, John Fraser, Anthony Quayle, Robert Morley, Barbara Windsor, Adrienne Corri and Judi Dench either slash or are slashed with abandon.

Murder by Decree's blending of Holmes and the horror, however, was even more seamless.

With Christopher Plummer cast as a startlingly suave detective, James Mason as his bumbling but likable sidekick Watson, and a supporting cast that includes David Hemmings, Frank Finlay (again), Donald Sutherland, John Gielgud and the radiant Geneviève Bujold, *Murder by Decree* opens early on in the life span of the citizens' committees, with just three murders (presumably Smith, Tabram and Nichols) on their mind.

Their initial approach is unsuccessful—Holmes turns them down, only to reconsider when he learns of a fourth killing. From there, the movie spools out equal parts wild fiction, considered theory and popular conspiracy, with the killer ultimately being traced to the highest echelons of British society, and the royal household itself.

The police, throughout it all, remained effectively ineffective.

Enter Leather Apron

The Whitechapel murders were not Scotland Yard's sole preoccupation that year. The previous summer, a well-organized protest movement saw Trafalgar Square, one of the centerpieces of the city, occupied by what polite society could only call the dregs of humanity.

In an attempt to draw attention to the appalling standards of living among the London slums, a vast army of homeless and unemployed men and women abandoned their customary haunts in the rookeries and took to sleeping out in central London instead.

It was, of course, an intolerable situation, and both Sir Charles Warren, who had been appointed commissioner of police just eighteen months previous, and Henry Matthews, the Home Secretary, moved swiftly to remedy it. No less than 2,000 police were stationed in the area, under the guise of maintaining public order, while emergency legislation outlawed all forms of protest marches and meetings in Trafalgar Square.

It was an unpopular decision, not only with the protesters themselves, but also with the left-wing media, which had hitherto treated Warren with a certain degree of respect. Purposefully flouting his authority, the Metropolitan Radical Association organized a protest of its own, calling a meeting in the square for November 13, 1887.

With other left-wing organizations swiftly flocking to the banner—including the Irish National League, protesting conditions in Ireland beneath British rule—the stage was set for a mighty confrontation, and that is precisely what took place.

A massive crowd of protesters attempted to storm the square, to do battle with the 2,000-strong human barricade Warren had established in readiness. Behind the scenes, 3,000 more police, together with an infantry battalion of the Grenadier Guard and a regiment of the mounted Life Guards, were readied to attack. Four

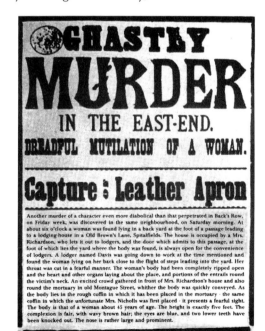

The Leather Apron scare was just the first of so many "named" manhunts. *Wikimedia Commons*

hundred people were arrested that day, and many more injured. Two police officers were hospitalized with stab wounds, and at least one protester was killed, run through with a bayonet. And this time, there was no question that it was wielded by a military man.

"Bloody Sunday" would be remembered as one of the most infamous days in the history of modern British law enforcement—at least until that same name was borrowed for an even more heinous overreaction in Derry, Northern Ireland, in 1972, when another protest was broken up with military gunfire.

Certainly it utterly shattered any semblance of a friendly relationship between the police and great swaths of the working-class public; and while the right-wing media continued to regard both Warren and Matthews with lickspittle admiration, a growing tide of socialist sympathies seemed dedicated to their overthrow.

The Whitechapel murderer played readily into their hands.

His latest victim, Annie Chapman, was barely cold on the slab before the *Pall Mall Gazette* admonished: "the triumphant success with which the Metropolitan Police have suppressed all political meetings in Trafalgar-square contrasts strangely with their absolute failure to prevent the most brutal kind of murder in Whitechapel."

> The Criminal Investigation Department under Mr. [James] Monro was so pre-occupied in tracking out the men suspected of meditating political crimes that the ordinary vulgar assassin has a free field in which to indulge his propensities. Whether or not this is the true explanation of the immunity which the Whitechapel murderer enjoys, the fact of that immunity is undoubted.

In fact, Monro had already resigned the previous week (ironically, on the same day Mary Nichols was killed), to be replaced by Dr. Robert Anderson, a lawyer with extensive experience in what we would now call counterterrorism, again in relation to Ireland. Which doubtless established once again the arena on which the CID's attention was most keenly focused, at the same time as it was guaranteed to outrage the East End's own vast Irish community.

But on the same day as the *Gazette* published its attack, Anderson too fled the scene. He had been suffering from exhaustion for some time now, and this latest assault was surely the final straw. Under doctor's orders, Anderson was dispatched to Switzerland to take in the air and fully recuperate.

The always sensationalist *Illustrated Police News* details Annie Chapman's murder.

The CID was effectively leaderless, and so, briefly, was Scotland Yard itself. Warren, too, was out of the office, away on holiday through the first week of September, and it would be another week before he turned his attention to the absurd situation in which the CID found itself—investigating a series of barbarous murders, with nobody to head up the investigation.

That, Warren believed, was why the killer had gone free for so long. "I am convinced," he wrote on September 15, "that the Whitechapel murder[s] . . . can be successfully grappled with if . . . systematically taken in hand." Indeed, he boasted, "I go so far as to say that I could myself unravel the mystery provided I could spare the time and give individual attention to it."

Unfortunately he couldn't, and so he recommended that another officer, Chief Inspector Donald Sutherland Swanson, be appointed to head up the investigation until Anderson should return. The first file the new man would have opened on his first day in the office would have been the murder of Annie Chapman.

If the newspapers were to be believed, there were several reasons for Swanson to be optimistic regarding his chances of solving the case, not least of all the fact that the murderer had left two items alongside the corpse—the knife, with which he had disemboweled the woman, and a leather apron, of the kind worn by slaughterhouse workers.

But even before fresh events unfolded, Swanson knew—or, if he didn't, the media swiftly informed him—that the latter, at least, could probably be discounted. For the past week, the trickle of information that had seeped out of the investigation had apparently focused upon their search for a man who was indeed known to local prostitutes as Leather Apron.

Details were surprisingly thorough. Although his name was apparently unknown, he was a familiar sight around the streets, and could often be found in the Princess Alice pub on the corner of Wentworth Street and Commercial Street.

He lived, it seemed, by extorting money from prostitutes, and seriously beating those who could not pay, while his nickname arose from one of the two garments in which he was most frequently seen—the other, with an irony Arthur Conan Doyle may or may not have appreciated, was a deerstalker hat.

However, he was not completely unknown to the police, as Sergeant William Thick was quick to point out. In the course of his own daily interactions with the populace, Thick had long been familiar with reports of Leather Apron, and he could even provide a name—either Jack, or maybe John, Pizer, or Piser.

He was short, no more than five-foot-four, and he was in his late thirties, a Polish Jew who worked as a boot finisher and lived on Mulberry Street. The search for Pizer had just begun when *The Star* splashed this latest development across its pages.

Leather Apron was, the paper shrieked, "a strange character who prowls about after midnight," inducing "universal fear among women." He wore soft-soled shoes and carried a knife. He was a Jew. And he was "The Only Name Linked with the Whitechapel Murders."

As is so often the case even today, when a hysterical news outlet shatters law enforcement's silence, *The Star* argued that its sole motive in publishing these details was to alert the populace to the monster in its midst—for who knew how many more women might meet their deaths before the police were ready to act on the information they had received? It certainly had nothing to do with beating their rival newspapers to a major scoop.

To the police, on the other hand, the headlines meant that days of patient investigation had been wasted, and Leather Apron himself now knew of their suspicions.

On September 10, two days after Chapman's killing, Sergeant Thick visited Pizer's home and escorted him to the police station. There, Pizer not only denied that he had ever been known as Leather Apron (a claim his friends and family agreed with), he also insisted that, while he owned such a garment, he had not worn it for some time, on account of being out of work. Again, friends and family could substantiate this.

Where was he on the night of Mary Ann Nichols's death? In a lodging house on Holloway Road in north London, which he left only to look at the glow of the docklands fire from a vantage point on the nearby Seven Sisters Road. He had even struck up conversation with a policeman, discussing the flames and hazarding guesses as to what might be burning. Once that constable was traced, Pizer had a cast-iron alibi.

He had another for the night of Annie Chapman's death, but perhaps he had not required one. The taunting souvenir the real killer had apparently deposited alongside Chapman's corpse left few observers in any doubt that he was a far cooler customer than the fidgety, frightened Pizer.

Cooler, too, than Edward Quinn, the Woolwich laborer who was sitting in a local pub, still recovering from a nasty tumble he had taken on the street outside, when "a big, tall man came in and sat beside me, and looked at me. He got me in tow, and gave me some beer and tobacco, and then he said, 'I mean to charge you with the Whitechapel murders'."

Another glimpse into the boundless imagination of the nineteenth century media.

Quinn thought he was joking, but his companion was in deadly earnest. Quinn's accident had left him with bloodstained face and knuckle, and though the man "then dropped the subject, [he] took me for a walk until we got to the police station, where he charged me with the Whitechapel murders."

In court the following week, on a charge of drunkenness, Quinn remained outraged.

"Were you not drunk?" asked the magistrate, Mr. Fenwick.

"Certainly not, sir," answered Quinn. And when the magistrate recommended he be remanded in custody until the following day, Fenwick's patience snapped.

"This is rather rough. I am dragged a mile to the station, and locked up, and [now] I am to wait another day with all this suspicion of murder hanging over my head?"

"I will take your own bail in £5 for your reappearance," conceded Fenwick, but Quinn was not satisfied.

"I object to the whole thing. Me murder a woman? I could not murder a cat." To laughter from the court room, the prisoner was released.

Annie Chapman's killer remained at large.

Annie Eliza Smith was born in 1841, the illegitimate daughter of George Smith, serving in the Second Regiment of the Life Guards and Ruth Chapman. They were a reasonably well-to-do family, and Annie was lucky in marriage too, wedding one of her mother's relatives, John Chapman, whose job as a coachman frequently saw him engaged by the higher echelons of London society. At one point, the couple called Bruton Mews home, and later, around 1880, they were living on the country estate of Sir Francis Tress Barry, in the small town of Clewer, in Berkshire, where John Chapman was employed as both coachman and stable boy.

Their happiness was to prove short lived. Annie was a drinker and a drunkard, prone to public outbursts that not only brought her to the attention of the police, but heaped embarrassment on the head of her husband's employer.

Finally, it seems, John offered her a choice. She could remain sober and stay in Clewer with her family—the couple had two children, a son and a daughter. Or she could continue drinking and go back to London.

Annie chose the latter.

She would not starve. John arranged to send her a weekly allowance of ten shillings, and though much of it went to alcohol, Annie continued to thrive. But on Christmas Day 1886, John passed away, felled by dropsy and cirrhosis of the liver, and Annie was suddenly destitute.

She took whatever jobs she could find. For a time, she made a meager living doing crochet work; she also became a familiar sight at Stratford Market, selling flowers, matches or anything else she could peddle.

A new man came into her life, a sieve-maker named Jack, and when they parted in late 1887, she fell in with a laborer she had first met during her days in Clewer, Edward "Ted" Stanley. Together, the pair drifted between the doss houses and cheaper lodgings of Whitechapel, just two more people doing their best to keep body and soul together.

In fact, Annie was seriously ill by now, rotting from the inside with both brain and lung cancer, although she had no way of knowing that. She was aware that something was seriously wrong, however, and on the Sunday before her death, she told a friend, Amelia Farmer, that she was considering checking herself into the casual ward at the hospital.

Three days later, on Wednesday, she did so, remaining there for two nights before returning to Crossingham's boardinghouse on Dorset Street, on Friday.

There she spent the evening, drinking with one of the other lodgers, but sometime after 1:00 a.m., the watchman, John Evans, asked her for the money that would pay for a bed for the night.

She didn't have it, but cheerfully explained that she could easily get it, and that Evans shouldn't let anyone else claim her bed. And then, chillingly replaying the last hours of Mary Ann Nichols's life, she stepped out onto Dorset Street. Evans, who had walked her to the front door, remained in the doorway watching as she turned into Little Paternoster Row, heading toward Brushfield Street.

By sunrise the following morning, she was lying dead in the backyard of a house on Hanbury Street. Her legs were drawn up, her feet on the ground and her knees facing outward. Her abdomen had been split open, and her intestines removed, then heaped behind one shoulder. Her uterus had been removed, together with the upper portion of her vagina and a part of her bladder—they never were recovered. The actual cause of death, again as with Mary Ann Nichols, was a gaping wound in her throat, deep and vicious enough that it all but decapitated her.

Hanbury Street had been busy that morning. John Fennell Richardson, a resident of nearby John Street, made a habit of dropping by the lodging house his mother ran, number 29, on his way to work every morning.

THE FRONT OF 29, HANBURY STREET.

THE REAR OF 29, HANBURY STREET.
(The + shows where the body was found.)

The murder scene on Hanbury Street. *Alamy*

It was, all agreed, a perfectly respectable business, its rooms let to long-term tenants who were in full-time employment. In fact, Richardson's only reason for visiting was that there had been a break-in a short while before, and he was anxious to prevent a repeat occurrence.

He arrived around 4:50 a.m. and, as was his custom, made certain that both the front and back doors were locked, and that nothing looked untoward around the property. Then he went on his way. Had there been anything unusual in the backyard, he was adamant, he would have spotted it.

Twenty-five minutes later, in the house next door, glassblower Charles Cadosch got up and prepared to begin his own workday, stumbling out into the predawn backyard on his way to the outhouse.

Now there *was* activity at number 29: muffled voices in the garden—a woman (or, at least, Cadosch thought it was a woman) saying "no," and then a gentle thump as though something had fallen against the fence. But he thought nothing of it. He left the house for work and, glancing up at the clock on Christ Church, saw it was precisely 5:32. Like Richardson, he was beginning just another normal day.

But turning into Hanbury Street just a couple of minutes before, as the Christ Church clock struck 5:30, a Mrs. Elizabeth Long saw a man standing talking to a woman outside number 29—"dark," like a foreigner, she said, wearing a dark coat and a brown deerstalker hat.

He looked to be around forty years of age, and as she drew closer, Mrs. Long heard the man ask, "Will you?" and the woman answer, "Yes." The man's face had been turned away from her, so Mrs. Long really caught but a glimpse of his profile. But when she was shown Annie's body at the mortuary, she had no hesitation in identifying it as the woman she had seen on the street.

Moments later, in number 29, one of Mrs. Richardson's lodgers came downstairs and discovered the front door wide open. Puzzled, he turned and walked toward the back door, and peered out into the yard. There lay Annie Chapman, in a pool of her own blood and guts.

A small crowd gathered, other passersby Davis called to look at the body. Then they scattered, in search of a policeman. It took time to find one—in fact, the first PC they met was on fixed-point duty at Spitalfields Market, and under orders not to leave his post. But another, Inspector Joseph Chandler, had been alerted by the sight and sound of four men racing excitedly out of Hanbury Street, and made his own way to the scene.

A nearby doctor, George Bagster Phillips, was called, and the body was transported to the morgue. Phillips estimated it would have taken the killer "the best part of an hour" to complete his barbaric dissection, but more importantly, he estimated the time of death at no less than two hours before he examined it. Which not only suggested that Annie was already lying there when John Richardson carried out his inspection, but calling into question, too, the events related by Cadosch and Long.

At the inquest, the coroner dismissed the doctor's estimate as being completely wrong. But the police stuck by his findings, and both of those testimonies were ignored.

Besides, this time the killer had left them some clues.

Or had he?

Despite the claims of the newspapers, there was no knife left behind at the scene, while the taunting leather apron turned out to be the property of John Richardson. All the police had to go on, once Cadosch and Long's statements were discarded, was the fragment of an envelope found among the dead woman's belongings, in which she kept the pills she'd been given

A local vigilance committee, in the pages of the contemporary press. *Wikimedia Commons*

that week in the casual ward. On the front, the postmark showed it had been mailed in London on August 28. On the back was the seal of the Sussex Regiment.

With inquiries into Martha Tabram's death still ongoing, and the military connection still not exhausted, this looked like a major breakthrough.

But it wasn't.

Visiting the town of Aldershot, where the Sussex was then based, detectives discovered not only that anyone passing through the camp could have laid their hands on such an envelope, but that anybody visiting the post office could have, too.

And though some detectives remained hopeful that the envelope might still have a story to tell them, even that soupçon of solace was snatched away when the police learned where Annie had got the envelope: from the floor of the boardinghouse where she spent her last evening, after the box in which she kept her pills accidentally got broken.

Once again, the murderer had vanished like the mist, leaving only mystery and mayhem in his wake, as the *Daily News* breathlessly reported:

> On Saturday one more crime was added to the ghastly series of Whitechapel murders. Just before six that morning a woman was found murdered and mutilated at a lodging house in Hanbury street, Whitechapel road. She was of the same class as Mary Ann Nichols, and she was butchered in much the same way. If there was a difference, it was in favour of the earlier victim. The head of Annie Chapman, the latest, had been nearly severed from her body by one stroke of a sharp knife, and her mangled remains had been disposed about her in a way that suggested a delight in the slaughter for the slaughter's sake.

The murderer had decoyed the woman into the house, slain her in the yard, robbed her of her sham rings, inflicted nameless indignities on the dead body, indignity upon indignity, horror upon horror, and got clean away. The house teemed with life; it was near the hour of rising for most of the inmates, yet no human being heard a cry or an alarm. The swiftness of it, the perfect mystery of it, are heightening effects of terror. The wildest imagination has never combined in fiction so many daring improbabilities as have here been accomplished in fact.

Discomforted policemen, a terrified populace, a string of gory murders and a killer who came and went like the wind. The press, the law knew, was having a field day. But at least the police had one consolation.

On September 8, as Annie's last movements were pieced together, and witness statements were being collected, they still had a suspect—Leather Apron.

By September 12, when John Pizer appeared at the inquest and was conclusively cleared of any involvement in the killings, the investigation was back to square one.

9

A Nineteenth-Century Identity Parade

Less a "Whodunit" Than a "Who-Is-Still-Doing-It?"

Let us assume for a moment that [the killer] was a man of prominence and good repute locally. Against such a man, in the absence of direct evidence, it is too much to expect that local police officers would hold such a terrible suspicion. And, assuming this to be the case, the man's amazing immunity can be more readily explained. The same qualities which silenced the suspicions of his women victims would keep him right with the police officers who knew and respected him.

—*Walter Dew*

Not every suspect was interviewed, not every one was even identified. On September 14, a short, dark-haired man with a mustache and false whiskers terrified the caretaker in the Tower Subway when he asked, "Have you caught any of the Whitechapel murderers yet?" Without waiting for a response, he then produced a foot-long knife with a cruel, curved blade, and snarled, "This will do for them."

And then he vanished.

No further sightings were made of the well-spoken gent who alerted the night watchman to the murder of Mary Ann Nichols; nor did anyone ever learn the identity of the suspect who one Detective Sergeant Robinson was pursuing through a cabyard in Phoenix Place, Clerkenwell, the day he was set upon by a gang of ruffians.

But doubtless they would have proved as useless as all the others.

Nevertheless, Walter Dew's words were chillingly accurate. A man of quality, or in a position of trust, could *probably* have got away with the murders.

Anyone with fine local credentials—a doctor, a mailman, a delivery-man, a newspaper vendor, or even a police officer—might easily have been behind the murders; indeed, tucked away among the myriad hoax letters the police received regarding (and even confessing to) the killings, at least one claimed to be from a serving policeman, and included the peculiar detail "I'm writing . . . this while in bed with a sore throat, but as soon as it is better I will set to work again." How many hours did the investigators waste, circulating their colleagues in search of a cop with a heavy cold?

Doctors, too, have endured more than their fair share of suspicion, with author Leonard Matters introducing the enigmatic Dr. Stanley to the cast in 1926.

Originally published as a magazine article, before being expanded (in 1929) into the book *The Mystery of Jack the Ripper*, Matters's narrative presented a new Ripper: an apparently respected physician who became an avenging angel after his beloved son contracted a fatal dose of syphilis from a prostitute. Then, with his rage finally sated, he retired to Argentina. (A stage play, *Murder Most Foul*, was based on this theory.)

Another doctor would be fingered in 1928, in author William Le Queux's *Things I Know about Kings, Celebrities, and Crooks*. Few researchers, however, have found even the vaguest semblance of reality in Le Queux's account of Dr. Alexander Pedachenko, a Russian secret agent who was sent to London to discredit the police; and our excursion through the world of potential killers could now easily slip into the realms of pure fiction—a process that itself is as old as the murders themselves.

On November 17, 1888, the *Star* newspaper teased its readers with an article headlined "A Fictional French 'Ripper,'" purportedly recounting a story "being widely circulated" . . .

> that the Whitechapel murders were possibly committed by a certain Nicholas Wassili, who is said to have been placed in an insane asylum in 1872, after he had committed a series of crimes in Paris similar to those that have been lately committed in the East-end of London.
>
> A certain amount of probability has been attached to this theory, in view of the fact that Wassili was, according to the reports, released from confinement last January.
>
> It is doubtful, however, whether such a man as Wassili ever existed. M. Macé, a former Chef de la Sûreté, who is thoroughly

posted in the criminal history of France, has said to an interviewer that no such person committed murders in Paris in 1872.

The only Parisian case in any way resembling the London assassinations was one which occurred about 1875. A certain individual terrified the women in the Rochechouart quarter by repeated assaults. He was captured after five or six of these outrages, and was pronounced insane. He was a foreigner, but not a Russian, and in any case he killed none of his *victims.*

The Killer Was a Clergyman. Maybe.

In 2016, novelist Alex Bell published the intriguing tale of a young Catholic priest sitting through the most horrendous confession he has ever heard, on the afternoon of September 30—only for both the confession and the confessor to take an even more horrific twist before the short story's end.

Published in editor David V. Barrett's 2015 *Tales From the Vatican Vaults* anthology, Bell's "The Confession" was initially inspired, says Bell, by "a book called *Jack the Ripper and Black Magic* by Spiro Dimolianis." The notion strengthened when Bell came across a report in the *Illustrated Police News*, dated 1899, in which a Church of England clergyman claimed the killer had confessed his crimes to a fellow priest a decade before. Bell's tale both builds on, and then deliciously twists, this tale, but she admits, "whether Jack the Ripper really was a priest or not, I'm afraid I'm just as clueless as you are!"

And as clueless as the police were, and other modern investigators remain. A full list of every suspect to have been named over the years would amount to a small telephone directory full of names, with the majority condemned less on the strength of any firm evidence, than they are on the findings of so-called psychological profilers—many of whom could probably fit any subject to any crime if they thought it might get them into a television documentary.

Even before that profession commenced its merry marriage of detail and distortion, however, a remarkable battery of suspects had been accumulated.

In 1908, Danish researcher Carl Muusmann pointed the finger at Alois Szemeredy, an Austrian whose travels also took him to Argentina and the United States, as well as to a stint in a lunatic asylum. There was no evidence ever to suggest Szemeredy visited England, in 1888 or at any other time, but the truth (as so many subsequent authors have demonstrated) rarely gets in the way of a good story.

David Cohen was an itinerant Polish Jew who was arrested in December 1888 and sent first to the workhouse, where he allegedly became violent, and then confined to the asylum at Colne Hatch, where he died the following December. Again, no link was ever made by the police, but author Martin Fido's *The Crimes, Detection & Death of Jack the Ripper* (1987) made a grand stab at proving how surviving records of this sad case could be shifted to fit certain of the descriptions that the police were working on at the time. With, of course, a century's worth of hindsight to back up the revelation.

German-born Carl Feigenbaum, executed at Sing Sing in 1896 for the brutal slaying of his wife, was implicated on the suspicions of his own defense lawyer, William S. Lawton.

According to Lawton, Feigenbaum apparently declared, "I have for years suffered from a singular disease, which induces an all-absorbing passion. This passion manifests itself in a desire to kill and mutilate every woman who falls in my way. At such times I am unable to control myself." Then, when Lawton tested him with the details of a couple of the Whitechapel killings, Feigenbaum fell silent.

A Norwegian sailor named Fogelma allegedly confessed to the crimes sometime around the turn of the nineteenth century, while being held in an asylum in New Jersey. Sadly, he passed away in 1902, and it was 1923 before one of his fellow inmates took the revelation to the press.

Ripperologists have even turned on one of their own. Robert Donston Stephenson was an amateur detective who wrote several letters to, and articles for, the press suggesting both motives for the killings and the means by which they might have been carried out.

He suggested the involvement of the occult (another theme that future authors would build upon); he petitioned the editor of the *Pall Mall Gazette*, W. T. Stead, for financial aid to help him catch the Ripper; and he even named his chief suspect, Dr. Morgan Davies of the London Hospital (where Stephenson was being treated for back pain at the time).

However, another amateur detective, George Marsh, believed Stephenson was also a likely candidate, and so both Davies and his accuser were investigated, before being cleared. According to Melvin Harris, author of *Jack the Ripper: The Bloody Truth*, however: "alone, of all the suspects, [Stephenson] had the right profile of the opportunities, the motives, and the ideal cover. His background, his personality, his skills, his frame of mind, all [equip] him for the fateful role." Stephenson remains among many people's primary suspects.

Another contemporary student of the crimes, L. Forbes Winslow, also boasted his way onto the law's list of suspects. A practicing alienist (as psychiatrists were then known), Forbes Winslow also fancied himself a brilliant detective, and became a familiar sight around Whitechapel, following up on his own theories and suspicions.

"The detectives knew me," he would later brag, "the lodging house keepers knew me, and at last the poor creatures of the streets came to know me. In terror they rushed to me with every scrap of information which might be of value. To me the frightened women looked for hope. In my presence they felt reassured, and welcomed me to their dens and obeyed my commands eagerly, and found the bits of information I wanted."

What, however, did he do with these alleged scraps? He *said* he took them to the police, and was confident enough in his own skills that he even took tales of his investigations to the press. It was one of these investigations that saw Winslow hauled in for questioning.

According to the amateur sleuth, G. Wentworth Bell Smith was a Canadian who rented a room in a lodging house in April 1888, and who baffled his landlord, a Mr. Callaghan, with his strange behavior.

Smith changed his clothes two, three times a day, and never went out without one of the three pairs of rubber-soled boots he owned. He was heavily armed—he possessed at least three revolvers—and his conversation rarely strayed from his favorite topic of hating whores. Indeed, he enjoyed nothing more than sitting his landlord down, and then reading from a great sheath of foolscap papers, fifty or more of the things, upon which he had set down his loathing of "dissolute women."

Matters came to a head on the night of August 7, 1888—the evening upon which Martha Tabram was killed. According to Mr. Callaghan, as quoted by Forbes Winslow, the mysterious Mr. Bell Smith arrived late home that night and, when the maid visited his room the following morning, she discovered bloodstains on his sheets.

He also seemed to have washed the cuffs of the shirt he'd been wearing (but only the cuffs), and soon after that, he left the lodging house, claiming he was returning to Canada.

He didn't. Some days later, Callaghan learned that Bell Smith was still in Whitechapel, and was now propositioning women on the street with the promise of vast riches—one woman claimed to have been offered one pound to join him in a darkened alleyway.

She refused, but that night there was another murder—presumably Mary Ann Nichols. This, too, Callaghan related to Forbes Winslow, who then repeated it to the *New York Herald Tribune*, together with a particularly

Anthony Perkins in *Edge of Sanity*, one of Hollywood's manifold attempts to identify the Ripper.   *Photofest*

damning allegation. Forbes Winslow claimed he had told all of this to the Whitechapel police, complete with explicit details of how and where they could apprehend Bell Smith. He also informed them that, if they did not act upon his suspicions, he would go to the press. They didn't, so he did.

Unfortunately, it was all a lie—or, as Forbes Winslow told Chief Inspector Swanson, a case of misquotation and misrepresentation. In fact, Forbes Winslow had not spoken a word to the police; he had not offered them a single piece of information. He even denied he had shown the visiting *Herald Tribune* journalist the pair of bloodstained rubber-soled boots that he claimed, and the writer had reported, had belonged to the Whitechapel murderer.

In fact, beyond wasting both the journalist's time and the police's, the only contribution L. Forbes Winslow made to the investigation was a vague theory revolving around an escaped lunatic—one which even the great alienist eventually abandoned.

As for the other men the police saw fit to investigate, they too fall by the wayside. Barely a day went by without another "arrest" being announced, but always, the suspect was cleared, be he the short, stout gent with a sandy beard and dark cap who was picked up on a charge of threatening to stab people in the neighborhood of the Tower of London; or Edward McKenna, a sandy-haired Scot, who was apparently pursued by down the street by a gang of youths, who were shouting, "Look what he has behind him!"—a knife. But it was a small knife, said the police, once they searched him; and besides, McKenna had an alibi for all the killings.

An escaped murderer named James Kelly, who knifed his wife in 1883 and escaped from the Broadmoor maximum-security mental institution in January 1888, was briefly linked to the investigation, but only as one of the many "loose ends" the police were then pursuing—any man with a history of violence toward women, and a mental disposition that marked him as dangerous, was considered a possible suspect.

Kelly's tale, however, is nonetheless a fascinating one. He was never recaptured; rather, he wandered the Western world, spending time in France, the United States and Canada, before finally surrendering himself at the gates of the very institution he had escaped from, in 1927. He remained there until his death two years later, and does not seem ever to have been questioned about the events in Whitechapel, forty years earlier.

A Foolish Man

In October 1888, one Alfred Blanchard loudly confessed to the crimes in a pub in Aston, near Birmingham, in the English midlands. He was a Londoner, possibly a traveling salesman, and his words were certainly taken seriously enough for him to be arrested. According to the *Birmingham Press Gazette* newspaper,

> Detective-sergeant Ashby said that on Friday night the prisoner was in a public-house in Newtown Row, and he told the landlord that he was the Whitechapel murderer. He repeated the statement to several people and witness arrested him. When at Duke Street Police Station he denied being the murderer, but witness thought proper to keep him in custody. The police had not yet had time to make inquiries, and knew nothing of the prisoner's antecedents.

> Richard King, landlord of the Fox and Goose, Newtown Row, said the prisoner came to his house about eleven o'clock on Friday morning, and remained till about a quarter past eight at night. During his stay in the house he drank about five and a half pints of beer.

> About half-past twelve o'clock he asked witness what kind of detectives they had in Birmingham. Witness told him he believed them to be very clever men. Prisoner said that it would be a funny thing if the Whitechapel murderer were to give himself up in Birmingham. Witness acquiesced, and prisoner continued, "I am the Whitechapel murderer." Turning round to an elderly gentleman sitting in the bar, prisoner said, "Look here, old gentleman; perhaps you would not think there was a murderer in the house." "I don't know about that," replied the customer; "you might not look unlike one." Prisoner said, "I am one, then."

> Later on the old gentleman asked prisoner had he got the knife with him, and he answered that he had left a long knife behind him. Someone asked prisoner how he did the murders without making the victims scream. He explained that this was done "simply by placing the thumb and finger on the windpipe and cutting the throat with the right hand." He said he had "done six of them in London." He was sober when he made this statement. Turning round to witness prisoner said, "You are a fool if you don't get the thousand pounds reward offered for me; you may as well have it as anyone else."

Once Blanchard was in court, however, it readily became obvious that he had been drinking for three days before he uttered his "confession," and he was swiftly dismissed with just one admonition ringing in his ears: "What a foolish man you have been."

Other confessions, too, were swiftly revealed to have been made in a state of drunkenness. At least four men—John Fitzgerald, Benjamin Graham, William Bull and one whose name was not recorded—informed the Whitechapel police that they were guilty of the murders, only to recant once they had sobered up. Still, the police were duty-bound to investigate their claims, again adding to a caseload that was already inhumanely overstretched.

Yet another confession shocked Whitechapel just two days after Mary Jane Kelly's slaughter in November. The *Pall Mall Gazette* reported, "A man with a blackened face who publicly proclaimed himself to be 'Jack the Ripper', was arrested at the corner of Wentworth-street, Commercial-street . . . ."

> Two young men, one a discharged soldier, immediately seized him, and the crowds which always on Sunday night parade this neighbourhood raised a cry of, "Lynch him". Sticks were raised, and the man was furiously attacked, but for the timely arrival of the police would have been seriously injured. The police took him to Leman-street station.
>
> He refused to give any name, but asserted that he was a doctor at St George's Hospital. His age is about thirty-five years, height 5 ft. 7 in., complexion dark, and dark moustache, and he was wearing spectacles. He wore no waistcoat but had an ordinary jersey vest beneath his coat. In his pocket he had a double-peaked light check cap, and at the time of his arrest was bareheaded. It took four constables and four civilians to take him to the station, and protect him from the infuriated crowd. He is detained in custody.

Somewhat more tantalizing is the anecdote spun by Montague Williams, a magistrate whose courts were very likely those to which any man charged with the Whitechapel murders would be assigned.

> I was sitting alone one afternoon, on a day on which I was off duty, when a card was brought to me, and I was informed that the gentleman whose name it bore desired that I would see him.
>
> My visitor was at once shown in. He explained that he had called for the purpose of having a conversation with me with regard to the perpetrator, or perpetrators, of the East End murders. He had, he said, taken a very great interest in the matter, and had set on foot a number of inquiries that had yielded a result which, in his opinion, afforded an undoubted clue to the mystery, and indicated beyond

any doubt the individual, or individuals, on whom this load of guilt rested.

My visitor handed me a written statement in which his conclusions were clearly set forth, together with the facts and calculations on which they were based ; and, I am bound to say, this theory-for theory . . . struck me as being remarkably ingenious and worthy of the closest attention.

Besides the written statement, this gentleman showed me copies of a number of letters that he had received from various persons in response to the representations he had made. It appeared that he had communicated his ideas to the proper authorities, and that they had given them every attention.

Of course, the theory set forth by my visitor may be a correct one or it may not. Nothing, however, has occurred to prove it fallacious during the many months that have elapsed since the last of this terrible series of crimes.

Williams could not, he said, divulge any further information, as, "possibly, in doing so I might be hampering the future course of justice. One statement, however, I may make, and, inasmuch as it is calculated to allay public fears, I do so with great pleasure. The cessation of the East End murders dates from the time when certain action was taken as a result of the promulgation of these ideas."

In fact, his visitor was a clerk named Edward Larkins, who had already contacted Scotland Yard with the name of one suspect, Antoni Pricha. But Pricha had an alibi and was released; now Larkins was pointing the finger at not one, but four men, a veritable conspiracy of Portuguese sailors named Manuel Cruz Xavier, Jose Laurenco, Joao de Souza Machado, and Joachim de Rocha.

Fortunately for them, but less gratifyingly for Williams, they too were swiftly proved innocent.

Maybe the Killer Was a Murderer?

If random suspicions and drunken stupidity could not provide the key to the mystery, perhaps purportedly similar cases might shed some light upon it.

In April 1889, one W. H. Bury was hanged in Scotland for the crime of uxoricide, having first strangled and then partially mutilated his wife, Ellen, and there were certainly several similarities between his crime and the

THE GREAT SYMBOL OF SOLOMON

Among the numerous theories was one that the Ripper was working to create a map of the Seal of Solomon, each murder site representing one of the six points of the star. *Wikimedia Commons*

Ripper's style. But though the London police did investigate, the evidence did not stack up.

Likewise, when one Frederick Deeming cut the throats of his wife and four children at their lodgings in Liverpool in July 1891, and then murdered his second wife in Perth, Australia, six months later, newspaper rumor was soon insisting that he had been sighted around Whitechapel three years earlier, purchasing knives and acting suspiciously.

Early suggestions that Deeming was in fact living in South Africa at the time have subsequently been demolished; researcher Robin Napper discovered that he was indeed in England, living in Liverpool but regularly traveling down to London, throughout the period in question.

Napper also unearthed evidence that Deemer had contracted syphilis from a prostitute sometime before the birth of his first son, and now nursed such a violent hatred for such women that he openly admitted that, should he happen to kill one, he would not consider it murder. He then proceeded to contradict this vow following his arrest in Perth, by confessing to two of the Whitechapel murders—albeit in a manner guaranteed to confound historians.

He claimed "the last two," but who were they? If canon is to be believed, it would have been Catherine Eddowes and Mary Jane Kelly. Or did he mean Rose Mylett and Elizabeth Jackson? Alice McKenzie and the Pinchin Street torso? Or another brace altogether?

Doubts and misgivings, of course, abound around Deeming, ranging from the distinctly different nature of the killings of which he is known to have been guilty, and those he is merely suspected of, through to the fact that the only time he seems to have positively been to Whitechapel, he was in the company of a woman who not only lived to tell the tale, but who also had never even considered him a likely suspect until she saw his picture in the newspapers after he killed his family.

Nevertheless, following his execution, the following verse was swiftly coined:

> On the twenty-first of May,
> Frederick Deeming passed away;
> On the scaffold he did say —
> "Ta-ra-da-boom-di-ay!"
> "Ta-ra-da-boom-di-ay!"
> This is a happy day,
> An East End holiday,
> The Ripper's gone away.

. . . while Scotland Yard's Black Museum, for many years, described a copy of Deeming's waxen death mask as the face of Jack the Ripper.

Of these suspects (and there are many more), all can be, and have been, dismissed without too much effort. But still, Holmes, in *Murder by Decree*, is surely hanging his head in shame. He unearthed only *two* Rippers.

10

The Devil Makes Work for Idle Hands

The Macnaghten Memorandum, and Other Blood-Red Herrings

> It seemed impossible he could be living in the very midst of us; and, seeing the Metropolitan Police had orders to stop every man walking or driving late at night or in the early morning, till he gave a satisfactory account of himself, more impossible still that he could gain Leytonstone, Highgate, Finchley, Fulham, or any suburban district without being arrested.
>
> —*Henry Smith, 1910*

In the face of so many possibilities, real and imagined, it is surprising that the law's own list of suspects was so short—or, perhaps, not so surprising. The full extent of the investigation has itself long been lost, damaged, destroyed or even stolen along with so many other early Scotland Yard cases.

For all we know, the police really did follow up every lead and pursue every avenue that could ever have been suggested to them, and it is our knowledge of those efforts that should be found wanting, not the efforts themselves. In 1910, Henry Smith—who served as acting commissioner of the Metropolitan Police during the latter stages of the Whitechapel investigation—published his memoir *From Constable to Commissioner*, and recalled:

> I made such arrangements as I thought would insure success. I put nearly a third of the force into plain clothes, with instructions to do everything which, under ordinary circumstances, a constable should not do.
>
> It was subversive of discipline ; but I had them well supervised by senior officers. The weather was lovely, and I have little doubt they thoroughly enjoyed themselves, sitting on door-steps, smoking

their pipes, hanging about public-houses, and gossiping with all and sundry.

In addition to this, I visited every butcher's shop in the city, and every nook and corner which might, by any possibility, be the murderer's place of concealment. Did he live close to the scene of action ? or did he, after committing a murder, make his way with lightning speed to some retreat in the suburbs ? Did he carry something with him to wipe the blood from his hands, or did he find means of washing them ? were questions I asked myself nearly every hour of the day.

Nevertheless, it must also be acknowledged that the paucity of usable evidence and the contradictory nature of a handful of descriptions both litigated against swift detection, while the sheer weight of information that flooded in from the public and the press saw an already overworked force stretched even further.

To that can be added the traditional distrust of the local populace toward the police, while future methods deployed by investigations—painstakingly interviewing every man in the neighborhood via assiduous house-to-house enquiries, for example—were hampered by the transience of so much of the population.

The boardinghouses kept no records of who stayed where on any given night; an outsider checking into such an establishment late one evening, and then departing early the following morning, would scarcely be noticed, as long as he paid his fourpence.

As for tip-offs from the public, the example of Leather Apron proved how unreliable they could be, no matter how persuasive they seemed. Indeed, Leather Apron simply added to the police workload, not so much because of the investigation, but through the hysteria it unleashed upon the streets.

For example, on September 1, the day after Mary Nichols's body was discovered, a local street criminal named George "Squibby" Cullen was shouting abuse at a police constable when a stone that he hurled missed its target and struck a passerby.

Squibby ran, but a week later, the day of Annie Chapman's murder, Detective Walter Dew spotted him and gave chase.

Soon a crowd had joined the pursuit—all convinced that the officer was pursuing the Whitechapel murderer. And with the crowd growing larger all the time, as fresh pursuers joined the chase and started to encircle him, Cullen—who was, in fact, wanted only on a charge of street gambling—must have been delighted to surrender to Dew's custody. He would have been torn to shreds if the mob had caught him.

On another occasion, in Islington, North London, the local police station came under siege from a crowd of some 2,000 people, all convinced that a man and woman who had been arrested for drunkenness on nearby Chapel Street were actually the Whitechapel murderer and his female accomplice—and that the police had already been warned, by letter, that the killer was intending to visit that neighborhood.

The anti-Semitism that was already a fetid undercurrent in Whitechapel life erupted onto the surface, all the more so after John Pizer was cleared. The notion that the murders had been committed by a Jew—if not *this* one, then another—seized the public imagination, fermenting in the cauldron of speculation that the media was stirring up.

The *Star* newspaper pointedly referred to Pizer as a "crazy Jew" and, while he was proven innocent, the remainder of his race remained under suspicion. Jewish businesses were attacked, and Jewish men were beaten up on the streets. Wild accusations were hurled at anyone who looked Jewish, or even vaguely foreign.

A bizarre form of patriotism gripped Whitechapel—bizarre because, in a slum where nobody could sink too low, the belief took hold that "no Englishman would commit such murders." It had to be a foreigner.

Entire professions came under suspicion: doctors, slaughterhouse workers, meat porters, even the local pork butcher, as one Jacob Isenschmid was to learn. That he was already known as the *Mad* Pork Butcher should not be held against him, however, nor should the fact that he was indeed mad and would subsequently be placed in an asylum.

That doesn't mean he was the Whitechapel murderer, any more than was the great London stage actor Richard Mansfield. Yet Mansfield, too, was interviewed by the police as a possible suspect.

That August of 1888, one of the most successful stage plays of the London season was an imported American adaptation of Robert Louis Stevenson's *The Strange Case of Dr. Jekyll and Mr. Hyde.*

The tale of a mild-mannered physician who, by quaffing a potion of his own invention, is transformed into a malevolent, murdering monster, *Jekyll and Hyde* created a sensation from the moment it opened at the Lyceum, on the Strand, on August 4.

But it was not the gripping presentation alone that attracted attention. The sickening realism of the murder scenes, too, grasped the headlines, first in the review sections and then on the front pages, after the goriest of them came brutally to life in Whitechapel.

Immediately, Mansfield, so convincing in the Lyceum play's title roles, found himself among the very first to fall under suspicion for the actual killings. Then, when his innocence was established to all, the play itself came under the spotlight for possibly inspiring the killer in the first place!

All across the East End, groups of self-appointed vigilantes took it upon themselves to investigate suspicious-looking characters—although it's certainly clear with whom this artist's sympathies lay.

Alamy

On October 12, long before demand for tickets had been exhausted, the *Daily Telegraph* reported that "the murderous Hyde will peer round the drawing-room windows and leap at his victim's throat for the last time during the forthcoming week. Experience has taught this clever young actor that there is no taste in London just now for horrors on the stage. There is quite sufficient to make us shudder out of doors."

Mansfield also promised to premiere a new play, *Prince Karl*, the following Friday, and to donate the full receipts to the Bishop of Bedford's Home and Refuge Fund for the Poor of the East-end of London. Few people, the *Telegraph* concluded, "will regret Mr. Mansfield's determination to show us, before he leaves England, a pleasant side of human nature in contrast to the monsters he has conjured up."

Not one of the disappointed cast members or ticket holders could ever have imagined that one day, the very same rampage that sounded the original play's death knell would be the opening act for a fresh rash of shocking plays, movies and even musicals!

Melville's Murderers

The best known, and best respected, repository of Ripper suspects lies within what is known as the Macnaghten Memorandum.

Although Melville Leslie Macnaghten had not been directly involved in the Whitechapel murder investigations (he joined the police force in April 1889, having spent much of his life in India), it is inevitable that the future chief constable would have had his own favored suspects for the case.

He might never have set them down for public perusal, however, had *The Sun* newspaper, in 1894, not reawakened old memories by pursuing a new so-called "lead," one that reached into the very heart of the Metropolitan Police.

Thomas Cutbush was the nephew of the Met's well-respected executive superintendent, Charles Cutbush. However, he was also regarded as a murderous lunatic, who had at least two vicious stabbings to his credit.

Without naming the felon himself—inference and innuendo did that job perfectly—*The Sun* appeared to be suggesting not only that Cutbush was the Whitechapel murderer, but also that Scotland Yard had been aware of the fact all along, and hushed it up to avoid embarrassment. The Yard responded by having Macnaghten first refute all of the newspaper's so-called evidence, and then by noting his own favored suspects, "any one of whom would have been more likely than Cutbush." (It was this same memorandum, incidentally, that instigated the canonical tally of five bodies.)

It is important to remember that none of the men named in the memorandum were officially suspected at the time of the crime—rather, it is an indication of just how much work the police continued to do after the murders stopped, and the weight of the inquiries they undertook.

A suicide named Montague John Druitt, whose drowned and weighted body was discovered in the River Thames on the last day of 1888, is frequently numbered among the leading suspects because Macnaghten wrote of his belief that the killer had committed suicide, and "did indeed at one time lie at the bottom of the Thames." He then named Druitt, and continued, "From private information I have little doubt that his own family suspected this man of being the Whitechapel murderer; it was alleged that he was sexually insane."

As for evidence, however, there is not a shred, and Druitt was never under any form of investigation during his tragically curtailed lifetime.

Similarly, the case against local cigar maker Hyam Hyams is based more on the fact that he fit another of Macnaghten's theories—that the killer was a low-class Jew—than on any surviving evidence.

That said, knowing glances have been cast at the fact that Hyams was known to be a violent man who spent his last years in and out of asylums, after he attacked and stabbed his wife. But one has to ask where a poor cigar maker would acquire the skill to disembowel his victims with the surgical precision the real killer exhibited.

More damning were Macnaghten's suspicions against Aaron Kosminski, a Polish Jew who "became insane owing to many years indulgence in solitary vices [a euphemism for masturbation]. He had a great hatred of women, specifically of the prostitute class, and had strong homicidal tendencies."

BLIND-MAN'S BUFF.

(As played by the Police.)

"TURN ROUND THREE TIMES, AND CATCH WHOM YOU MAY!"

From the pages of *Punch* magazine, a comment on the law's apparent blindness.

Wikimedia Commons

A well-dressed stranger, a foggy night . . . the Ripper could have been anyone, anywhere.

J. R. Pepper

Kosminski was finally committed to Colney Hatch lunatic asylum in March 1891, after attacking his sister with a knife, but the law had been watching him long before that.

A barber by trade, who arrived in England as a refugee of the Russian pogroms of the early 1880s, Kosminski has always been high up on the list of likely suspects, both at the time of the killings (Robert Anderson was among those who agreed with Macnaghten) and subsequently—indeed, in 2014, author Russell Edwards's *Naming Jack the Ripper* appeared to confirm Kosminski's guilt once and for all.

Edwards's proof was based upon analysis of DNA evidence discovered on the shawl that Catherine Eddowes was allegedly wearing the night she died. Edwards, however, believed the shawl belonged to the killer—that it was of far too fine a quality to have been the possession of a Whitechapel street-walker—and this assumption appeared to be vindicated by the revelation that it was of Russian manufacture, probably from around Saint Petersburg.

Within a month of Edwards's book's publication, however, the scientist who carried out the DNA analysis was shown to have made what was described as an "error of nomenclature"—he had misread the DNA database used to calculate the chances of a genetic match. Which didn't mean that Kosminski had been proven innocent, just that he was no more guilty than he had ever been.

In other words, the investigation was back where it started, although suspicions regarding Kosminski live on—both as a possible Ripper and also, in the pages of novelist Sarah Pinborough's *Mayhem* (2013) as the hand behind the so-called Torso Murders (see Chapter Thirteen).

Macnaghten's third and final suspect was Michael Ostrog, described in the memorandum as

> a mad Russian doctor and a convict and unquestionably a homicidal maniac. This man was said to have been habitually cruel to women, and for a long time was known to have carried about with him surgical knives and other instruments; his antecedents were of the very worst and his whereabouts at the time of the Whitechapel murders could never be satisfactorily accounted for.

All of which sounds rather promising.

Subsequent researches, however, have proved that while Ostrog may have been mad, and had in fact spent some time in prison, his "homicidal mania" was more likely wishful thinking on Macnaghten's part. The man's only convictions had been for fraud, and the theft of such items as a gold chain, a metal tankard, some books and a microscope. He was not a doctor, either, although he had posed as one on occasion. Just as none of the police's other suspects, including those who confessed, were really aspiring mass murderers.

Abberline Takes the Case

The Killing of Elizabeth Stride

The Police have done nothing, they have thought of nothing, and in their detective capacity they have shown themselves distinctly inferior to the bloodhounds which a few years ago, in the provinces, tracked the mysterious murderer of a little girl to his doom. The trail must run true and clear from Berner-street to Mitre-square, and beyond, for those who have the true instinct of the detective calling. None of the accepted apologies for the shortcomings of the force will cover their repeated failure in these extraordinary cases. The inadequacy of their numbers, though it is absolute in regard to the Metropolitan district taken as a whole, is but relative in regard to the limited area which is the scene of these crimes.

—Daily News, *October 1, 1888*

Punch magazine had never been a friend of the police—or if it had, it was one that proved as willing to mock their frailties as it was to praise their strengths.

In 1863, the magazine published what it called "A Detective's Diary," a lengthy diatribe that purported to recount the daily life of a practicing policeman, but which overflowed with mundanity and even absurdity.

The detectives are on the hunt for a housebreaker, described as being around five-foot-eight in height and having light-colored hair. "We are on the track!"

April 4. [Suspect] examined. Said he hadn't done it. Asked him how it was he came to have light hair and be five feet eight? Was confused. Found out that he'd only just arrived from Birmingham where he had lived all his life. Cautioned and discharged him.

April 5. Saw a man in the street, very tall and dark-haired. [Sergeant] Dodgett said that was his cunning. Took him up. Asked him why he hadn't light hair, and why he wasn't five feet eight inches? He was dum-founded.

Now a quarter of a century later, a second diary appeared in *Punch*.

Monday—Papers full of the latest tragedy. One of them suggested that the assassin was a man who wore a blue coat. Arrested three blue-coat wearers on suspicion.

Tuesday—The blue coats proved innocent. Released. Evening journal threw out a hint that deed might have been perpetrated by a soldier. Found a small drummer-boy drunk and incapable. Conveyed him to the Station-house.

Wednesday—Drummer-boy released. Letter of anonymous correspondent to daily journal declaring that the outrage could only have been committed by a sailor. Decoyed petty officer of Penny Steamboat on shore, and suddenly arrested him.

Thursday—Petty officer allowed to go. Hint thrown out in the Correspondence columns that the crime might be traceable to a lunatic. Noticed an old gentleman purchasing a copy of *Maiwa's Revenge* [a then-popular novel by H. Rider Haggard]. Seized him.

Friday—Lunatic dispatched to an asylum. Anonymous letter received, denouncing local clergyman as the criminal. Took the reverend gentleman into custody.

Saturday—Eminent ecclesiastic set at liberty with an apology. Ascertain in a periodical that it is thought just possible that the Police may have committed the crime themselves. At the call of duty, finished the week by arresting myself.

It was in the midst of this mockery that a new face joined the investigation—or, depending upon your view of affairs, allowed himself to be added to the long line of hapless faces at which the press felt free to take potshots.

Inspector First-Class Frederick Abberline had enlisted in the Metropolitan Police in 1863, quickly rising up the ranks to become a sergeant in 1865 and inspector in 1873, just three days before he was posted to Whitechapel from his earlier beats in north London.

He remained there for fourteen years, until 1887, from all accounts being regarded as "a good copper" by the locals and a knowledgeable one by his colleagues. It was these attributes, after just a year spent at the Metropolitan Police's central office in Scotland Yard, that saw him return to Whitechapel in early September 1888. His understanding of the area,

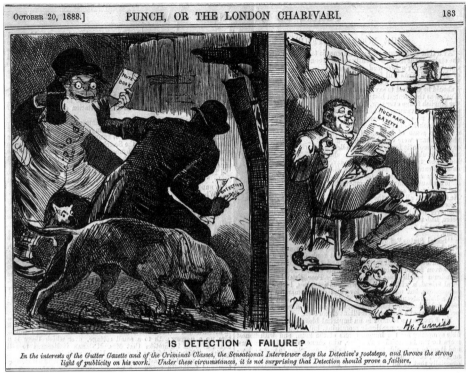

IS DETECTION A FAILURE?

In the interests of the Gutter Gazette and of the Criminal Classes, the Sensational Interviewer dogs the Detective's footsteps, and throws the strong light of publicity on his work. Under these circumstances, it is not surprising that Detection should prove a failure.

From lamentable to laughable—the police's increasingly inept-seeming attempts to capture the Ripper provoked any number of satirical comments and cartoons.   *Alamy*

and his expertise in dealing with the local underworld, established him as an ideal candidate to lead the investigation "on the ground."

Abberline arrived at the height of the furor surrounding Leather Apron and the opening investigations into the death of Annie Chapman, although among his earliest tasks was contending with suggestions that the killer had moved to the country's far northeast, after the mutilated remains of twenty-seven-year-old Jane Beadmore were discovered in the village of Birtley, near Gateshead.

The nature of the attack was certainly suggestive. According to the local *Durham Chronicle & County Gazette*, reporting from the inquest:

> There was a wound on the right side of the face made by a down stroke; a second wound on the left side, behind the ear, made by a sweeping stroke, and the force with which it would be inflicted would stun the deceased and knock her down. Neither of these wounds were mortal.

There was a severe wound in the lower part of the body, inflicted, he thought, when the deceased was down; another wound, an inch or two in length into the abdominal cavity, inflicted by a knife held with a cutting edge upwards; and a third wound, within the abdominal wall, was produced by the withdrawal of the knife or instrument used.

This was undoubtedly a fatal wound, and death would result in a short time. There would be no time for the screaming or struggling—not more than a minute would elapse between the infliction of the wound and death. The intestines protruded from the lower wound, but none were missing, and no attempt had been made to remove them.

Death arose from internal and external hemorrhage from a wound in the lower part of the body.

Of course there was no link to the Whitechapel Murderer; a former boyfriend, William Waddell, was quickly charged and ultimately executed. Disturbing, however, was Waddell's response when he was asked what made him undertake such a savage assault. According, again, to the local paper:

> [He] attributed the crime to his having been so drunk as to having entirely lost his mind. He also stated that he had been reading the accounts of the Whitechapel murders in London, and his mind must have been deranged.

Abberline also needed to investigate charges against one Charles Ludwig, a German barber who was caught red-handed on Leman Street waving a razor and attempting to assault a prostitute named One-Armed Liz Burns, just eighteen years old, but already a familiar (and, as her nickname attests, readily identifiable) sight on the streets.

Ludwig would be in trouble again soon enough; he also attacked the owner of a coffee stall on Whitechapel High Street. But though he was clearly a menace, he was no murderer. In court, he "fully accounted for himself on the nights of the Whitechapel murders" and was discharged.

Another startling development, however, was on the horizon.

At least one and possibly more letters had already been received by the investigators, claiming to have been written by the killer. They were quickly dismissed as hoaxes—like the fake confessions with which the police were now so wearingly familiar, taunts and mockery were also part and parcel of the investigation.

By the time the investigations were over, and on into the next decade, various interested parties had received over 200 different communications, all claiming to be from the killer, posted from all over the country and as far afield as the United States.

On September 27, 1888, however, Scotland Yard was apprised of a letter intended not for law enforcement, but for the media. Addressed to "The Boss, Central News Agency, London City," and again purporting to be the

The infamous "Dear Boss" letter.   *National Archives/Public Domain/Wikimedia Commons* handiwork of the murderer, this particular missive was probably no more or less convincing than its predecessors.

Yet it was destined to change the very iconography of the murders for all time. They were no longer the wicked slashings of a mysterious stranger. They were the methodical work of Jack the Ripper.

> Dear Boss,
>
> I keep on hearing the police have caught me but they wont fix me just yet. I have laughed when they look so clever and talk about being on the *right* track. That joke about Leather Apron gave me real fits. I am down on whores and I shant quit ripping them till I do get buckled. Grand work the last job was. I gave the lady no time to squeal. How can they catch me now. I love my work and want to start again. You will soon hear of me with my funny little games. I saved some of the proper red stuff in a ginger beer bottle over the last job to write with but it went thick like glue and I cant use it. Red ink is fit enough I hope *ha. ha.* The next job I do I shall clip the ladys ears off and send to the police officers just for jolly wouldn't you. Keep this letter back till I do a bit more work, then give it out straight. My knife's so nice and sharp I want to get to work right away if I get a chance. Good Luck.
>
> Yours truly
> *Jack the Ripper*
>
> Dont mind me giving the trade name

A postscript, written at right angles to the letter's main text, continued, with the same disdain for punctuation, "PS Wasnt good enough to post this before I got all the red ink off my hands curse it No luck yet. They say I'm a doctor now." There then followed one final piece of mockery, boldly underlined for emphasis: "ha ha."

But it was the writer's "trade name," not his grammar, that attracted the most attention.

Jack the Ripper! It truly was too perfect.

Why Jack? One theory is that the writer took his inspiration from an equally shadowy character who had transfixed west London half a century previous. Spring-heeled Jack was a monstrous fiend (some reports described him as "an immense baboon, six feet high," others as a ghost or devil with iron claws) who preyed upon lonely travelers, tearing or cutting at their clothes, but generally leaving them unharmed, if utterly terrified.

But Jack was also a common name, and a familiar one. It emphasized the sheer ordinariness of the life and surroundings that he was assaulting.

It was neutral—it had no religious or political connotations. It was very English—as if to deny the insistence that the killer must be a foreigner. It was even a little playful, conjuring nursery images of so many favorite fables and verses: Jack Sprat, who could eat no fat. Jack, the nimble and quick, who leapt over the candlestick. Jack Shepherd, the boy escapologist, long since raised from petty crook to penny-dreadful hero. Jack the Giant Killer.

Even when it was flipped to darker reflections—Jack Ketch, the hangman; Jack Frost, freezing the poor in their sleep—there remained something almost childlike about his choice of name. And that might have been the most horrifying aspect of the entire affair.

Besides, what else *could* he have called himself? A few chapters into Louis Bayard's monumental *Mr. Timothy* (2003), a Dickensian labyrinth of London alleyways, murders and mystery, we meet Willie the Slasher, and that name is one of the only false steps—if not the only one—in the entire novel. What kind of killer would call himself something so drab, so labored and, though that story is set twenty years before this one, so obviously indebted to the name of the master?

At the same time, however, it can't be easy coming up with the ultimate name for the ultimate killer, and one cannot help but wonder whether, in some dusty forgotten drawer someplace, there lies a yellowed, mildewed scrap of paper upon which the killer tried out a few other identities?

James the Stabber.

Charles the Dicer.

Sebastian the Cutter-Upper.

Albert the Very-Handy-with-a-Sharp-Blade.

One sincerely hopes there isn't.

The news agency itself did not initially use the letter in its reportage, not out of respect for the writer's request that they "keep this letter back till I do a bit more work, then give it out straight," but because they, too, believed it to be a hoax. And so it would appear to have been, as no fewer than three journalists have since been identified as likely authors of the letter.

In 1913, Chief Inspector John Littlechild wrote of his suspicions regarding the Central News Agency's general manager, Charles Moore, and editor Thomas Bulling, while *The Star*'s Frederick Best has also been named as a likely candidate.

This page and next: Spring-heeled Jack, real-life bogeyman turned Penny Dreadful hero.

SPRING-HEELED JACK,
THE TERROR OF LONDON.

THE WINDOW SHIVERED AS SPRING-HEELED JACK LEAPED BODILY THROUGH IT.

If it was a hoax, however, the promise with which the letter ended, the wish to "get to work right away," must rate among the most precise prophecies in the history of crime. Three days after the letter was received at the Central News Agency, and just twenty-four hours after it was forwarded on to Scotland Yard, the killer struck again.

And he did so not once, but twice.

The Murder of Elizabeth Stride

Elisabeth Gustafsdotter arrived in London from her native Sweden sometime following her mother's death in 1866, when Elisabeth was twenty-three.

Although her local police had known her as a prostitute, and she was no stranger to the hospital, where she was treated for venereal disease, she had most recently been working in Gothenburg as a maid, and she seems to have continued in this profession after she moved and anglicized her first name.

She married in 1869 and with her husband, John Stride, opened a coffee shop in Poplar, in east London. By 1881, however, Long Liz—as she was known among her friends—was on her own again, and living in a doss house on what seems as though it was the most inappropriately named road in all of Whitechapel, Flower and Dean Street—but which was, in fact, named for the men who first laid it out in the seventeenth century, John Flower and Gowen Dean.

Like so much of the district, Flower and Dean Street has altered beyond all recognition over the past 130 years. It was largely boardinghouses back then, huddled side by side along the north side of the street, facing onto the minatory tenements that made up the Charlotte de Rothschild Dwellings.

Urban renewal tore down some, the Blitz of World War II destroyed others, and modern gentrification has since completely reshaped not only this street, but its neighbors, too.

But Flower and Dean Street retained its grotesque cachet at least into the mid-1970s, when author Patrice Chaplin published the novella *By Flower and Dean Street*, the supremely eerie tale of a modern-day housewife being pursued by, and finally succumbing to, the supernatural echoes of Long Liz's final hours.

Voices first, and shadows. Hallucinations—cutting meat for her family's supper, she is suddenly overwhelmed by the sight of blood. Bathing her children before bed, she is overcome by a terror of water . . . Long Liz used to claim that she lost her husband and children in the *Princess Alice* disaster of 1878, when a pleasure steamer packed with East End day-trippers was accidentally rammed by a coal boat and sank within minutes.

Over 650 people died in the filthy river waters, and subsequent researches have cast considerable doubt upon Long Liz's tale—there were no victims named Stride among the dead, and husband John would live on until heart disease took him in 1884. But that is not to say she did not have friends, or even loved ones, aboard the doomed steamer and, even if her story was a fiction, still its reappearance in the novella is effective.

Snatches of conversation, odd flashes of impossible knowledge. Glimpses of gaslit streets and cobblestoned alleyways. So many incidents and instances

WHERE THE CORPSE WAS FOUND IN BERNERS STREET.

Berners [sic] Street, where Elizabeth Stride met her murderer. *Alamy*

pile atop one another as the book drives toward its sudden, horrifying denouement. Amidst the sheer plethoric confusion of Jack the Ripper's fictional life, *By Flower and Dean Street* stands among his most evocative manifestations.

Like so many of the Whitechapel murderer's victims, Long Liz was a drinker. Her boyfriend over the final three years of her life, waterside laborer Michael Kidney, spoke at the inquest of their frequent separations, saying, "It was drink that made her go away."

Her taste for alcohol ensured that she was familiar, too, to both police and magistrates, again on charges of being drunk and disorderly.

Kidney himself was no angel. On at least one occasion, Long Liz accused him of assaulting her, but she failed to turn up at the hearing, presumably because the pair had reunited again. Just a few nights before her death, however, Long Liz told a friend, Catherine Lamb, that she had left Kidney once again.

Long Liz returned to her old boardinghouse at 32 Flower and Dean Street (she had previously been living with Kidney) and appears to have been a model guest. The house's owner, Elizabeth Tanner, spoke of Long Liz's willingness to do whatever work she could find, while another of the lodgers, Mrs. Ann Mill, insisted that "a better hearted. more good-natured cleaner woman never lived."

Which might well be something of an exaggeration, born out of the Victorian tradition of never speaking ill of the dead. But it also suggests a woman who genuinely struggled against her lot in life, only to be pulled back down by her love of drink.

She was certainly a friend to many of the younger women on the streets, including One-Armed Liz—Long Liz might even have been among the friends who comforted the terrified teen following the drunken Charles Ludwig's assault.

Likewise, Long Liz spent the day of her death patiently cleaning the common sleeping rooms at number 32, for which she was paid sixpence and, perhaps, guaranteed a bed for the night.

The money did not last long. She spent some time at the Queen's Head pub, and after a swift visit back to the boardinghouse, might well be the woman who was seen kissing and cuddling with a particularly well-dressed, respectable looking gent in the doorway of the Bricklayer's Arms.

Two of the men who saw the couple, and who later visited the mortuary where Long Liz's body awaited identification, were certain it was the same woman, and their description of her companion was certainly striking. He was around five-foot-five, in a smart black suit and coat, with a black bowler hat and a thick black mustache. They were also adamant that he possessed not a single other strand of facial hair, and that included eyebrows.

Long Liz may have been sighted again sometime between eleven and midnight, purchasing grapes from a shop on Berner Street. The store owner's description of her companion, however, portrayed a taller gentleman, middle-aged and stoutly built, at the same time rekindling memories of the man who had attacked Ada Wilson in her home earlier in the year, by recalling his wideawake hat. The storekeeper also noticed that the woman had a white flower pinned to her bosom.

Around the same time, a few houses up the street, another local resident, William Marshall, also saw a man and woman standing in the road. Now the man, although he remained middle-aged and stout, was wearing a dark jacket and light-colored trousers, and wearing a peaked cap similar to those sported by sailors. Marshall strained to overhear their conversation, but caught just one phrase, spoken by the man: "You would say anything but your prayers."

The pair then walked away toward Fairclough Street.

Also sometime around 11:45, further down Berner Street, one Morris Eagle left the meeting he had been chairing at the International Working Men's Education Society, "Why Jews Should Be Socialists," and saw nothing to attract his attention on the street.

Twenty-five minutes later, another man left the club to deliver some literature to the offices of *Arbeter Frainti* (*Worker's Friend*), a radical Yiddish newspaper whose headquarters lay alongside the club. He, too, saw nothing on either his way out, or when he came back a short while later. Neither did Charles Letchford, a young man returning to his home at number 30; nor his sister, who was waiting for him in the doorway of their house.

But PC William Smith, as his beat took him down Berner Street at 12:35, definitively saw a man and woman on the pavement outside the club. She had a flower pinned to her jacket, he was clean-shaven, around five-foot-seven, in a dark overcoat and dark trousers, and was wearing a deerstalker hat. He also held a parcel wrapped in newspaper in his hand.

Smith passed them by. No doubt he had his suspicions as to the manner of transaction taking place, but orders made it clear that it was no concern of his. Besides, the gent looked respectable enough. Smith continued on his beat, passing out of sight of the club even as Morris Eagle returned to it. Again, all was calm and it remained so for a few minutes more—time enough for one James Brown to step out of his house on Fairclough Street, on his way to buy some food from a nearby chandler's shop.

He picked up his groceries and returned home. A man and woman were standing against the wall of the Board School, the woman with her back to the wall, the man partially screening her with one arm also against the wall. He wore a hat of some kind, said Brown, but (perhaps mercifully) he wasn't able to describe it. He also wore a long dark coat that reached almost to his ankles. The woman was saying, "No, not tonight. Some other night." The man's response, if there was one, went unheard. Brown continued on his way.

Another man stepped onto Berner Street. Israel Schwartz, a Hungarian refugee, was walking home when he saw, ahead of him, a man approach a woman who was standing outside the club, pause to speak to her and then, clearly not liking her reply, attempt to pull her into the street, before hurling her to the ground.

Schwartz's path took him right alongside the couple; he crossed the street to avoid them, and spotted another man standing in a nearby doorway, in the act of lighting his pipe.

A cry of "Lipski!" from this second man sent Schwartz hurrying on his way. The previous June, Whitechapel had been horrified by a gruesome murder committed by one Israel Lipski, a Polish-Jewish umbrella salesman who forced his pregnant neighbor, Miriam Angel, to drink nitric acid, and then attempted to commit suicide by the same means.

Or so said the prosecution. Lipski claimed the pair had been attacked by two men he had recently hired, as they attempted to rob him; when he protested that he was penniless, they forced a piece of wood into his mouth and said, "If you don't give it to us, you will be as dead as the woman." They then forced the acid into his mouth.

He was not believed. While there was never any explanation of why Lipski was in Ms. Angel's room in the first place (robbery or rape were considered the most likely motives), a jury took just eight minutes to return a verdict of guilty, and Lipski was sentenced to hang.

Neither could a major press campaign, and even the alleged disapproval of Queen Victoria, force the authorities to reconsider. Lipski was executed on August 21, 1887, and, since that time, his name had been considered one of the most appalling insults to shout at any Jew.

Schwartz certainly felt the cry was aimed at him, particularly when he perceived the second man to be following him. He ran home and locked the door tight. But he was able to give the police a description of the man

ISRAEL LIPSKI'S MURDER OF MIRIAM ANGEL; PORTRAIT OF THE MURDERER AND SOLICITOR, AND SCENE OF THE CRIME—(See "Law and Police.")

Israel Lipski—the killer whose name became a common insult on the streets of Whitechapel.

Alamy

who was assaulting the woman—around five-foot-five, with fair hair and a fair complexion, a small brown mustache, dark jacket and trousers, and a black peaked cap. He also had very broad shoulders.

The discrepancies between these descriptions should not be surprising. Almost any detective could tell you of the number of times he has been sent out to apprehend a tall short man with black blond hair, clean-shaven with a beard and mustache, wearing light dark clothing and seemingly changing his hat and shoes between every fresh encounter.

All of the sightings were made in darkness, and few lasted more than a moment or two—sufficient time in which to store a few impressions, perhaps, but scarcely any that could ever be considered accurate in themselves.

What *was* important was the composite picture that could be drawn—a man between five-foot-five and five-foot-seven in height, smartly dressed either in black or dark clothing, wearing some kind of hat and, more likely than not, sporting a mustache.

It wasn't much to go on, the police knew that. Hundreds of thousands of men in London fit so vague a description—in fact, one of them was arrested in Borough, south of the river, the following day. A tall, dark man wearing an American hat had drawn the attention of his fellows at a lodging house by making what a newspaper described as "certain observations . . . regarding the topic of the day."

The police were called, and "shortly before midnight a man whose name has not yet transpired was arrested in the Borough on suspicion of being the perpetrator of the murders in the East-end."

> On the arrival of the officer the stranger was questioned as to his recent wanderings, but he could give no intelligible account of them, though he said he had spent the previous night on Blackfriars Bridge. He was conveyed to Stone's End Police-station, Blackman-street, Borough.

And that was the last to be heard of him. He may have been tall, he may have owned a hat. But he was not a murderer.

So yes, there were a lot of people who fit the wanted man's description. But there were many more who *didn't*. Scotland Yard still didn't know whom they were looking for, but they had a good idea now of whom they weren't.

While Israel Schwartz was running for what he perceived was his life (he later added a very visible knife to the second man's personal description), back on Fairclough Street, James Brown was just finishing his supper when the night air was rent by an ear-piercing cry of "Police! Murder!"

Long Liz's body was discovered by Louis Diemshitz, the steward of the club against whose wall the corpse lay. He was returning from an outing in his pony and cart when the beast suddenly shied at something on the ground. Diemshitz dismounted and lit a match.

His first thought was that a local drunk was sleeping off her latest excesses, but something about the woman's unearthly stillness gave him pause. Running up the stairs into the club, he told his wife, "There is a woman laying in the yard, but I cannot say whether she is drunk or dead."

A few of the menfolk followed him back downstairs, and another match was struck. Now the scene was clearer, particularly the great puddle of blood which pooled across the sidewalk and ran into the gutter.

Diemshitz and another man rushed off to find a policeman—it was their cries that James Brown heard as he finished his meal, and their commotion that drew another bystander, Edward Spooner, to the murder scene.

It was Spooner who confirmed that the woman was dead, but that her murder could only have just occurred; her body was still warm, and blood was still flowing from her neck wound. He also noted the flower pinned to her jacket.

PC Henry Lamb arrived moments later, and, having arranged for the gates into the alleyway to be closed, he proceeded to question everybody who had been on the club premises at the time, inspecting their hands and clothing for any sign of blood. He found none.

Meanwhile, the doctor, Edward Johnston, had arrived. He placed the time of death at between twenty-five and thirty minutes previously—right around the time that Israel Schwartz would claim to have seen a woman being assaulted on almost the exact same spot. He would also outline Long Liz's injuries.

A modern marker remembers Elizabeth Stride's grave.
© *Maciupeq/ Wikimedia Commons*

She was lying on her left side, her face turned toward the wall. She still clutched a packet of cachou breath-fresheners in one hand; a few of the tiny tablets lay in the gutter close by. Her throat had been gashed open, a six-inch slash that tore through artery, cartilage and muscle alike. As with previous victims, the cause of death was glaringly obvious.

Closer examination of the body, however, revealed that to be the woman's sole injury. There was evidence that some weight, perhaps her killer's hands, had been exerted on her chest, but there was no mutilation, no surgical incisions, no suggestion in any way that Long Liz's death had been the all-too-grotesquely familiar handiwork of the Whitechapel murderer.

Stabbings and slashings, after all, were a common means of assault at that time; that very same day at Bow Street Court, evidence was heard against an army reserve man named Henry Taylor, charged with assaulting one Mary Ann Perry in Clare Street Market, and threatening her with a three-inch clasp knife.

He might even have carried out his threat had a crowd not gathered around, and Taylor backed away, still wielding the knife and threatening to stab anybody who came close. At which point the cry went up of "Leather Apron!" and Taylor was forced to flee for his life—straight into the arms of a passing policeman.

Long Liz's murder was horrifying, then, but it was not horrif*ic*, not in the sense that the Whitechapel murderer's last two slayings had been, and it would have been easy enough for history to file it away as one more unsolved (if not unsolv*able*) murder, a john going off with a doxy while his companion waited in a nearby doorway, and then slashing out at her when she refused to offer him whichever service he required.

This was certainly Walter Dew's opinion, and several other investigators', too, and their opinion might have carried even greater weight were it not for events elsewhere in Whitechapel that same night.

For they suggested something far worse than a random stabbing gone wrong. They suggested that Long Liz had been the Ripper's intended victim that night, but that something—probably the approach of Louis Diemshitz's pony and cart—had interrupted him as he prepared to start work, and so he had hurried off to find a replacement.

Or, as the *East London Advertiser* put it, "It is announced by the police that in all probability the wretch was disturbed in his work, and made off in the direction of the City with the ghoulish thirst for blood still blazing within him; that he beguiled another hapless victim into a dark secluded spot, and then again fell to his butchery."

12

The Double Murder (Continued)

The Death of Catherine Eddowes

> Half the victim's missing kidney restored. The other half eaten by the cannibal assassin.
>
> —Evening News, *October 1888*

I f it was, as Walter Dew later suggested, nothing more than hysteria (and, perhaps, convenience) that saw the two murders committed in Whitechapel that evening linked to the same devilish butcher, it was nevertheless an understandable response.

With the area already poised on the brink of communal panic, absolutely any act of violence against women was instinctively placed at Jack the Ripper's door, as Henry Taylor had discovered that day in Clare Street Market.

Two killings in one night, particularly two carried out so close together, may have been a coincidence. But they also suggested the Ripper was upping the ante.

Next time, would it be three?

The second body was found in Mitre Square, the same patch of darkened, warehouse-shadowed cobbles that the mythical Fairy Fay had traversed on her last night on earth.

Back on Berner Street, Long Liz's body was still cooling in the alleyway, awaiting the cart that would convey her to the morgue; some forty-five minutes had elapsed since her corpse was discovered, but the excitement had not yet communicated itself to those folk who were out and about around Mitre Square—a night watchman in a counting house that looked out onto the cobbles, firefighters on duty at a nearby station. So far as they were concerned, the night was quiet and peaceful. Nobody heard a thing.

THE SCENE OF THE MITRE SQUARE MURDER.

Mitre Square, where the body of Catherine Eddowes was discovered.   *Alamy*

But things were happening, all the same. Under a cloak of silence so profound as to be supernatural, a woman first had her throat cut and then, as her body surrendered the final vestiges of life, the killer set to work.

Her abdomen was slit open and her intestines removed. The majority were positioned over the woman's left shoulder, but one smaller piece was very deliberately laid between in the space between her left arm and her torso.

Her left kidney was missing, and the majority of her uterus as well. Her face had been cut, a pair of inverted Vs on her cheeks, beneath her eyes, and tiny nicks on the eyelids.

The tip of her nose had been removed, and her right ear was cut so badly that several pieces fell out of her clothing as the body was being undressed at the mortuary. A handful of the dead woman's possessions were scattered around her—her bonnet, soaking in a pool of blood; some buttons and a thimble; and a mustard tin containing a couple of pawn tickets.

Again, there were several witnesses—not to the killing itself, but to events that perhaps led up to it. Shortly before 1:25, the night watchman's solitude had been briefly interrupted by a respectably dressed man who asked if the watchman had seen a man and a woman enter nearby Church Passage, which led into Duke Street. The watchman hadn't, and the man walked away.

However, Joseph Lawende, passing by the passage on Duke Street itself, as he and two friends left the Imperial Club, *did* see a couple in the darkness, the woman in a black jacket and dark bonnet laying her hand on her companion's chest. The man was taller, and wearing a cloth cap with a peak, but Lawende paid them little heed. Such sights were scarcely uncommon on any city street, much less around these parts.

At 1:30, PC Edward Watkins passed through the square as he did every night, shining his lantern into the darkened corners and ensuring that all was well. Nobody was in sight. Another constable, PC James Harvey, was also on Duke Street, around five minutes after Lawende and his friends; he saw nobody in the passage and did in fact walk down the narrow alleyway as far as its entrance into Mitre Square. All was as it should be.

But at 1:44, PC Watkins turned back into the square from Mitre Street, and witnessed a sight that would remain with him for life.

"She was ripped up like a pig in the market," he told a journalist from *The Star*. "I have been in the force a long while. but I never saw such a sight."

Quickly, he hurried to the Kearley and Tonge grocer's warehouse, where a former policeman, George Morris, was now employed as night watchman. It was Morris who summoned help, racing out onto Mitre Street and then onto Aldgate, blowing on his old police whistle.

Two more constables, PCs Harvey and Holland, responded immediately; Harvey ran to join Watkins at the murder scene, while Holland raced to awaken Dr. George Sequeira at his surgery on Jewry Street.

The inevitable crowd began to form, policemen for the most part—three plainclothes detectives who happened to be in the area, an inspector from nearby Bishopsgate police station and so forth. All were sickened by the sight that awaited them.

The police surgeon, Dr. Gordon Brown, was on the scene by 2:20 and estimated that the body had laid there for around forty minutes—meaning that Watkins, had he been just a minute or two earlier, might have caught a glimpse of the murderer himself. The doctor also noted, once again, that the killer had more than a passing knowledge of human anatomy—the kidney, he said, is especially difficult to locate unless one knows precisely what to look for.

Again, the shadow of either a medical man or a butcher loomed over the investigation and, in many ways, that only increased the panic that gripped the neighborhood as word of the murder began to seep out.

A frenzied attacker, hacking at random, was awful enough to contemplate. But a cold, calculating killer who knew precisely what he was doing was worse, all the more so since those two professions were both such a part of the daily life. Everybody had cause to visit a doctor at some point in their life; everybody had cause to visit a butcher's store as well. The realization that the skills with which a man earned his living could then be turned *against* the living was simply too terrible to contemplate.

Neither was the fear confined to Whitechapel, or even the East End alone. Author M. V. Hughes, as described in her delightful memoir *A Victorian Family*, was living in faraway West London at the time, all the way over on the other side of city.

But she recalled:

> I was afraid to go out after dark, if only to post a letter. Just as dusk came on, we used to hear down our quiet and ultra-respectable Edith Road, the cries of the newspaper boys in tones made as alarming as they could: 'Another 'orrible murder! Whitechapel! Murder! Disgustin' details! Murder!'
>
> One can only dimly imagine what the terror must have been in those acres of narrow streets, where the inhabitants knew the murderer to be lurking.

A reporter for the *Evening News* captured the mood of the crowd that gathered both on Berner Street and in Mitre Square:

> I found the street literally packed with people of both sexes, all ages, and nearly all classes. Clubmen from the West-end rubbed shoulders with the grimy denizens of St. George's-in-the-East: daintily dressed ladies, whom a wondering curiosity had drawn to the spot, elbowed their way amid knots of their less favoured sisters, whose dirty and ragged apparel betokened the misery of their daily surroundings.
>
> Policemen were there in great numbers, jealously guarding the approach to the yard in which the murdered woman was found. I may mention that the same thing (the number of police on duty) struck me in passing Mitre-square, reminding one irresistibly of the old adage about locking the stable door after the steed has been stolen.
>
> It's a pity some of you fine chappies wasn't about 'ere larst night," said a morose individual who had been ordered to move on. "You'd a-done a deal more good than shovin' innercent folks hoff the

pavement this arternoon." Then, in a jeering tone, "When do you expect you'll ketch the murderer, sonny?"

"Ketch the murderer?" laughed another dilapidated onlooker. "Not till they puts a 'bobby' to sit upon hevery doorstep in Vitechapel. And then 'alf on 'em will be asleep."

No Double Negative Is Not Nothing Not to Be Sneered At

Rumors flew.

According to the *Daily News*, it was being said that the murderer, "having committed the dastardly deeds, inscribed in chalk on the brick wall words calculated to provoke local antagonisms."

The report continued, "It was added in this connection that Sir Charles Warren when he saw the writing on the wall early on the Sunday morning, ordered it to be washed out, and that the direction was followed out by the police. A careful examination of the wall, however, clearly establishes the fact that the whole story is a fabrication."

In fact, the story was true. Just before 3:00 a.m., PC Alfred Long was walking up Goulston Street when he spotted a piece of apron lying on a stairway that led into dreadnought hulk of Wentworth Dwellings, another of the model homes that had been built in recent years. It had not been there when he passed by a little over half an hour earlier, and when he bent to pick it up, he noticed that one corner was both damp and stained.

Then he looked up at the wall. In three lines of white chalk, each letter a little less than one inch high, were written the words "The Juwes are the men that will not be blamed for nothing."

Another constable was called over to guard the scene, while Long checked the rest of the stairway to make certain that no further surprises awaited him. He then returned to the police station to report his discoveries.

The precise meaning of the graffiti has never been unanimously agreed upon, beyond the fact that its ambiguity was not necessarily deliberate. But the general consensus, as further police arrived to view the words, was that it could not help but stir up further anti-Semitic sentiment in the area.

Latter-day scholars have seized upon the spelling and determined, among other explanations, that the word "Juwes" could as easily have Masonic, Manchurian or even magical connotations as Semitic ones. And perhaps it did. But to a local populace who knew nothing of such things, but were capable of reading words for themselves, it could have only one interpretation.

The mysterious message found daubed on a wall at Wentworth Dwellings.   *Alamy*

That was why Warren, arriving on the scene around 5:00 a.m., ordered the writing to be erased. He knew he was destroying a potentially valuable piece of evidence. But he also knew what the mob would do if that evidence ever became public—as it very swiftly did. But even *The Star*, traditionally so critical of everything that Warren said and did, mitigated what it called his "blundering haste" with the concession "his motive seems to have been just a trifle more creditable than usual."

Goodnight, Old Cock

Meanwhile, the gruesome business of identifying the Mitre Square corpse was under way, although it turned out to be somewhat easier than in the past.

Famously, Elizabeth Stride's identification had been thoroughly thrown into disarray by the insistence of one woman that the corpse belonged to her sister, Elizabeth—who was also known to her friends as Long Liz. (This is not as coincidental as it sounds—"Long Liz" was a nickname commonly applied to any taller-than-average woman.)

But in this latest case, they needed simply ask at Bishopsgate Police Station, for it was there that forty-six-year-old Catherine "Kate" Eddowes spent her last evening alive—albeit under an assumed name.

Earlier in the evening of Saturday, September 29, "Mary Ann Kelly" was booked for public drunkenness, a display that included performing a raucous impression of a fire engine, and placed in a cell to sleep it off. A few hours later, at 12:55 a.m., she had sobered up sufficiently to be released. Her last words to PC George Hutt as he held open the door for her were a friendly "Good night, old cock."

Kate was born in Wolverhampton, in the English midlands, but moved to London with her family while she was still a child. It was there that both her parents died, her mother when Kate was thirteen, in 1855, her father two years later.

The girl returned to Wolverhampton to live with an uncle and aunt, but left to live with another uncle in nearby Birmingham after she was caught stealing from her employer.

Early in the 1860s, she met a former soldier named Thomas Conway, and the pair set up business as the writers, publishers and sellers of chapbooks—small, sensationalist booklets that purported to tell the truth behind famous crimes and criminals.

They probably made a reasonable living at it. Just as a police investigation can be divided into so many different parts—the crime, its discovery, its solution, its consequences—so the publishers of chapbooks followed a similar course.

The first publication would detail the crime in all its awful glory (for only the awful crimes were worth reporting in this manner), and do so within hours of its discovery; a second edition might dog the footsteps of the investigating policemen. If a murder had been committed, a third would report on the inquest, and one more on the victim's funeral. Others would document the perpetrator's arrest and trial, and finally the series would close with his or her execution, and a glorious last-minute confession.

And, of course, if the actual details of all of these things were not immediately forthcoming, the most enterprising publishers would simply make them up, and then challenge others to prove them wrong.

Neither would there be any shortage of sensational crimes during the years that the Eddowes's were producing their booklets. Indeed, according to an article in the *Pall Mall Gazette*, published in 1865, that decade had already proven the most murderous in living memory.

The newspaper's outrage was stirred by the trial of twenty-one-year-old Constance Kent. She had confessed to the murder of her half brother Frances four years earlier—and, in the process, laid bare such a rich seam of family scandal that her story is still being told today. Kate Summerscale's *The Suspicions of Mr. Whicher or The Murder at Road Hill House* (2008) is only the most recent of the books to have told her story; Charles Dickens and Wilkie Collins simply the most literate of Constance's contemporary supporters. The chapbook and broadside authors had a field day with her case.

Kent, though found guilty and sentenced to death, eventually had her sentence commuted to life imprisonment and was, in fact, released after twenty years. That, however, was not the object of the *Pall Mall Gazette*'s concern. Far more pressing was the awful knowledge that there were so many murders being committed, full stop.

> "The multiplicity of murders among us is growing into a very grave matter. That they are increasing, and increasing at a rapid rate, there can be no question. Nearly every day brings to light some fresh homicide. They are often horribly brutal, often strangely melodramatic – sometimes awfully deliberate, sometimes mere ebullitions of momentary bad temper; while in not a few cases the victims are so numerous as almost to elevate murder into massacre.

But the most common and noticeable, and in our view the most alarming feature about them is the weakness of the motives, and the slightness of the provocations which are sufficient to produce them.

It would almost seem as if the very smallest inducement and the scantiest irritation were enough, in the morbid condition of mind prevalent among certain classes, to lead to the greatest of crimes.

Now it is a sister who murders a brother merely because she has a grudge against him. Now it is a man who kills his companion simply because the idea of the homicide has got into his head, and he cannot get it out again. Now it is a hag who smothers any number of babies at two-and-threepence a head. Now it is a suitor who shoots his mistress, with every circumstance of cool deliberation, because she will not have him. Now it is a wife who murders all her children to spite her husband; now a husband who repeats the tragedy because he is ill off in the world, and he fears or fancies his children will be worse off still; now a brute who beats out the brains of the woman who cohabits with him because his supper was not ready and his room not clean.

Finally, in the course of one week – and by no means for the first time – one soldier slays his superior officer because he is a strict disciplinarian, and another shoots his sergeant because the sergeant had ordered him two days' extra drill.

In a word, it would seem as if with some people, and with a great variety of people – at least with people in very various positions in life – anything was enough to produce murder, and nothing was enough to prevent it.

Neither was that the end of the editorial. The public's hunger for the most sordid details of each successive slaying was castigated as readily as the criminals who committed them; unspoken, but doubtless on the author's mind was Thomas De Quincey's then forty-year-old observation that, while nobody would want to find the remains of their sweetheart bubbling in the tea urn, little was more pleasurable than reading about *someone else's* sweetheart being discovered there.

Murder made money, and while the *Pall Mall Gazette* was as guilty as any other periodical of profiting from the grisly crime (and would continue to be so), still that did not excuse the public its hunger.

We are convinced that, if it were not for the utterly irrational set of opinions and the utterly immoral set of feelings which, in reference to these subjects, have lately got hold of the public mind, three-fourths of the murders which are now half horrifying and half edifying us day after day would never have been perpetrated;

they would have died away as inchoate temptations, and never have ripened into concrete facts.

How ironic, that writer would surely have proclaimed, that one of the very people who did make a living from other people's deaths should herself be destined to headline the kind of publication that she once produced so carelessly.

The Eddowes's had several children, but their relationship was tempestuous, apparently marred by Kate's temper and love of drink, and her habit of simply walking out of the house and effectively disappearing for weeks, even months, at a time.

Kate left her husband for the final time around 1880, moving to London to live with one of her sisters while she looked to secure an address of her own. She found it, ironically, at 55 Flower and Dean Street, just a few doors up from Elizabeth Stride's favorite boardinghouse, and it was there she struck up a relationship with one John Kelly.

He worked, when he could, as a laborer in nearby Spitalfields Market; Kate, for her part, took on cleaning jobs and the like, and late every summer, just as autumn touched the air, the pair would join the exodus of East Enders who made their way eastward into the county of Kent, to pick up casual work picking hops for the brewery industry.

Modern romance depicts hop-picking, like so many other now-lost occupations, among those charming aspects of "old England" that progress and machination should never have been allowed to sweep away. The image of trainloads of happy Cockneys piling into bucolic fields, there to gather nature's bounty for a red-cheeked farmer, is as much a part of the country's tradition as Robin Hood, Sherlock Holmes or, indeed, Jack the Ripper.

In fact, as George Orwell wrote some fifty years after the Eddowes's were making the journey, "hop-picking is far from being a holiday, and, as far as wages go, no worse employment exists."

> The process is extremely simple. The vines, long climbing plants with the hops clustering on them in bunches like grapes, are trained up poles or over wires; all the picker has to do is to tear them down and strip the hops into a bin, keeping them as clean as possible from leaves.

But, "the spiny stems cut the palms of one's hands to pieces, and in the early morning, before the cuts have reopened, it is painful work; one has trouble too with the plant-lice which infest the hops and crawl down one's neck."

Accommodation was provided, but it was rudimentary to say the least. In Orwell's day, the workers slept four, even eight, to a hut, just ten feet across and with no furniture beyond a heap of straw for a bed, and no bedding beyond an old sack.

The windows were unglazed and, depending upon the weather, sundry other holes and fissures ensured that wind and rain were constant companions. And this, said Orwell, was *after* "a whole tribe of Government officials" descended to oversee the conditions in which the workers were kept. "What it can have been like in the old days is hard to imagine."

A lot like the lodging houses and dormitories that the pickers had left behind in London, probably.

But still they came. The work was regular, the exercise was welcome, and the fresh air must have felt heavenly after a year spent breathing the gases of London.

This year, however, a cold, wet summer had all but wiped out the hops crop, and on September 28, Kate Eddowes and John Kelly returned to London, penniless. They scraped together the money for a bed for the night—they pawned John's boots, and then Kate decided to make her way to Bermondsey, just a few miles distant, to see if she could borrow some money from one of her daughters.

Apparently, the last thing Kelly said to her as she set out was to beware of the Whitechapel murderer—words one can imagine every local speaking to a loved one as she prepared to leave the house.

"Don't you fear for me," Kate replied. "I'll take care of myself and I shan't fall into his hands."

In the event, she didn't go to Bermondsey. Instead she got drunk and wound up in a cell. Then, following her release, she set out in the direction of Duke Street. The following day, a postcard received at the Central News Agency seemed to confirm all of the police's suspicions.

> I was not codding dear old Boss when I gave you the tip, you'll hear about Saucy Jacky's work tomorrow double event this time number one squealed a bit couldn't finish straight off. ha not the time to get ears for police. thanks for keeping last letter back till I got to work again.

Once again, the missive was signed "Jack the Ripper."

13

Not So Quiet on the West End Front

The Whitehall Mystery and Other Thameside Torsos

> The trunk was without head, arms, or legs, and presented a horrible spectacle. Dr. Bond, the divisional surgeon, and several other medical gentlemen were communicated with, and from what can be ascertained the conclusion has been arrived at by them that these remains are those of a woman whose arms have recently been discovered in different parts of the metropolis.
>
> —Pall Mall Gazette, *October 1888*

Scotland Yard was moving house.

The nerve center of London's Metropolitan Police was originally opened on Whitehall, in the very center of London, in 1829. But it was the street the premises backed onto which would give the new building its name—Great Scotland Yard.

As the force grew alongside the city it served, however, that original edifice quickly began to feel quite inadequate. Over time, the police found their operations spreading far beyond their original offices, first into the adjoining buildings, and then farther up the street, out onto Great Scotland Yard itself, and even into local stables. Finally, in 1887, ground was broken on a new headquarters, to be named, appropriately, New Scotland Yard.

Even more appropriately, the new site was set to become a crime scene.

Around mid-afternoon on October 2, 1888, less than forty-eight hours since the discovery of the so-called Double Murder in Whitechapel, carpenter Frederick Windborn was on his way to retrieve some tools he kept on a shelf in one of the new building's underground vaults.

Normally, and despite the darkness, he could lay his hands on them without a thought. This morning, however, he felt something else on the shelf, and he struck a match.

There he saw a neatly wrapped parcel measuring around two by two and a half feet, and he seems to have assumed that one of his workmates had placed it there. The following day, however, he mentioned it to one of his fellows, and they decided to take another look—in other words, to open it and satisfy their curiosity as to what it might contain. Somebody's forgotten lunch was probably their best guess.

And so it initially seemed. Or at least, that's what Windborn first thought as the newspaper was peeled away. A side of old bacon.

Which, on closer inspection, somebody had wrapped up in what looked like a black petticoat, and then tied with string. It was also crawling with maggots, and suddenly it did not look quite so much like bacon. It was the fast-decomposing remains of a woman.

Over a century later, the modern face of New Scotland Yard.   *Solid Web Designs/Shutterstock*

Immediately the two workmen's thoughts turned to the Whitechapel murders—of course they did. The newspapers had been filled with little else since the end of August. Others who heard of the discovery—their fellow workers, the first press men on the scene, and the police as well—doubtless joined them in such speculation.

The killer had, after all, already proven his disdain for the police. Then, as now, the vast majority of people remembered only the shocking headlines they read, as opposed to the more nuanced denials and explanations that frequently followed them.

No matter that the police believed the letters that named the killer as "Jack the Ripper" were hoaxes; the public believed he had written them. No matter that the presence of the leather apron beside one of the corpses had been a coincidence; the public believed he had planted it. No matter that the writing on the wall had been dismissed as a rumor; the public believed it existed.

The mystery of the Ripper has seldom ceased to fascinate the movie world, as this 1960 epic reminds us.
Alamy

Time and again, the murderer had displayed a love of taunting and tormenting his pursuers. What more fitting way to really humiliate them could there be, then, than for him to scale the eight-foot hoardings that surrounded the slowly growing new building; to pass through the deserted darkness of the site at night; and then to deposit the grisly remains of another victim right beneath the commissioner's nose?

The police investigation turned up little to contradict this impression. They established that the vault had last been visited on September 29, and that the parcel had not been noticed on that occasion. But the presence of maggots, not only on the parcel but on the walls and shelf as well, suggested it had been there for several weeks, while the newspaper used to wrap the remains was dated August 24—that is, two weeks after Martha Tabram was killed, and a week before Mary Ann Nichols.

The *Pall Mall Gazette* detailed the discovery.

> Dr. Nevill, who examined the arm of a woman found a few weeks ago in the Thames, off Ebury Bridge, said on that occasion that he did not think that it had been skilfully taken from the body. This fact would appear to favour the theory that that arm, together with the one found in the grounds of the Blind Asylum in the Lambeth-road last week, belong to the trunk discovered yesterday, for it is stated that the limbs appear to have been taken from it in anything but a skilful manner.
>
> The body is pronounced by medical men to have been that of a remarkably fine young woman. The lower portion from the ribs has been removed.

The search for any further remains that might have been left on the building site went on into the following day. None were forthcoming, but the notion that the entire affair had somehow been orchestrated by a murderous genius was in no way stilled when, with the detectives still in the vault, a massive piece of machinery, a four-ton steam crane, suddenly fell from the 150-foot-high platform upon which it had been set and crashed to earth—onto the exact same spot where the package had been discovered.

The detectives escaped unhurt; in the time it took for the crane to reach, and then crash through, the ground, the cries of warning from outside had alerted them. Nevertheless, to any reader blessed with even a soupçon of imagination, no deadlier a booby trap could ever have been designed.

Neither had the site surrendered all its secrets, although it would not be the police who made the next discovery. Rather, and even more humiliatingly, it was a journalist who took it upon himself to visit the scene some fifteen days later, accompanied by a sniffer dog, a Russian terrier.

Alerted to a recess on quite the opposite side of the site from where the torso had been discovered, the journalist watched as the police procured candles to see by and began excavating. They discovered a left leg and a left arm.

They had a body, and they certainly had their suspicions. But the police were nevertheless lacking one crucial thing. They had no evidence the woman had actually been murdered.

Clearly, she had died, but all the signs pointed to her dismemberment having occurred following her death. Decomposition, however, and the nature of that dismemberment, disguised any signs there may have been of some earlier, fatal violence.

But neither was there any evidence she had died from disease. As *The Times* explained, police and inquest alike "had before them the surmise that no one would so mutilate a body except for the purpose of concealing an identity, which once established might lead to the detection of a terrible murder." But they could not prove it.

The best that the experts could say, both in private and at the inquest, was that she had died, a determination that left the inquest with no alternative but to return one of the least helpful verdicts in its entire repertoire: "Found dead."

Attempts to identify the woman's remains continued. Missing-persons records were combed and, for a time, there was the possibility that the remains were those of seventeen-year-old Lilly Vass, missing since July 17, when she had left her home amid the splendid terraces of Tetcott Road in Chelsea, ostensibly to return to the house in Wandsworth, where she was a servant.

But her mother viewed the clothing that was found with the body, and it was not Lilly's; neither, the mother said, was the torso itself.

Other leads likewise led no place. No identity was ever forthcoming, and therefore no proof of murder. The so-called Whitehall Mystery remains just that . . . a mystery.

A River Full of Remains

Such a grisly discovery, and frustrating mystery, was not, however, unprecedented.

Back in 1873, a similarly dismembered body had washed up in three different places on the banks of the Thames, and the following year, a second turned up in Putney. And little more than a year before the Whitehall discovery, another was found, carved into no fewer than twelve pieces distributed between the Thames Estuary, Regent's Park Canal and the riverbanks at Temple and Battersea.

All were women, all had limbs removed, all were headless. At least some of these corpses, certain researchers have theorized, could have been the remains of a fresh cache of Ripper victims, disposed of not by the killer but by members of their own community. The law, however, shrugged away such suspicions. Rather than assign the Whitehall mystery to the continuing depredations of Jack the Ripper, the police preferred—unofficially, at least—to align it with these earlier cases, all of which bore far more similarities to one another than to anything that had occurred in Whitechapel. And, in the process, they created a *second* monster to roam the streets of the city, one who appears no less shadowy and mysterious than the Ripper, and who might well have shared his sense of humor.

The following summer, the similarly mutilated remains of a prostitute named Elizabeth Jackson were discovered in Chelsea, in the gardens of a house that once belonged to Mary Shelley, the creator of *Frankenstein*. Like the Whitehall mystery, the placement of the remains screams its scorn at the hapless lawmen.

Again the police shrugged aside suggestions that the Whitechapel murderer had ventured west. But at least one contemporary student of the murders, the aforementioned Robert Donston Stephenson, expressly believed the Whitehall mystery was actually the first of the Whitechapel murders.

And September 1889 delivered what some researchers consider to be the last of them, when yet another headless, legless torso was discovered, this time beneath a railway arch on Pinchin Street, off Backchurch Lane in Whitechapel (see Chapter Sixteen).

The Investigation Goes to the Dogs

A journalist's use of a terrier to sniff out the final remains of the Whitehall mystery torso was not mere caprice. It also reminded the public that, in the other great investigation of the day, the police had defiantly resisted employing dogs of any description to aid them in the hunt for the killer.

So far, anyway. Now, however, plans to do just that were under way. On October 10, the London *Echo* newspaper reported that Sir Charles Warren had recently arranged for a trial of bloodhounds in Hyde Park, and "seemed pleased" with the results.

With the press having been howling for weeks for such an innovation to be introduced, the trials should have gone some way toward redeeming Warren's reputation, at least so far as the Whitechapel killings were concerned.

Instead (but perhaps inevitably), the use of bloodhounds was seized upon as another example of the man's lack of imagination. Bloodhounds, the *Echo* continued, "are scarcely what is required. There are hounds in London which have been trained to follow a trail through a street, and these are the animals that are required."

Damned if he did, damned if he didn't, Warren assured newsmen that, although the dogs were still in training, "should they be required to aid in the work of detecting fresh crimes, [they] will be despatched to any spot in London with the utmost speed."

But even his own men were apparently divided over the usefulness of the dogs. An unnamed CID man told the paper, "If the murders had taken place in any of the parks, the hounds would have been there as soon as the police. But with hard, stony ground, and the many other obstacles to scent a trail, it is not thought they will be of any use."

Nevertheless, there clearly was some sympathy for the beleaguered investigators, as another news item revealed.

> Inspector Reid, Inspector Abberline, Inspector Chandler, and other of the chief officers are pursuing their investigations with the utmost rigour. Indeed, since the commission of the murders the detectives have been at work almost night and day. Many of them are heavy pecuniary losers, having in their zeal to find a clue, paid money which, even under the head of "extraordinary expenses," the Receiver would not sanction. Some of this money had been given to women who either associated with or knew the victims. The ordinary routine in the detection of criminals has been departed from, and any suggestion, however novel, is discussed by the authorities, and acted on if at all of a feasible character.

The weeks passed. The inquests into the deaths of Long Liz and Kate Eddowes came and went, and their bodies were laid to rest. The Whitehall mystery hogged the headlines for a few days, but that, too, soon passed.

Fear continued to percolate, but with every passing day bringing no fresh outrage, life in Whitechapel began to return to a semblance of normalcy—at least among those people who remained there.

As one newspaper reported, "Trade in many callings has been seriously affected, and some of the common lodging-houses are now almost denuded of female occupants of a certain class, the police having had direct information that unfortunate women who lately resided in Whitechapel and Spitalfields, are now residing at Battersea, Hammersmith, Notting Hill, Chelsea, and other populous suburban parishes."

By the third week in October, however, the Ripper had been silent for longer than at any time since his reign began. Even the newspapers, to whose circulation the murders had been a positive gold mine, were taking a hit. Over the past couple of months, *The Star*'s circulation had soared to over a quarter of a million copies a day. Now it was plunging back again, and its rival rags could all tell a similar sorry tale.

There was just one fresh outrage to report—a second letter, addressed to George Lusk, head of the Whitechapel Vigilance Committee, and delivered on the evening of October 16.

The letter was utterly unequivocal in its horror. In the top right-hand corner, in the place where the average correspondent would inscribe their address, this writer chose to scrawl, merely, "from hell."

He then continued,

> Mr Lusk, Sir, I send you half the Kidne I took from one woman and presarved it for you tother piece I fried and ate it was very nise. I may send you the bloody knif that took it out if you only wate a whil longer

> signed

> Catch me when you can Mishter Lusk

And true to the letter-writer's word, there was indeed another enclosure in the package—one half a kidney that itself was swiftly confirmed to be human by the medical examiner. Which left the authorities only to argue over whether it was actually the organ removed from Kate Eddowes's body. Some said it could be, others were adamant that it wasn't, that it was too healthy to have been pulled from a long-term alcoholic's body.

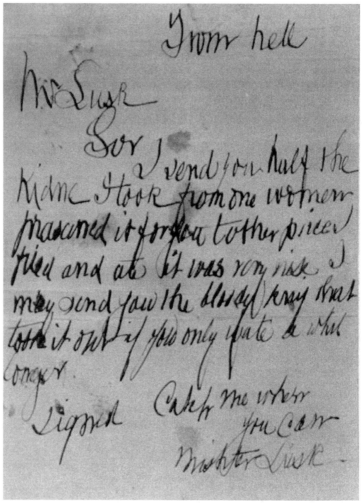

"Catch me when you can"—another taunting letter from the Ripper.
Wikimedia Commons

At least so far as the surviving evidence and records are concerned, however, everybody seemed to be missing one crucial point. If the kidney was not Kate's, then where did the sender get it from? Medical students were briefly suspected; so were mortuary attendants. But one fact remained. Past letter-writers had been dismissed as cranks. This one cast a considerably more sinister shadow.

14

The Dover Street Demon

Black Magic in the White Chapel

> Did the murderer . . . designing to offer the mystic number of seven human sacrifices in the form of a cross—deliberately pick out beforehand on a map the places in which he would offer them to his infernal deity of murder? If not, surely these six coincidences are the most marvellous event of our time.
>
> —*Robert Donston Stephenson, 1888*

S till, October passed slowly for the investigators. Already they were dispirited by their absolute failure to make any headway in the case, and the murderer's silence also played on their nerves, leaving them not only wondering and worrying about when he might strike again, but also perhaps hankering for the wildfire of adrenaline they knew would awaken them *when* the next murder was reported.

A multitude of researchers, both amateur sleuths and professional agencies, have produced psychological profiles of the Ripper over the years, mapping out the kind of man he was from what is known of his methods and behavior.

What they rarely consider is that the Ripper himself was employing a form of psychological profiling, if not outright psychological warfare. Effortlessly, he had analyzed his pursuers' state of mind; now he was inciting in them the same doubts, uncertainties and boredom that afflicted so many armies as they became bogged down in those periods of inaction that characterized the great European wars.

He was lulling them not into a false sense of security, but into a very *real* state of disillusion—never knowing when he might strike again, and with every passing day, wondering *if* he would. And while they watched and waited for something to happen, the media's speculation—which was not dulled by inaction—went into overdrive.

More than one supernatural theory was raised, and long before author Ivor Edwards published *Jack the Ripper's Black Magic Rituals* in 2002, the belief that there was an occult element to the killings had permeated the popular imagination.

In 1973, *True Detective* magazine published an article by researcher Leonard Gribble, which demanded "Was Jack the Ripper a Black Magician?" And three years later, discharged with offhand nonchalance in Patrice Chaplin's *By Flower and Dean Street*, is the observation that "the Ripper *was* a magician. He had to do five murders—the number five formed a pentagram—and then he'd be immune from discovery."

Ivor Edwards's researches, however, turned up even more esoteric shocks.

First, he told the *Guardian* newspaper, "I found that by joining some of the [murder] sites together, you created two equilateral triangles; a sacred symbol which, in occult doctrine, Satan devised to be used in worship of him."

But then he examined one further victim, and realized that "by joining the sites together, it was possible to create the Vesica Piscis, a fish-like symbol

"HE TURNED AND LOOKED AT ME."

The slightest glance from a stranger could provoke a new Ripper sighting, as this contemporary magazine illustration proves.   *Alamy*

worshipped by the early Christians. By murdering his victims and leaving their bodies in that way, the killer intended a tribute to Satan."

And who was his primary suspect? Robert Donston Stephenson, the London Hospital patient who himself had nursed many far-fetched theories regarding the Ripper—including his own insistence that black magic lay at the heart of the mystery. No less than today, where the Ripper is concerned, no theory was too far-fetched to be reported, and no methodology either.

In December 1888, the *Pall Mall Gazette* published a piece written by Stephenson ostensibly dedicated to proving that "the Whitechapel Demon" was a Frenchman.

It was credited to "One Who Thinks He Knows," and it discusses a French grimoire, *Le Dogme et Rituel de la Haute Magie,* a two-volume work published by Eliphas Levi (actually, a Parisian shoemaker named Alphonse Louis Constant) , within whose pages, Stephenson believed, could be found a recipe for conjuring demons.

In fact, Levi was firmly opposed to any such practice, describing it as "an epidemic of unreason." Nevertheless, Stephenson wrote,

> It is in the list of substances prescribed as absolutely necessary to success [in the conjuration of devils] that we find the link which joins modern French necromancy with the quest of the East-end murderer.
>
> These substances are in themselves horrible, and difficult to procure. They can only be obtained by means of the most appalling crimes, of which murder and mutilation of the dead are the least heinous. Among them are strips of the skin of a suicide, nails from a murderer's gallows, candles made from human fat, the head of a black cat which has been fed forty days on human flesh, the horns of a goat which has been made the instrument of an infamous capital crime, and a preparation made from a certain portion of the body of a harlot. This last point is insisted upon as essential and it was this extra-ordinary fact that first drew my attention to the possible connection of the murderer with the black art.

Stephenson also points out that of the *seven* murders the Ripper was known to have committed, the first six could be united to form the shape of a cross—"a form which he intended to profane." He seems, too, to insist that what we regard as the final Ripper killing, Mary Jane Kelly's, was not the same man's work at all—Stephenson's seventh corpse was "the mutilated trunk found in the new police-buildings, which was probably the first of the series of murders, and was committed somewhere on the lines of the cross, the body being removed at the time.

The Dead Woman's Last Embrace

Stephenson was not the first person to introduce the supernatural to the case, however. That honor belonged to one of Long Liz's sisters, when she stood before the inquest into her sibling's demise and testified that "about twenty minutes past one on Sunday morning I felt a pressure on my breast and heard three distinct kisses."

But were they actually kisses? The *East London Advertiser*, thrilled by her testimony, pointed out that "this was just about the time at which the sister was giving up her life under the hands of the awful being in Berner-street."

> It was more than probable that Judas-like he first betrayed his victim with a kiss, and the pressure on the breast is what would naturally occur as he knelt over to cut her throat.
> Here then we have a representation of what was happening to the murdered woman reproduced at the same time in the mind of her sister.

Emboldened by the introduction of supernatural evidence into a legal inquiry, spiritualism raced to the cause. The movement had been gathering pace in the United Kingdom for several years; four decades after the Fox sisters introduced communing with the dead to American society, British mediums were finally making their own presence felt. The Whitechapel murders offered them their grandest stage yet.

In early October, it was widely reported that a renowned spiritualist in the northern city of Bolton had staged a séance, specifically to learn the identity of the Whitechapel murderer.

According to a report in London's *Evening News*, "the spirits revealed a vision of a man having the appearance of a farmer, but dressed like a navvy with a strap wound his waist and peculiar pockets. He had a dark moustache and scars behind his ears, besides other marks. He will commit one more murder and be caught red-handed."

Another medium in Cardiff contacted her local police to say she had contacted the spirit of Long Liz herself, who not only described her killer, but also named him, gave his address as a certain house on Commercial Road, and said he was a member of a gang of twelve men.

A third clairvoyant, one Mrs. Charles Spring, was adamant that the killer was an Italian. "Go to Florence," she implored the investigators. "We do not know his name but there are more than one in hiding now. He goes in and comes out of his home like a gentleman, and sometimes has a disguise like an old woman, going about."

> They go away out of London soon after the deed is done, back to their homes to carry on their business as usual through the week . . . They use chemicals to wipe off spots of blood from their clothes. They are too respectable-looking to be suspected by those who know them. Foreigners quick with knife and sure not to make a blunder. How they plot and plan: But look to military medicals, bad fallen ones now they cannot get bodies from the hospital so soon after death. They have a particular purpose. They want to find something.

It is uncertain whether or not the police followed up on Mrs. Spring's warnings. But they certainly had very little patience for another medium, Robert James Lees, when he paid the Whitechapel police a personal visit on October 2, to offer his services in the investigation. According to Lees's diary, he was "called a fool and a lunatic."

Nevertheless, upon visiting the murder site on Berners Street, he "got the trace of a man" and, the following day, he returned to the police station. This time they called him a madman *and* a fool, but Lees was not disheartened.

One day he and his wife were riding an omnibus from Shepherds Bush into the West End, when a man boarded the vehicle at Notting Hill. He was, Lees was convinced, the murderer, and when the man left the bus on Oxford Street, Lees was right behind him, pointing him out to a policeman and telling him, "That's Jack the Ripper."

The policeman didn't believe him.

Neither was this was Lees's only direct encounter with the killer, although it would be 1895 before he was prepared to publicly reveal his knowledge—to a newspaper, of course. That year, the rudiments of his tale appeared in the Chicago *Sunday Times-Herald*, and it would be another thirty-six years before "the full story" was published, serialized by the *Daily Express* over three days in March 1931.

Resplendent beneath a headline proclaiming him to be "[the] Clairvoyant Who Tracked Down Jack the Ripper," Lees first detailed how a vision warned him of Catherine Eddowes's death, which he described as the *ninth* killing; and that no fewer than seven more murders were committed before finally Lees led the law to the "west end mansion" that was the lair of Jack the Ripper.

There they confronted, and arrested, a once celebrated physician, now worn down by madness and guilt. The man would live out the remainder of his life in a private insane asylum, where he lived beneath the pseudonym of Thomas Mason. And it is from this story that researcher Stephen Knight spun his own determination that the madman was actually Sir William Gull, Royal Physician in Ordinary or, in common terms, the Queen's personal doctor.

The jury remains out on Lees. He was apparently well-known in spiritualist circles of the time, and his efforts to aid the investigation do appear genuine—at least, there is no evidence that he sought either financial gain or the glare of publicity when he made his offers to help; had there been, he certainly would not have waited seven years before selling his story to the press.

But just as contemporary police officers held different beliefs as to who "the Ripper" killed, so contemporary mystics held different theories over who "the Ripper" was.

The era's greatest occultist took center stage. Aleister Crowley, the self-proclaimed "wickedest man in Britain," allegedly claimed on several occasions to know the identity of the Ripper, and interestingly, he too appeared to suggest that it was Robert Donston Stephenson—even publishing an anecdote that might well speak volumes.

Stephenson at the time was sharing a house with both his former lover, Mabel Collins, and her sapphic mistress, the Baroness Vittoria Cremers. Both women were leading lights in the Theosophical Society, the occult movement founded by the legendary Russian mystic Madame Helena Petrovna Blavatsky, and it is probably worth noting that there was little love lost between the society members and Crowley himself.

Nevertheless, Crowley's story does have a ring of truth to it.

> One evening, [Stephenson] had just come in from the theatre—in those days everyone dressed, whether they liked it or not—and he found the women discussing [the Whitechapel murders].
>
> He gave a slight laugh, went into the passage, and returned in the opera cloak which he had been wearing to the theatre. He turned up the collar and pulled the cape across his shirtfront, made a slight gesture as if to say: "You see how simple it is;" and when a social difficulty presented itself, he remarked lightly: "Of course you cannot have imagined that the man could be a gentleman," and added: "There are plenty going about the East End in evening dress, what with opium smoking and one thing and another."

Crowley appears, too, to verify Stephenson's published theories about ritual magic, and the process by which "a sorcerer could attain 'the supreme black magical power' by following out a course of action identical with that of Jack the Ripper."

A chilling modern depiction of a Ripper-style murder.   *KUCO/Shutterstock*

Certain lesser powers [would be] granted to him spontaneously during the course of the proceedings. After the third murder, if memory serves, the assassin obtained on the spot the gift of invisibility, because in the third or fourth murder, a constable on duty saw a man and a woman go into a cul-de-sac. At the end there were the great gates of a factory, but at the sides no doorways or even windows. The constable, becoming suspicious, watched the entry to the gateway, and hearing screams, rushed in. He found the woman, mutilated, but still living; as he ran up, he flashed his bullseye in every direction; and he was absolutely certain that no other person was present. And there was no cover under the archway for so much as a rat.

It is not a precise description of Kate Eddowes's death, but, as Crowley expressly states, he was writing from a memory that he admitted might not be accurate. But it is instantly identifiable, regardless, and if one accepts the validity of the occult theory to begin with, it also seems perfectly reasonable.

"The Ripper" *did* disappear on the night of the double murder. And he had barely been seen or heard from since.

15

A Violet Plucked from Mother's Grave

The Ripping of Mary Jane Kelly

Of the latest, but not the last, of the murders in the East-end we need say little. The murderer seems on this occasion to have selected a younger victim, and to have profited by the security of a locked room to indulge to a much greater extent than on any previous occasion in his mania for mutilation. Short of absolutely skinning his next victim from head to heel, it is difficult to see what fresh horror is left for him to commit.

There is, of course, absolutely no means of preventing such a murder as this in the little room of an unfortunate. The woman invites the murderer into an apartment into which no one has a right to intrude. The certainty that no one will interfere, no matter what shouts and shrieks may be heard, is one of the indispensable conditions for carrying on her ghastly business, and in all probability she herself locked the door before reducing herself to the position of a living victim ready for this fiend's post-mortem.

—Pall Mall Gazette, *November 10, 1888*

Not all of the women ensnared within what the popular press called "the white slave trade" did so unwillingly, at least if Mary Jane Kelly was to be believed.

Deep into the night with her lover, Joseph Barnett, Mary would weave the tale of a blue-eyed blonde from Limerick, in Ireland, whose family—including six brothers and a sister—moved to Wales when she was young, where her father got a job at an ironworks.

She married at sixteen, but her collier husband was killed in a mine explosion just a couple of years later, and she moved to Cardiff to stay with a cousin. It was there, desperate for work, that she first fell into the world of prostitution, and when she moved to London, she readily found similar employment, in a high-class bordello (a "gay house" in the terminology of the age; and its employees were referred to as "gay women") among the upper-class homes on Cleveland Street in Knightsbridge.

There, she would entertain only the wealthiest of clients; was dressed in the best finery; and traveled around in a carriage. The madam of the establishment was French, as were many of the clientele, and on at least one occasion Mary traveled to that country with one such gentleman, presumably to work in a brothel there.

France was a frequent first stop for women being taken further afield against their wishes, but Mary seems to have made the trip of her own accord, and when she tired of it (she told Barnett she didn't like it the country), she returned to London. Her only lasting souvenir of the visit was to give herself a new middle name, the exotic-sounding "Jeanette," and even that was corrupted to "Jane" in the mouths of her new neighbors.

Back in London, life had certainly taken a turn for the worse. She did not return to the West End, at least for any amount of time; instead, she drifted into its mirror-image East End, and a boardinghouse close to the dockyards. She had just turned thirty and, by all the standards of the day, her best years as either a prostitute or a potential wife were behind her. She was drinking heavily and had a foul temper.

For a while, though, she seemed to find her feet, moving in with one Joseph Fleming, who worked in the building trade, and who did apparently propose to her. But they argued constantly, and Mary moved out of his Bethnal Green home to take up with a man named Morganstone, living in the shadow of Stepney Gasworks.

But that relationship, too, was doomed, and by 1886, she was living in Cooney's Lodging House on Thrawl Street in Whitechapel. She must have felt that she'd fallen as far as she could—nobody would ever have asked for a "tuppenny upright" in Knightsbridge.

Mary and Joseph

On Good Friday 1887, Mary met Joseph Barnett, a porter at Billingsgate fish market, who also worked as a fruit seller on Commercial Street. They went for a drink and arranged to meet again the following day, when he invited her to move in with him. Mary agreed, and with Barnett bringing in a steady wage, the couple rented a room on George Street.

They moved house a couple of times, first to a room on Little Paternoster Row, then to Brick Lane and, finally, to Dorset Street, where their tiny room at the back of number 26 looked out onto Miller's Court.

Sixpence a week bought them around twelve square feet, barely furnished with a bed, a table, a chair and a tin bath that was kept beneath the bed. The sole source of illumination was a candle seated atop a broken wineglass. A print of a woman mourning the death of her fisherman husband hung over the fireplace—widows were a popular theme with a lachrymose Victorian public, even in the depths of the Whitechapel slums

For Dorset Street was indeed a slum. Once, when it was known as Datchet Street, it had been quite glorious, at the heart of the weaving and silk-making industry that had built Spitalfields up in the first place. At one point, the street even housed one of Thomas Wedgwood's flagship pottery showrooms.

But the Industrial Revolution had destroyed the weaving trade, even as the neighborhood's reputation as a voracious employer boomed. People had long since grown accustomed to turning toward Spitalfields in search of jobs, and for many years, the trade had obliged. Now it was struggling to survive, but still the flood roared in.

As enterprise declined, so did the street, its reputation corrupting as fast as its name. By 1888, it had been Dorset Street for as long as anyone could remember, and the once proud houses had decayed just as long ago.

In the street's prime, those homes had been more than serviceable, even boasting private back gardens. As the more respectable tenants moved away, however, the entrepreneurs moved in, purchasing each house at knockdown prices and preparing to make a fortune in return.

Almost every home on the street was now a lodging house, the original, spacious rooms divided and divided again, until cheap wooden or even paper partitions were all that stood between one family and their immediate neighbors. When reformer Charles Booth set to work on his monumental "poverty map" of London, color-coding every neighborhood according to his studies of them, Dorset Street was shaded as black as night. It was "vicious," he said, "and semi-criminal."

Other observers concurred. But to Mary Jane and Joseph, it was home.

Miller's Court itself owed its existence to the voracity of local landlords. John Miller had owned a butcher's shop at number 30, and when two nearby properties, numbers 26 and 27, came up for sale, he purchased them.

He promptly set to work developing the gardens, paving them over and then building three cottages around the ensuing courtyard, each with one room upstairs, one downstairs. He called it, appropriately enough, Miller's Rents, and then proceeded to add three further cottages, for a total of six—each one as poorly built and maintained as the other.

The development, which he then renamed Miller's Court, was entered via an arched passageway just short of halfway down Dorset Street, adjacent to the Britannia public house (one of three pubs on the street at that time—the others were the Blue Coat Boy and the Horn of Plenty).

The court itself was tiny, fifty feet by ten, and clustered not only by those half dozen so-called homes, but also three communal toilets, a large public trash can and a single water tap. These utilities were the sole source of hygiene for the thirty or so residents of Miller's Court, and while Miller had long since moved on, the court's new owner had done nothing to improve his tenants' lot.

John "Jack" McCarthy was proprietor of the grocer's shop a few doors down, but landlord, too, of houses up and down Dorset Street, and across the rest of the area as well.

Mary Jane Kelly and Joseph Barnett were the kind of tenants McCarthy liked—Barnett had a job and Mary Jane . . . well, let's just say that she had the means to earn money as well. More than a few local landlords not only turned a blind eye toward such activities, they also actively encouraged it—it meant their female tenants would rarely be short of money, and also allowed the landlord to add a little extra to her rent, by way of "danger money."

That was not, apparently, the case with Mary Jane and Barnett, at least at first. The couple seemed to be genuinely fond of one another, but they fought regularly and violently, and it was one such row that ensured Mary Jane would be, if not alone in her room on the night of November 8, then at least in the company of a male stranger.

The fight itself occurred on October 30. Barnett moved out, but he would visit as often as he could, and when Mary Jane needed money, he'd give it to her. He was, in fact, there on the evening of November 8, arriving at 7:30 and staying for around half an hour.

His movements for the remainder of the evening, of course, would be checked by the police, but Barnett was never more than a "person of interest" in the inquiries that followed. Not until the late 1970s was his possible involvement in his partner's murder reawakened, through the work of novelist Mark Andrews (*The Return of Jack the Ripper*, 1977) and researcher Bruce Paley (*True Crime* magazine, 1982). Few other researchers, however, agree with their suggestions.

The Absent Heart

The minutiae of Mary Jane's itinerary, on the other hand, proved more elusive. Police inquiries revealed a possible sighting in the Britannia around 11:00 but it was not until almost midnight that she was spotted with any kind of certainty, when another local woman, Mary Ann Cox, saw her turning into Miller's Court with a strange man.

She and Mary Jane said good night to one another; Mary Jane was already roaring drunk, Cox thought, but her companion had slammed the door behind them before Mary Jane could say much more. Her last words to Cox were "I'm going to have a song," and sure enough, once inside, she started to sing, a popular Irish ballad called "A Violet from Mother's Grave."

Scenes of my childhood arise before my gaze,
Bringing recollections of bygone happy days.
When down in the meadow in childhood I would roam,
No one's left to cheer me now within that good old home,
Father and Mother, they have pass'd away;
Sister and brother, now lay beneath the clay,
But while life does remain to cheer me, I'll retain
This small violet I pluck'd from mother's grave.

Her companion was not an especially handsome fellow. Mid-thirties and stout, he was shabbily dressed in black, with a lengthy dark overcoat and a felt billycock hat. But his face was pale and blotchy, and a thick ginger mustache only accentuated the stains. Cox knew, however, that beggars could not be choosers, particularly in Mary Jane's line of business, and put him out of her mind.

Half an hour passed and Mary Jane was still singing, the same refrain echoing across the court, and the neighbors were getting sick of it. There were, they knew, all manner of reasons a woman might take a strange man back to her room in the middle of the night, but an impromptu drunken concert was probably not among them. One resident, a flower seller named Catherine Pickett, was even prepared to go and complain, but her husband, Dave, dissuaded her.

"You just leave the poor woman alone," he told her, so "I stopped where I was . . . and goes to bed," said Pickett later. "Worse luck for the poor dear soul. I should have come out of my room and caught the white-livered villain."

In fact, she wouldn't have. By 1:00 a.m., all was silent in the room, but at two, Mary Jane was on the move again, or so said another neighbor, George Hutchinson, who passed her on Commercial Street.

She stopped for a moment and asked if he could lend her some money; Hutchinson couldn't—in fact, he'd just had to walk home from Romford, thirteen miles distant, so penniless was he.

But there was another man on the street, and he seemed more amenable to Mary Jane's request. As Hutchinson passed by, he heard Mary Jane say, "All right," and the man reply, "You will be all right for what I have told you." He then draped an arm across Kelly's shoulders and they walked back toward Dorset Street.

Hutchinson was concerned. So much time had passed since the last of the murders, but the killer's shadow still hung over the streets. He'd noticed how, as he looked toward Mary Jane and her new companion, the man had pulled the brim of his dark felt hat down over his eyes, as if to thwart any attempt at seeing his face, and that aroused Hutchinson's suspicions.

What he did see, however, intrigued him. Past descriptions of the murderer were notoriously contradictory. But this man clearly was not a local—a long dark coat trimmed in astrakhan opened to reveal a dark jacket and a light waistcoat. A thick gold chain glinted across the man's chest, with a large seal and a red stone sunk into it. He wore a horseshoe tie pin, a white linen shirt, button boots and gaiters, and in his hand he held kid gloves and a small parcel wrapped in oilskin.

Hutchinson decided to follow the pair from a distance, remaining in the shadows as they stopped at the entrance to Miller's Court and straining to hear their conversation.

It was difficult, though. Only one sentence really sank in, Mary Jane telling the stranger, "All right, my dear, come along. You will be comfortable." And then they kissed.

Still beset by doubt, Hutchinson remained at his station, watching Miller's Court, for the next forty-five minutes. But all was quiet. Finally, at 3:00 a.m., he turned for home, just missing Mary Ann Cox as she returned from a late-night errand, and still all was silent.

It is the sheer detail contained within Hutchinson's testimony that has aroused suspicion—not so much at the time, but certainly later. The police certainly had no problem in believing Hutchinson's account. But Stephen Wright's *Jack the Ripper: An American View* (1999) looks more closely at this desperately concerned citizen, a man who waited *forty-five minutes* outside

Mary Kelly's house in a driving rainstorm, and whose description of the man he'd seen her with was far too detailed to be true.

Anybody could have determined the man's height, hat and clothing. But Hutchinson's observations would have put Sherlock Holmes to shame—gold chain, red stone, horseshoe tie pin . . . all seen and minutely described from across a darkened street at two in the morning!

It was all too good to be true, and Wright is not alone in suspecting Hutchinson of having made up the entire tale, to draw suspicion away from his own activities. Ben Court and Caroline Ip, writers of the British TV series *Whitechapel*, are likewise supporters of the belief that the Good Samaritan was responsible for at least one of the Whitechapel murders—the one a number of other investigators have suggested was not a part of the existing sequence in the first place.

At 4:00 a.m., two of Mary Jane's neighbors—Elizabeth Prater in the room upstairs, and Sarah Lewis across the way—distinctly heard a scream, and a cry of "Murder!" Both turned over and went back to sleep—fears of the Jack the Ripper might have been rife, but if the average Whitechapel resident paid attention to every cry of "murder" they heard in the night, nobody would ever get any sleep.

Maybe if the cry had been repeated, or there had been other sounds, the women might have acted. But silence fell again, and it remained undisturbed till dawn, when the first locals began stirring for a new day.

Elizabeth Prater was up at five, heading down to the Ten Bells for a breakfast glass of rum. About forty-five minutes later, Mary Ann Cox heard what sounded like a man's footsteps out in Miller's Court, but she ignored them.

The morning had dawned cold and wet, so one of Mary Jane's friends, Catherine Pickett, knocked on her door to ask if she could borrow a shawl. She got no reply, and continued her search elsewhere. Not until around 10:30 did anybody else call on Mary Jane—the rent collector, Thomas Bowyer, or "Indian Harry," as he was known around the streets.

He, too, knocked, but received no reply. He tried the door; it was locked. So he went stepped around the cottage and looked through the window, pushing aside the rags that had been wedged in to replace a pane broken during one of Mary Jane and Joseph's recent fights.

His cry of shock and horror could have wakened the dead. But it did not awaken Mary Jane.

Police Surgeon Thomas Bond's description of what Indian Harry glimpsed, and the police soon saw, makes lengthy—and appalling—reading.

The body was lying naked in the middle of the bed, the shoulders flat but the axis of the body inclined to the left side of the bed. The head was turned on the left cheek. The left arm was close to the body with the forearm flexed at a right angle and lying across the abdomen.

The right arm was slightly abducted from the body and rested on the mattress. The elbow was bent, the forearm supine with the fingers clenched. The legs were wide apart, the left thigh at right angles to the trunk and the right forming an obtuse angle with the pubes.

The whole of the surface of the abdomen and thighs was removed and the abdominal cavity emptied of its viscera. The breasts were cut off, the arms mutilated by several jagged wounds and the face hacked beyond recognition of the features. The tissues of the neck were severed all round down to the bone.

The viscera were found in various parts viz: the uterus and kidneys with one breast under the head, the other breast by the right foot, the liver between the feet, the intestines by the right side and the spleen by the left side of the body. The flaps removed from the abdomen and thighs were on a table.

The bed clothing at the right corner was saturated with blood, and on the floor beneath was a pool of blood covering about two feet square. The wall by the right side of the bed and in a line with the neck was marked by blood which had struck it in a number of separate splashes.

The face was gashed in all directions, the nose, cheeks, eyebrows, and ears being partly removed. The lips were blanched and cut by several incisions running obliquely down to the chin. There were also numerous cuts extending irregularly across all the features.

The neck was cut through the skin and other tissues right down to the vertebrae, the fifth and sixth being deeply notched. The skin cuts in the front of the neck showed distinct ecchymosis. The air passage was cut at the lower part of the larynx through the cricoid cartilage.

Both breasts were more or less removed by circular incisions, the muscle down to the ribs being attached to the breasts. The intercostals between the fourth, fifth, and sixth ribs were cut through and the contents of the thorax visible through the openings.

The skin and tissues of the abdomen from the costal arch to the pubes were removed in three large flaps. The right thigh was denuded in front to the bone, the flap of skin, including the external organs of generation, and part of the right buttock. The left thigh was stripped of skin fascia, and muscles as far as the knee.

The left calf showed a long gash through skin and tissues to the deep muscles and reaching from the knee to five inches above the ankle. Both arms and forearms had extensive jagged wounds.

The right thumb showed a small superficial incision about one inch long, with extravasation of blood in the skin, and there were several abrasions on the back of the hand moreover showing the same condition.

On opening the thorax it was found that the right lung was minimally adherent by old firm adhesions. The lower part of the lung was broken and torn away. The left lung was intact. It was adherent at the apex and there were a few adhesions over the side. In the substances of the lung there were several nodules of consolidation.

The pericardium was open below and the heart absent.

Indian Harry ran first to fetch John McCarthy from his store nearby, and the pair hurried to Commercial Street police station, from whence Inspector Walter Beck and the young PC Walter Dew accompanied them back to Miller's Court.

The door to number 12 remained locked—the bloodhounds were coming, it was said, and instructions had been received to keep the room undisturbed until they had arrived, to avoid confusing the scents. Even the doctor who joined the group, George Bagster Phillips, made his initial examination through the dirty window pane.

It was 1:30 before the gathering crowd was informed the dogs were not available after all, and finally the door could be forced—John McCarthy took a pickax to it, perhaps giving the lie to the belief that everything in his properties was cheap and nasty. If that had truly been so, the door, and its lock, would have succumbed to the lightest kick. One can imagine (and many subsequent authors have) the response of the men who now pushed through the shattered remains of the door, into the charnel house that unfolded before them.

By now, the scene outside was pulsing with onlookers—a police cordon placed at the Commercial Street end of Dorset Street was barely able to contain the heaving mass, all the more so after a horse and cart arrived, bearing with it the coffin in which Mary Jane would be transported to the mortuary.

And even after her remains had left the premises and the room had been firmly padlocked, the crowds continued to mill around Dorset Street.

Author Margot Asquith was among the people who flocked to the East End to "visit what journalists called 'the scene of the tragedy.' It was strange watching crowds of people collected daily to see nothing but an archway." As if she were doing anything different!

All manner of rumor and speculation was abroad, but one thing seemed fixed to everybody's lips: This was Jack the Ripper's most gruesome killing yet.

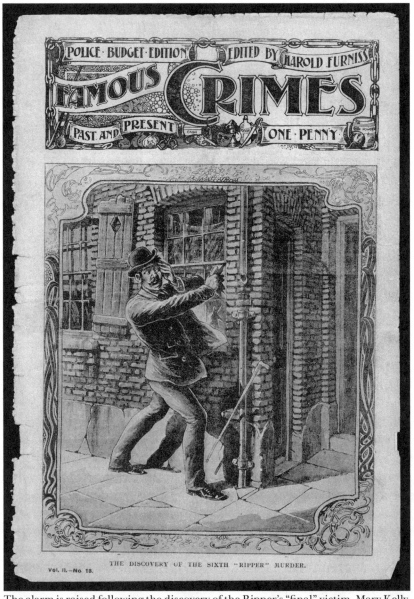

The alarm is raised following the discovery of the Ripper's "final" victim, Mary Kelly.

Alamy

Kelly was buried in St Patrick's Roman Catholic Cemetery, Leytonstone, on 19 November 1888. Unlike the other victims, however, her remains may not be permitted to rest in peace. In March 2017, author Patricia Cornwell announced her intentions to locate that grave (its precise whereabouts are long forgotten), exhume the remains, and run DNA tests, seeking not only clues as to Kelly's background, but also seeking any surviving traces of her killer. "[The Ripper] spent more time with her body than any [of the others]," Cornwell explained. "In addition we could give her the dignity she deserves and perhaps, through DNA, satisfy claims that she has descendants alive today."

Chasing Ghosts

Again, the police launched into the business of investigating every lead, following every suggestion, scraping every barrel. Sir Charles Warren even, finally, overcame the policy of no longer offering rewards for material evidence, when he let it be known that "the Secretary of State will advise the grant of Her Majesty's gracious pardon to any accomplice not being a person who contrived or actually committed the murder, who shall give such information and evidence as shall lead to the discovery of the person or persons who committed the murder."

It was a unique document—never before in the annals of British crime had a royal pardon been offered for a capital crime (nor ever since). But it was not without its critics. After all, beyond the testimony of Israel Schwartz and the two possible gang assaults all those months before, there had never been any concrete suggestion that the killer even had an accomplice. The suspicion quickly, and understandably, arose that the pardon was issued more in the hope of silencing the police's critics than of flushing out any possible partner in crime.

Besides, even if there were two people involved, why would either of them want to turn themselves in now? If the police hadn't caught them yet, they probably never would.

They were too busy arresting other people.

In a beer-house on Fish-street-hill, as a group of friends discussed the latest murder, one of their number, a Mr. Brown (who actually lived on Dorset Street) pointed to a stain on a stranger's coat and declared that it looked like blood.

The stranger insisted it was paint, but there were further, similar stains on his shirt, and when Brown continued to press him, the man took off.

Brown followed, convinced he had discovered the Ripper, and then hauled him into Bishopsgate police station. But of course the stranger had an alibi—he'd spent the night of the murder in a cell in Shadwell, ironically enough on a charge of behaving suspiciously. He was released.

So were two men spotted loitering around Dorset Street in the early hours of the morning—nothing unusual, one would assume, in the light of the furor that had still to die down, but sufficient to arouse the suspicions of a couple of nearby residents.

One of the men, the more foreign-looking of the pair, apparently, even sported a pointed mustache, a long black overcoat and a deerstalker hat, and when the police searched him, he was found to be carrying what was known as a pocket medical chest, containing small bottles of chloroform.

The killer?

No. He was a medical student from Pimlico, drawn to the area by the same curiosity that everybody else was exhibiting. He was released.

A third man was arrested after one Peter Maguire saw him try to pick up a girl in the Clean House pub, and then walk out onto the street with what one can only imagine was sufficiently suspicious a demeanor that Maguire felt a pressing need to follow him.

The stranger led Maguire toward Spitalfields Market and there, suddenly realizing he was being followed, began running. But Maguire kept on his trail, and became even more convinced he'd cornered the killer when the man entered a darkened street, took off the pair of gloves he'd been wearing and put on another.

At this point, we might assume that Maguire had simply been reading too much cheap fiction, but the chase was only beginning.

The stranger boarded an omnibus. Maguire followed, looking all the while for a policeman who would stop and search it. One refused, but another agreed, and there was the suspect, sitting up in one corner of the vehicle.

Off to Commercial Street station he went—from whence he was almost equally promptly discharged. Even at the height of the murder investigation, talking to girls, changing your gloves and running when a stranger started to follow you were not indictable offenses.

These were not isolated instances. Across Whitechapel, throughout the East End, all around London, and the rest of Britain too, every report, every glimmer of suspicion, every tiny hint had to be followed up, for who knew when a passerby's observations might triumphantly turn up the right man?

Other theories were followed. Could the schedule of the killings be applied, perhaps, to the comings and goings of ships at the docks? A Manchester-based correspondent to the *Pall Mall Gazette* certainly thought so.

Apparently, he had recently met an English seaman who said that, visiting an East End music hall sometime after August 13, he'd met a Malay cook who claimed to have been robbed of two years' savings by "a woman of the town."

He was now searching for her, but said that should he fail to find the guilty doxy, "he would murder and mutilate as many of the class as he could lay his hands on." Find a ship whose schedule coincided with the killings, explained the letter-writer, search its crew for an angry Malay cook, and you would find your killer.

The calendar was consulted and consulted again. The murders, it had long been apparent, seemed only to occur on weekends and holidays—even the psychic Mrs. Spring had picked up on that: Emma Smith on Easter Monday; Martha Tabram on the night of bank holiday Monday; Mary Ann Nichols on a Friday that also saw the city celebrating Lord Mayor's Day; all the others on a Saturday night or Sunday morning. The newspaper in which the Whitehall mystery was wrapped was dated August 24—a Friday.

Any man whose livelihood took him out of London throughout the week (or, contrarily, took him into London at weekends) was now an automatic suspect.

So were the crews of the cattle boats that reliably docked on Thursday nights and then left with the tide on Mondays.

But there were no vast databases of names, addresses and occupations the police could call upon; no registry of voters, or Social Security records. Few employers even kept a written record of the men they employed.

People lived in a world absolutely devoid of what we might call a paper trail, free from any kind of official scrutiny beyond that they brought upon themselves. Even arrest records were next to useless—false names and addresses fell easily from a felon's tongue, and the police knew it.

Only the national census, conducted once every ten years, could even pretend to offer up a reliable accounting of every man, woman and child in the land, but the most recent one was seven years old, and even that detailed only where each person was on the night it was taken.

There were approximately 70,000 people living in Whitechapel in 1888. Almost half a million in the East End as a whole, five million throughout London in its entirety, and more than twenty-five million across the entire

United Kingdom. And the authorities knew next to nothing about any of them.

Did they really want to start adding foreign seamen to the list?

The sheer ordinariness of the killer rendered him utterly invisible. As journalist George Sims later wrote,

> He rode in tramcars and omnibuses. He travelled to Whitechapel by the underground railway, often late at night. Probably on several occasions he had but one fellow-passenger in the compartment with him, and that may have been a woman. Imagine what the feelings of those travellers would have been had they known that they were alone in the dark tunnels of the Underground with Jack the Ripper! Some of us must have passed him in the street, sat with him perhaps at a cafes or a restaurant. For a whole year at least he was a free man, exercising all the privileges of freedom. And yet he was a homicidal maniac of the most diabolical kind.

This realization must have played on many a mind, including that of Her Majesty Queen Victoria herself.

The monarch had already signaled her dissatisfaction with the situation in meetings with the Prime Minister, Lord Salisbury. But now, she let him have it with both barrels.

The modern debate over how many women the Ripper killed is not, in fact, new. A period map of Whitechapel and Spitalfields, showing the locations of seven suspected murders.

Wikimedia Commons

The queen was at her Scottish castle of Balmoral when she heard the news of Mary Jane Kelly's murder, and she dashed off a telegram almost immediately:

> This new and most ghastly murder shows the absolute necessity for some very decided action. All these courts must be lit [a reference to the darkness that was endemic to the city's alleyways and yards], & our detectives improved. They are not what they should be.

She closed with a stern admonishment: "You promised when the 1st murders took place to consult with your colleagues about it." Unspoken was the accusation that clearly, he had not.

16

The Horror Never Stops

The Ripper Rips On

Shortly before 1 o'clock this morning a constable on his beat, while passing through Castle-alley, in Whitechapel, noticed the form of a woman lying in the shadow of a doorway. He at first thought it was one of the wanderers so numerous in the neighbourhood, especially at this season, and was about to rouse the woman, when he was horrified to discover that she was dead, blood flowing from a wound in the throat.

The body was in a pool of blood, which flowed from a gash in the stomach, evidently inflicted with a sharp knife or razor. The officer at once gave the alarm and within a few minutes several other constables were on the spot. The officials at the Commercial-road Station were informed of the discovery, and the superintendent in charge at once despatched a messenger in a cab for the divisional surgeon. From what could be ascertained in the neighbourhood the murdered woman seemed to be about 40 years of age, and seemed to have belonged to the unfortunate class. The neighbourhood is closely watched by police, but no one had been arrested up to 2 o'clock

—The Times, *17 July, 1889.*

Canonical history informs us the barbaric butchering of Mary Jane Kelly was the last of the Ripper murders. But just as police and citizens alike lived the six weeks between the fourth and fifth deaths in a state of constant alertness and fear, so the weeks that followed the slaughter in Miller's Court themselves percolated with dread and anticipation.

The *Pall Mall Gazette* was certainly not alone when it predicted that this latest slaughter would not be the last; nobody who had paid the slightest attention to the killings could believe the Whitechapel murders would simply stop.

And they would be correct.

On November 21, Whitechapel awoke to the news that another woman had been killed; "another murder and mutilation," as the *Evening News* put it, "similar to those which have already been perpetrated."

> The Central News learns that another terrible murder was com-mitted, last night, near Flower and Dean-street, Spitalfields. The murder took place in a lodging house, the unfortunate woman having her throat cut, and being otherwise shockingly mutilated. The murderer again escaped, leaving no trace behind.

In fact, she hadn't. A woman *had* been attacked, apparently by the man with whom she intended spending the night. They had taken a bed at a common lodging house on George Street, close by Flower and Dean Street, around 8:00 p.m. but ninety minutes later, her screams aroused the entire building.

As her companion rushed out, seemingly unhindered, the woman, Annie Farmer, was found with her throat cut open, but still alive. She was able to describe her assailant, and apparently name him, too, and she lived.

The media was swift to describe her as "the latest victim of Jack the Ripper." But the police were less convinced. Despite the copious amounts of blood, Annie Farmer's wound was more or less a superficial one.

Furthermore, while she allegedly insisted she'd been attacked by Jack, she also acknowledged that she was well acquainted with the man, and . . . yes . . . well . . . maybe . . . the attack had not been wholly unjustified. She was attempting to rob him at the time, and had hidden his money in her mouth.

As for the man's hasty departure, nobody could be surprised at that. With Annie screaming the name of the Ripper, he'd have been sized by the lynch mob before the police could even put their boots on.

Again the streets fell silent—or, at least, as silent as they ever could with a major murder investigation still under way, and the alleyways as alive as ever with vice, and countless other crimes, too. Maybe the girls were more cautious than before; maybe they worried, as they went about their business, that the next john might turn out to be a Jack. But they had to eat, they needed to sleep. So they trusted their luck and got on with their lives.

Besides, November was turning into December, the promise of Christmas was in the air, and though that was scarcely a cause for celebra-tion among many of Whitechapel's most unfortunate residents, still there

With the right lighting, the grimmer aspects of the modern city can still convey the mood of its Victorian counterpart.   *Pyty/Shutterstock*

would have been a certain gaiety abroad as the days tumbled into weeks and the Ripper maintained his silence.

There was one scare just before Christmas, however, when the body of another prostitute, Catherine "Rose" Mylett, was found in Clarke's Yard, just off Poplar High Street.

She appeared to have been strangled—no fewer than four doctors stepped forth at her inquest to say so; and it was unlikely, all agreed, that the killer was Jack. There were no other injuries, no signs of further violence or even a struggle; and the only witness to anything untoward that evening was adamant that he'd seen Rose in the company of two sailors.

> It was about five minutes to eight o'clock on Wednesday night, when I was going to my work. Upon going up England row [nearly opposite Clarke's yard] I noticed two sailors. The shorter one was speaking to the deceased, and the tall one was walking up and down. So strange did it seem that I stopped and 'took account' of

them. Then I heard the woman say several times "No! no! no!" and the short sailor spoke in a low tone.

The tall one was about 5ft 11in. He looked like a Yankee. The shorter one was about 5ft 7in. It struck me that they were there for no purpose, and that was the reason I took so much notice of their movements. I have been to the mortuary, and seen the deceased. She is the same woman, and she was sober when I saw her with the sailors.

Again, it appeared that the Ripper was exonerated. But the police were not satisfied. Instead, there seemed to be a concerted effort on behalf of the authorities to remove Rose from the annals of the year's murder cases altogether.

A policeman, Sergeant Golding, testified that there was a spotted handkerchief around the dead woman's throat, but that it had neither been tied nor pulled tightly against the flesh.

Much was made, too, of the fact that there was no sign of a struggle. "The yard was not paved," explained one expert, "but was composed of earth, and would show signs of a struggle had once taken place. [The] witness's first impression was that deceased had been leaning against some posts near the wall and had fallen down."

When a fifth doctor, Thomas Bond, stepped forward to say his own examination of the body suggested death by natural causes, the coroner was disposed to agree with him.

A verdict of "willful murder against some person or persons unknown" *was* eventually arrived at. But such a level of uncertainty had been introduced into the popular narrative that, as the bloody year of 1888 finally shuddered to a close, the Ripper remained at least out of sight, if not wholly out of mind.

Except he wasn't.

Throughout the last half of the year, a number grief-and-gore-packed chapbooks (of the kind that luckless Kate Eddowes once produced) had inevitably been published to keep the public up to date with the saga, and that flow had scarcely been stanched by the killer's months of inactivity.

More learned treatises, too, had appeared, while the letters columns of the press continued to overflow with theories and possibilities. Less than a year after the killings commenced, the story of Jack the Ripper was already stepping out of the pages of the newspapers and into the realms of folklore—the eternal whodunit.

Moves were even afoot to bring the tale to the stage. French playwrights Xavier Bertrand and Louis Clairan were preparing to debut their play

Jack l'Eventreur at the Chateau d'Eau Theatre in Paris, and the *East London Observer* confirmed the killer's newfound status when it remarked, "The legendary Jack will assuredly be wanting in ordinary human curiosity if he fails to avail himself of one of the numerous cheap trips to the French capital, in order to see for himself what a couple of ingenious French playwrights, well versed in the physiology of crime and criminals, have made for him."

The *legendary* Jack. He must have been so proud.

Proud enough to provide the play with an encore?

Jack's Back

On July 17, exactly three weeks shy of the first anniversary of Martha Tabram's death, PC Joseph Allen was enjoying a remarkably peaceful beat.

Stepping off Whitechapel High Street, he made his way up Castle Alley, a narrow passageway that only unwillingly broadened into a wider thoroughfare, dark in the shadows of the Brooke Bond tea company's warehouses, and the back wall of the Whitechapel Wash House—the only source of hot water and soap for so many of the area's residents.

He paused beneath a gaslight and ate whatever light snack he had brought along with him. A brewer's dray and a scavenger's (road cleaner's) wagon were parked by the curb, but there was nothing unusual about that. The alleyway was quiet, so he finished his meal and moved on. It was 12:30 a.m.

A few minutes later, a second constable entered the alley, PC Walter Andrews. He, too, saw and heard nothing, and said as much to Sergeant Edward Badham, whom he met a little further along. Andrews continued on his beat and, less than thirty peaceful minutes later, he was back on Castle Alley, approaching it this time from the opposite direction.

And there he saw it, lying between the same two carts beside which PC Allen had eaten his snack: the body of a woman, her clothing and limbs so grotesquely arranged that it was impossible not to see what had been done to her.

Some of it, anyway.

As in every previous killing, the woman's throat had been cut first, severing the carotid artery. Again, there was evidence of the killer kneeling, or at least putting his weight on her chest while he did so. A seven-inch gash extended from below her left breast to her navel, and seven or eight more traveled between her naval and her genitalia, which had also been cut.

It was not evident at first, nor would it become so until the inquest. But where these wounds differed from the Ripper's traditional assault was in their severity.

According to the evidence, "the mutilations were mostly superficial in manner, the deepest of which opened neither the abdominal cavity nor the muscular structure." The wounds also suggested that the killer was left-handed (the Whitechapel murderer was believed to be right-handed), and that the "sharp-pointed weapon" he deployed seemed smaller than the one the police believed was traditionally favored.

It was for these reasons that Dr. George Bagster Phillips declared, "I cannot satisfy myself, on purely anatomical and professional grounds, that the perpetrator of all the [Whitechapel] murders is our man. I am, on the contrary, impelled to a contrary conclusion in this, noting the mode of procedure and the character of the mutilations, and judging of motive in connection with the latter."

He might also have pointed out that, for the first time, the killer had struck on a day that was neither holiday or weekend.

Hardly surprisingly, the media disagreed wholeheartedly with his conclusions. The *East End News* declared,

> There is apparently reason to believe that the murder committed shortly before one o'clock on Wednesday morning in Castle-alley, Whitechapel, is the work of the same hand that has already slain seven women in the locality.
>
> The recent crime indeed possesses nearly all the features of those that have gone before. The weapon has been handled with the same dexterity and muscular force; again a woman has fallen the victim, and again apparently the deed has been perpetrated in profound silence, and the murderer vanished as if miraculously.
>
> Only a short time before the crime was committed a policeman stood eating his supper on the very spot where the victim was afterwards found. At all surrounding points during the night constables had been passing to and fro at brief intervals.
>
> In a room overlooking the scene of the crime several persons were assembled at the time it is known that the assassin must have been at work. They are positive that they would have heard any noise in the road-way; and yet, as a matter of fact, they heard nothing.

Dr. Thomas Bond, too, was adamant:

> I see in this murder evidence of similar design to the former Whitechapel murders, viz. sudden onslaught on the prostrate woman, the throat skillfully and resolutely cut with subsequent

mutilation, each mutilation indicating sexual thoughts and a desire to mutilate the abdomen and sexual organs. I am of opinion that the murder was performed by the same person who committed the former series of Whitechapel murders.

Another conflict arose over the cause of five strange marks on the left side of the body. Dr. Philips thought they were the impression of the killer's right hand; Dr. Bond disagreed.

The dead woman was identified. Forty years old, Alice McKenzie had grown up in Peterborough and moved to the East End around 1871, when she was around twenty-two.

Her friends knew her as "Clay Pipe Alice," on account of her rarely being seen without such an implement to hand, but she was not an unattractive woman, despite the noticeable scars on her forehead, and the loss of part of one thumb, both the legacy of an accident at work.

Little is known of her life prior to around 1885, when she took up with an Irish porter named John McCormack. Together, they became a familiar sight around the local lodgings and doss houses, but they were most recently resident at Mr. Tenpenny's lodging house on Gun Street (the owner was actually named Tempany).

It was there that McCormack saw her for the last time, on the afternoon of July 16, when he returned home after a morning's work.

He was exhausted, so he handed Alice their rent money—eight pence—plus ten pennies more to spend as she wished. He then went to bed.

Alice did not pay the rent. Instead, she seems to have gone out soon afterward and, while she may have been sighted in one of several pubs, it was not until mid-evening that she was definitely seen again, when she returned to Mr. Tenpenny's.

She soon headed out again. A friend, Margaret Franklin, saw her shortly before midnight on Flower and Dean Street, hurrying down the road toward Brick Lane. Franklin, who lived on that street, greeted her, but Alice didn't slow down. She simply replied, "All right, can't stop now," and kept going.

She was running, it transpired, toward her death. Alice's body was discovered just one hour later.

A few paces behind him, PC Andrews heard a man approaching—Isaac Jacobs, a bookmaker in the employ, curiously enough, of Alice's landlord.

While Jacobs waited by the body, Andrews blew his whistle to summon aid. Sergeant Badham was the first to respond; he, in turn, sought out PC Allen and dispatched him back to Commercial Street police station with the news.

Both ends of the street were blocked off and Dr. Phillips was sent for. After so many past occurrences, the operation ran like a well-oiled machine. And it ran into exactly the same breakdown as usual. There simply was nothing for the investigators to grab onto. Or, in the words of what was once a well-known pun, it was as if a thief had stolen all the toilets from the police station: The cops had nothing to go on.

The media, on the other hand, had a field day, with the *East London Observer* most pointedly reminding officialdom that, almost a year into their supposedly thorough investigations, nothing had changed.

> The murder fiend is at his terribly ghastly work again. Countless pens are taken up again to write up the details of a mysterious and horrible crime in Whitechapel; and the heart of the nation is again harrowed by revolting stories of murder and mutilation. But what is there new to be said? Everything is on the same lines with the series of barbarous atrocities of last year—so nearly, indeed, does the crime tally with its ghastly predecessors that for all purposes we might as well tear out from the journals of that date a column or two describing one of last year's murders, alter a name here and a street there, and the sad tale would be complete.

Even more alarmingly, several newspapers reported that the police had been warned to expect such an attack, that they had, "during the past few weeks received letters, signed 'Jack the Ripper,' intimating that he would recommence his horrible work in July."

Another such note, allegedly, had been delivered to one of the leaders of the vigilance groups just three weeks earlier.

Had there been any increase in patrols? Had there been any warning issued to the public? Had there been any sign at all the police even cared that Jack was back?

So far as the press could see, not one.

We will never know for certain whether Alice McKenzie was truly a victim of the Ripper, or whether she fell prey to some kind of copycat killer.

Certainly there are many authors and researchers who believe she was—among them author Colin Wilson, whose acclaimed writings on, and fascination with, such diverse themes as crime, philosophy, the occult and sexuality met in tumultuous climax in his 1960 novel *Ritual in the Dark*.

The story itself is set in the modern era, with Wilson's narrator, Gerard Sorme, first befriended by the fascinatingly urbane Austin Nunne, and then drawn inch by inch into the parallel universe of sadism, deviance and violence being played out on the streets of mid-1950s Whitechapel by a man the press consider a living reincarnation of the Ripper.

It is there, where he is visiting a friend, that Sorme comes face to face with the living relative of one of the original killer's victims. "The last victim."

"The woman who was killed in the room in Miller's Court?" asks Sorme.

"No, there was another one. She was killed under a lamp post in Castle Alley. That was Great Aunt Sally McKenzie."

The name is slightly off (although it was not uncommon for Alices to be nicknamed "Sally"), but the insinuation is made regardless.

The canon was wrong.

The Pinchin Street Torso

If the Ripper had returned, however, he was certainly operating on a very different schedule than before. The remainder of July passed by without incident, and the whole of August, too. Rumor ran rife through Whitechapel as the anniversaries of the earliest killings came into view, but both passed by uncelebrated, at least by the killer. And, so it appeared, did the next date, recalling the September 7 killing of Annie Chapman.

Three days later, that belief was thoroughly disavowed by the discovery, beneath a railway arch in Pinchin Street, of what passing PC William Pennett initially took to be a mere bundle of rags.

Only when he walked over and leaned in closer to inspect it did he realize what was lying there. It was the naked torso of a woman. Both her head and her legs were missing.

The term "damage control" had yet to be coined in 1889, but that is precisely the policy the police decided upon.

Without even a hint of flippancy, it was pointed out that the Metropolitan Police were hardly unfamiliar with limbless, decapitated torsos turning up around the city, from the banks of the river, in a garden in Chelsea, even on the site of their own new headquarters.

Beyond the fact that this later corpse was discovered in Whitechapel, there was no evidence whatsoever to link this latest grisly exhibit with the depredations of the Ripper—aside, perhaps, from the date on which the woman died.

Dr. Phillips estimated she had breathed her last less than twenty-four hours prior to the body being discovered. But even that science was in its infancy, with no hard-and-fast methods by which a guess could be confirmed—into the early twentieth century, many doctors still relied on rigor mortis to answer any questions surrounding the time of death, with no regard whatsoever for those external factors (temperature, weather, storage conditions) that a modern lab considers of such vital importance.

She could easily have perished on the anniversary date, and it was just bad (or, given the hysteria that would have been occasioned, good) luck that the corpse laid undisturbed a few days more.

There was no doubt, however, that the victim—tentatively identified as a local prostitute named Lydia Hart—had been subject to a most Ripper-like assault.

Not only was the woman's abdomen seriously mutilated but, according to at least one report, her womb was also missing, along with her head and legs.

Some comments were made regarding the absence of any wounds to the woman's genitalia, but such details were beyond the reporting capabilities of the majority of period news journals. In this case, and many others, any injury below the abdomen would generally be referred to simply as "the lower part of the body."

Nevertheless, a panic approaching hysteria gripped the streets. Once again, the local mortuary found itself the epicenter of a vast crowd of spectators; and, once again, the police found themselves seeking a military man.

Two days before the torso was discovered, a newspaper vendor named John Arnold visited the London offices of the *New York Herald* to report a new Ripper murder. Traced by the police following the find, he explained that he heard the news from "a man in uniform" in Fleet Street. This man was never discovered.

But there was another side to the slaughter, too, one that Sir Melville Macnaghten recalled in his memoir, and which perhaps left him even more despairing than anything the killer could throw at him.

He was visiting a doss house at the time, visiting the common area in which the inmates were permitted to do their cooking.

> The code of immorality in the East End is, or was, unwashed in its depths of degradation. A woman was content to live with a man so long as he was in work, it .being an understood thing that, if he lost his job, she would support him by the only means open to her.
>
> On this occasion the unemployed man was—toasting bloaters, and, when his lady returned, asked her "if she had had any luck." She replied with an adjective negative, and went on to say in effect that she had thought her lucky star was in the ascendant when she had inveigled a "bloke " down a dark alley, but that suddenly a

detective, with indiarubber soles to his shoes, had' sprung up from behind a waggon, and the bloke had taken fright and flight.

With additional adjectives the lady expressed her determination to go out again after supper, and when her man reminded her of the dangers of the streets if " he " (meaning the murderer) was out and about, the poor woman replied (with no adjectives this time), " Well, let him come-the sooner the better for such as I." A sordid picture, my masters, but what infinite pathos is therein portrayed!

Author Chrissie Bentley would present a chilling variant on this same dreadful death wish in her 2010 short story "Again Last Night," her heroine a Whitechapel prostitute who purposefully courts an encounter with the Ripper, in the hope that she might become his next victim.

Alarming, too, was the revelation that the attack had again been carried out in complete silence. Then as (so sadly) today, railway arches were a favorite resting place for the city's homeless and indigent, and there were indeed three sailors asleep in the arch next to the murder scene.

The trio were promptly taken in for questioning, but they had heard nothing, and neither had any other regular denizens of the arches the police were able to track down.

Ultimately, the police's view of the murder became the official one: that the murder should be aligned with, if not directly linked to, all the other torso mysteries that lay unsolved on the files. There would be no suggestion, however, that the same killer might be responsible for all of those, though.

The term "serial killer" was another that had yet to be invented in 1889—indeed, although he most certainly wasn't, Jack the Ripper is often described as the world's first practitioner of that particular dark art, at least from a media perspective. The idea that there were two homicidal maniacs stalking the streets of London side by side was one nobody was willing to contemplate.

The Last Face in the File

One final killing is occasionally laid at Jack the Ripper's door, albeit one that occurred some sixteen months after the Pinchin Street slaying, and almost a year and a half after the death of Alice McKenzie.

On February 12, 1891, a twenty-nine-year-old prostitute named Frances Coles—"Carroty Nell" to her friends—was found with her throat cut in Swallow Gardens, close by Leman Street police station.

She was still alive, albeit barely, when PC Ernest Thompson came across her, and protocol demanded that he remain with her while he waited for help to arrive. Which meant, in turn, that he could not pursue the man he heard escaping down Mansell Street.

Had he been able to, Thompson believed until his death in 1900, he might have apprehended the Ripper, and that knowledge haunted him, too. In his own memoir, colleague Frederick Wensley recalled, "I fancy that the lost opportunity preyed on Thompson's mind, for I heard him refer to it in despondent terms more than once, and he seemed to regard the incident as presaging some evil fate for himself.

"By an uncanny coincidence, his forebodings came true. The first time he went on night duty, he discovered a murder; the last time he went on duty, some years later, he was murdered himself." (PC Thompson was killed by a knifeman at a coffee stall on Commercial Road.)

PC Thompson might have been the man to unmask Jack the Ripper. Or, more likely, he might simply have apprehended James Sadler, the fifty-three-year-old merchant seaman with whom Coles had spent a recent night or two, before an argument saw her storm away, leaving Sadler very drunk, and very vengeful.

Nothing about the murder echoed the Ripper. Even the fatal wound was inexpertly done, and there were no further injuries. But the case remains unsolved because, although the police quickly picked up Sadler, there simply was no evidence. Four days after the inquest returned the now wearily familiar verdict

A shadow on the cobblestones—the Ripper is nigh.
J. R. Pepper

of "Willful Murder against some person or persons unknown," all charges against Sadler were dropped.

And while different authors, with different theories, have suggested that the Ripper simply continued his career in other lands (the United States is always a popular choice), there is even less firm evidence for that supposition than there are for any of the myriad suspects whom the past 130 years have pinned, as though they were exhibits in some vast, vile butterfly collection, to the crime.

The fact is, the Whitechapel murders were finally over. Jack the Ripper was finally silent. And, the following year, the investigation was officially closed. Whitechapel and the police could breathe again.

Unless, of course, he—or she—started again.

17

Jill the Ripper

The Lady Was a Sociopath

Mary Ann Cotton
She's dead and she's rotten
She lies in her bed
With her eyes wide open
Sing, sing, what can I sing?
Mary Ann Cotton is tied up with string
Where, where?
Up in the air
Selling black puddings a penny a pair

—Children's skip-rope rhyme, circa 1870s

In the end it was not, as a twenty-first-century television documentary insisted, the discovery that "rocked" Ripperology "to its foundations."

But when DNA was extracted from the back of the postage stamp used to mail one of the 200 or so Ripper letters received during the original investigations, and revealed the sender (or, at least, the stamp licker) to have been female, it at least reminded historians of one of the more outlandish theories to have abounded around the Ripper.

Indeed, of all the solutions that have been posited, and the eminent names that have suggested them, there are few who have been so widely quoted as Sir Arthur Conan Doyle, the creator of Sherlock Holmes and, almost equally famously, the man credited with gifting Ripperologists a *heroine* who might have been even blacker than Holmes's traditional nemesis, the archfiend Moriarty.

Could Jack the Ripper have really been Jill the Ripper?

The stamp proved nothing. The letter was addressed to Dr. Thomas Horrocks Openshaw, who at that time was curator of the Pathology Museum at the London Hospital Medical College in Whitechapel. It was he who examined the kidney received in the mail by Mr. Lusk, and who pronounced it to be from the left side of the body. And, at the end of October 1888, he received the following letter:

Old boss you was rite it was the left kidny i was goin to hoperate agin close to your ospitle just as i was going to dror mi nife along of er bloomin throte them cusses of coppers spoilt the game but i guess i wil be on the job soon and will send you another bit of innerds

Jack the Ripper
O have you seen the devle
with his mikerscope and scalpul
a-lookin at a kidney
with a slide cocked up.

The 2015 documentary *Jack the Ripper: Reinvestigating the Evidence and Suspects* was nominally an attempt to prove (or at least suggest) that Frederick Deeming (see Chapter Nine) should be given more credibility among the lineup of Ripper suspects than he usually was. And the means of doing this, apparently, was to analyze the DNA evidence left on the back of the postage stamp.

This sample would, it was hoped, equip investigator Robin Napper with the proof he required, even though the same letter had already been tested once before, during author Patricia Cornwell's attempts to place the artist Walter Sickert in the frame. (This fact was, oddly, not included in the finished documentary.)

Cornwell's attempts proved nothing. Napper's turned up a more intriguing possibility, albeit one that again proved nothing. Yes, the DNA belonged to a woman. But more than one psychological profile has suggested the Ripper was married, even if his wife was more likely completely unaware of his activities.

Maybe it was Mrs. Ripper who licked the stamp?

Still, the possibility that Jack was Jill is one that has exercised many minds over the years. Sadly, at least one facet of that fascination turns out not to have been true after all.

Conan Doyle actually suggested nothing of the sort. According to his son Adrian:

> More than thirty years having passed, it is difficult to recall [Sir Arthur's] views in detail on the Ripper case. However, I do remember that he considered it likely that the man had a rough knowledge of surgery and probably clothed himself as a woman to avoid undue attention by the police and to approach his victims without arousing suspicion on their part.

"Clothed himself as a woman." The psychic Mrs. Spring had suggested as much, and other observers too. In fact, it was Inspector Abberline who first voiced the possibility of a female killer, after studying the testimony offered by one Caroline Maxwell, at the time of Mary Kelly's death.

According to Maxwell, she had seen Kelly on a couple of occasions on the morning of November 9; the first, sometime around 8:30, standing by

Mary Ann Cotton—the original Jill the Ripper.

the Miller's Court entrance to Dorset Street, and then again about an hour later, talking to a man outside the Britannia pub.

What was interesting—indeed, perplexing—about this statement was that, although the body had not yet been discovered, Mary Jane was certainly dead by that time.

The witness was unshakable, however. It was true, she conceded, that she had neither spoken to Mary Jane, nor taken a long, hard look at her face—but, in truth, how many people *would* do that, should they happen to see somebody they knew on the street?

But she recognized the woman's clothing, in particular the maroon shawl Mary Jane had wrapped around herself that cold, wet morning. The same shawl, in fact, that Mary Jane's neighbor, Catherine Pickett, had been hoping to borrow a little earlier that morning.

What if, Abberline mused, they had been looking not for the wrong man, but for the wrong gender all along? What if the killer were a woman who, knowing that the streets around were coming to life, had simply disguised herself in the dead woman's clothing, knowing that anyone who glimpsed her would just assume it was Mary Jane, on her way to wherever?

Which, of course, is precisely what did happen.

Dr. Thomas Dutton, with whom Abberline had this discussion, was not convinced. But, willing to play devil's advocate, he suggested one particular area of inquiry that would rope in the most likely suspects—midwives.

Midwifery was not necessarily among the most blameless professions of the age. Not only were midwives present at the birth of babies, they were also frequently implicated in their deaths, too, smothering unwanted or deformed children at birth, and performing illegal abortions.

They administered medicines that were known to be harmful; they paid little heed to even the rudiments of hygiene that were now present in hospitals and among authorized medical staff; and many of them knew no more about the art they professed to practice than their patients did.

But some were also highly skilled, with a more than prodigious knowledge of anatomy, and bags full of surgical instruments as well. They would also know how to render a patient, or a victim, almost instantly insensible, simply by exerting pressure on particular points of the body.

The more Abberline thought about it, the more appealing this theory became. He was well aware that a murderous midwife had been among the suspects in the slaying of Emma Smith earlier in the year, regardless of the motives that had been assigned to her. But there was more to it than that.

The mystery of how the Whitechapel murderer was able to pass unseen through the crowds, for example. Midwives were as familiar on the streets at night as by day, for newborn babies don't care a hoot for the hour at which they make their appearance; and if you should see a midwife making her way home, her clothing or even flesh stained with blood, you would scarcely give her a second glance.

The somewhat sentimental insistence that women rarely killed for kicks, too, could be undone by a swift glance through the annals of recent murder; and, as for female spree killers, it was less than twenty years ago that Mary

Johnny Depp as Inspector Abberline in the movie *From Hell*.

Photofest

Ann Cotton had been hanged for the murder of anywhere up to twenty people—her own children, family members and a couple of luckless lodgers among them.

The difference was, Cotton—and most of the other fatal femmes Abberline could think of—had chosen poison as the method of death. The Ripper, if Jill she were, represented a very different breed of butcher.

Having lain fallow for fifty years, the notion of a female Ripper was rekindled by author William Stewart in his 1939 investigation *Jack the Ripper: A New Theory*.

The previous year had seen the publication of Edwin Woodhall's *When London Walked in Terror*, in which the already common tale of a grieving father avenging the death of a son from syphilis was twisted—now it was a grieving woman, Olga Tchkersoff, whose sister Vera had been lured onto the streets by Mary Jane Kelly, and subsequently died from sepsis following a botched abortion.

Neither Olga nor Vera Tchkersoff have ever been proven to have existed, relegating Woodhall's tale to the realms of Ripper fiction.

But what, asked Woodhall, if it were Mary Jane who'd been pregnant, and who was seeking an abortion?

According to Woodhall, she was three months pregnant at the time of her death, a state that—if left unattended—would not merely have impaired her ability to make what little money she could. It was also something she simply could not afford. It was hard enough to make the rent on her lodgings as it was. Another mouth to feed would have pushed her straight back onto the streets, and that other mouth would still have been demanding food.

So she chose the only option the laws of the time made available—what we would term a "back-street abortionist."

Selective evidence from the murder room itself appears to back up this theory, although only if one disregards other possibilities.

For example, Mary Jane was naked on the vermin-ridden bed, with her clothing nearly folded on the chair, as though she was indeed presenting herself for a medical procedure. Or, perhaps, she had undressed for her client, and was simply fastidious about her clothes; she had precious few, after all and, unless she wanted to walk around in rags, she needed take care of those she did have.

Nevertheless, if she *did* have an abortion, then the operation was a success—so much so that when Dr. Thomas Bond's postmortem notes were discovered in 1987, he had clearly found no trace of pregnancy. Neither was there any evidence of a baby once the police arrived in the room. But neither would have there been one if her killer had been a man who simply attacked her unpregnant corpse with a blade.

It's a weak theory, then, and while subsequent authors have been able to run with it, advancing it to the point where one particular suspect has been named—Mary Pearcey, hanged in 1890 for the cutthroat murders of her lover's wife and child—the sheer weight of supposition, guesswork and fact avoidance that must be borne for the idea to stand upright is far too great.

Considerably more glamorous than most traditional descriptions, a modern Jill the Ripper in period garb.   *Nando Machado/Shutterstock*

Indeed, even in fiction, the switch is unreliable. On the one hand, there is the 1971 movie *Dr. Jekyll and Sister Hyde*, in which the good physician's potion transforms him into a murderous female with a taste for Whitechapel whores; but on the other, there is Dolph Lundgren's *Jill the Ripper* (2000), in which a female Ripper kills only male victims, and about which little more needs to be said.

Again, then, you could drive a coach and four through the Jill the Ripper theory, but the same can be said for almost every subsequent attempt to bring Jack the Ripper to posthumous justice. Is "the mad midwife," as Ripperologists like to refer to her, any more ridiculous than claims that the killer was Lewis Carroll? Sir William Gull? Pseudonymous Walter? Sir Charles Warren?

It could have escaped nobody's notice, after all, that no sooner had Warren resigned as commissioner of Scotland Yard on November 8, 1888 (the day of Mary Jane Kelly's murder), the canonical killings stopped dead.

Exhausted by his constant sparring with the Home Secretary, resentful of the mockery and disrespect heaped upon his shoulders by the media, overwhelmed by the sheer impossibility of keeping London's streets crime-free—why shouldn't he have finally cracked beneath the pressure, and set out to give his detractors something that really *was* worth complaining about?

We just need to know what he was supposedly doing on the nights that the Ripper was ripping . . . .

18

Frequently Unanswerable Questions

A Twenty-First-Century Identity Parade

> I am troubled by the intestines. Just the thought of them . . . it keeps
> me awake at night. There was nowhere for them to go. Once I'd
> pulled them all out, I couldn't get them back inside so I arranged
> them beside her along the ground, but the mess . . . .
>
> —*Alex Bell, "The Confession" (2016)*

O f all the reasons the Whitechapel murders continue to fascinate,
the greatest is *not* that the police were never able to name the
man who committed them. It is that a wealth of subsequent
researchers, students, historians and amateur detectives believe that they
can and, in so doing, have laid bare a plethora of suspects, each of them
fingered on what appear to be startlingly convincing evidence, but every
one of them no more than conjecture.

American journalist Amy Hanson examined such theorizing in her
article "Bloody Fodder for the Pen" in 1998 (since when, any number of
further theories have naturally arisen). "By the late 1970s and 1980s it
seemed everybody was publishing an opinion about the identity of the
killer," she wrote.

Author Paul Begg had already explained, "When an historical event is
used for fiction, the fiction can rapidly enter the popular imagination as
fact. When the reality becomes submerged under fiction, it can often prove
impossible to raise the truths from the depths."

But not, continues Hanson, "from a lack of imaginative theories [that
range] from the breathtakingly daring to the plain daft, for as long as new
'evidence' surfaces, it seems, new 'suspects' will continue to be found."

She continues, "*Psycho* author Robert Bloch tackled the 'whodunnit' question in *The Night of the Ripper* (Doubleday, 1984), which ties together all the then current biographical theories and also brings in the likes of Conan Doyle and Oscar Wilde to help solve the puzzle."

For fans of *Murder by Decree*'s daring solution, French author Philippe Jullien was the first to point the finger of suspicion at Prince Albert Victor Christian Edward, Queen Victoria's grandson and child of the future Edward VII. That was in 1962, since when a variety of other authors have added their own research to the theory.

Basically, the story goes, the prince entered into a secret marriage with a woman he had met on one of his nocturnal visits to the whorehouses of Whitechapel. The union produced a child, but it also unleashed a tsunami of outrage once the prince's parents and grandmother came to hear of it. It was imperative that this stain be removed from the family name, and so the order went out: Every witness to the marriage, of whom there were five (you can probably guess their names), must be murdered.

Different authors have delivered takes on this basic scenario, introducing other names into the plot, and often disagreeing over who the actual killer was. (The queen's physician, Sir William Gull, is the most popular.) But the essential conspiracy remained undented; indeed, so pervasive did this theory become that even the general public began coming forward with "fresh evidence."

In 1976, for example, during an investigation into the so-called House of Suicides in Ealing, west London, ghost hunter Andrew Green was contacted by one of the house's former maids, a Mrs. Laycock.

In 1922, she wrote, she had been clearing old boxes from the lumber room when she chanced upon a loose floorboard. Prizing it up, she discovered a case emblazoned with the royal crest and the words "Kensington Palace"; opening it, she found four cutthroat razors with gold and tortoise-shell handles, each one wrapped in newspaper articles from 1888, detailing the Ripper murders.

Green dismissed her story, as most people dismissed the entire theory, but it remained (and remains) a popular one. In 1978, the *Los Angeles Times* described author Frank Spiering's *Prince Jack* (Jove, 1978) as a book that finally "exposed . . . the royal cover-up, a kind of century-long Rippergate." It was, wrote Amy Hanson, "the zenith—or nadir?—of all the far-flung theories."

More recently, author Chrissie Bentley implicated the prince in her erotic parody of the Sherlock Holmes stories, *The Complete Adventures of*

The ghost of the Ripper was still being invoked two decades on, in this French cartoon condemning the Entente Cordiale agreement between Britain and France.   *Alamy*

Ambrose Horne (2015), but slyly admits, "I did so knowing that it could not have been him."

But still Prince Albert made a distinguished addition to a company that ranges from the highest in the land to the lowest of the low.

Could it have been a convicted poisoner named Dr. T. Neill Cream, who is said to have confessed to the killings just as the noose was placed around his neck in 1892? Probably not; he was in prison in Joliet, Illinois, between 1881 and 1891.

Perhaps it was Sir John Williams, a volunteer at the Whitechapel Infirmary, who is said to have been especially interested in the female reproductive system. Could he, author Antonia Alexander asked in 2013, have selected his victims from his patients, and then killed them on the street to gather specimens to work with? It will, after all, be remembered that the murderer "collected" both wombs and uteruses during his mutilations.

Even more damningly, Alexander's Williams also had an interest in Bright's disease, a kidney disease from which Catherine Eddowes suffered—and, of course, her killer took one of her kidneys. The same author also paints a portrait of Mary Jane Kelly as this eminent gent's secret lover, incidentally.

Was it Robert Mann, the mortuary attendant at the Whitehouse Infirmary when Annie Millwood arrived there following her attack, and who also received the corpse of Mary Ann Nichols? Or any of the many other men who witnessed the bloody aftermath of other early attacks, and felt something shift in their cold, diseased minds?

Could it have been mild-mannered Thomas Barnardo, founder of the nationwide network of children's homes that bear his name? He was a regular visitor to Whitechapel; is known to have identified Elizabeth Stride as one of the "unfortunate women" with whom he once spoke; and was a familiar enough face around the streets that nobody would have thought twice about spending some time alone with him.

Add him to the list, and then throw in a full-blown Masonic conspiracy, revealed *to those in the know* by the arcane mysteries of the symbols the killer left strewn around and carved into his victims' bodies. It could have been *anyone*.

The Poet, the Painter and Pooh

Lewis Carroll, author of *Alice's Adventures in Wonderland*, is one of the most unexpected suspects. In 1996, Richard Wallace published *Jack the Ripper,*

Prince Albert, every detective's favorite Royal Ripper. *Public Domain/ Wikimedia Commons*

Light-Hearted Friend, in which he based his suspicions on the discovery that Carroll's work contained any number of potent clues, including this damning paragraph from *The Nursery "Alice":*

> She wriggled about so! But at last Dodgson [Carroll's real name] and Bayne [his colleague Thomas Vere Bayne] found a way to keep hold of the fat little whore. I got a tight hold of her and slit her

throat, left ear to right. It was tough, wet, disgusting, too. So weary of it, they threw up—Jack the Ripper.

Only that is not quite what Carroll wrote. The actual paragraph reads: "So she wondered away, through the wood, carrying the ugly little thing with her. And a great job it was to keep hold of it, it wriggled about so. But at last she found out that the proper way was to keep tight hold of itself foot and its right ear."

But if you rearrange the letters of each of those words, you come remarkably close to forming the decisive sentence—a few letters must be discarded, a couple more need to be substituted. All of the key words, however, are there, including the pertinent names and the "confession" itself.

Indicating . . . not much, beyond the fact that, like statistics, you can prove anything with anagrams. It is true that another Carroll creation, "Marchioness of Mock Turtles," can be rearranged as "o fuck mother's incest morals," and the first verse of "Jabberwocky" might well disguise an ode to both masturbation and bestiality.

Interestingly, however, you can also play the anagrammatical game with Richard Wallace's own writings. Chapter Three, "A Life of Motive," thus becomes "I violate . . . me off"; Chapter Eight, "The urge to Tell," disguises the confession "thug let eel rot"; and the author's own name wryly drops two letters before conceding "a liar crawled." The book's title, incidentally, admits "I held frightened rat."

Finally, similar confessions can, and have, been drawn from the writings of William Shakespeare, Charles Dickens, and even A. A. Milne, whose murderous predilections were revealed by author (and Lewis Carroll authority) Karoline Leach by the simple expedient of upending the familiar "Here is Edward Bear coming downstairs now," to read "Stab red red women! CR is downing whores—AA"—CR being Christopher Robin, and "AA" representing author Milne's own signature.

The poet James Kenneth Stephen and the artist Walter Sickert are among the other figures drawn in by the so-called royal conspiracy, with the purported evidence against Sickert then mounting ever higher as subsequent authors, researchers and even novelists (Paul West's enthralling *The Women of Whitechapel and Jack the Ripper*, published in 1991) began delving into his story.

It was not Sickert's actions or even a confession that implicated him, however. It was his talent as an Impressionist painter, condemned by author Patricia Cornwell for displaying just a little too much intimate knowledge of the Whitechapel slayings; and the unsubstantiated rumor that he made on-the-scene sketches of the murders themselves. The novel *What Alice Knew*, by Paula Marantz Cohen (2010), even details how this sickened Sickert might have been caught at the time. Admittedly, it requires the additional recruitment of novelist Henry James, his bedridden sister and his psychologist brother to the detective team, with guest appearances from Oscar Wilde and Mark Twain. But they still catch him.

Another poet (albeit a failed one), former medical student Francis Thompson, has been implicated, largely on the grounds that from the boardinghouse where he most commonly stayed, at 50 Crispin Street, he could see the building in which victim Mary Kelly met her end, and that he may even have known the woman. Or he may not. We really don't know.

But he did possess some skill in the realms of dissection, and he was believed by at least one friend to carry a dissecting knife with him when he went out. He may have been a religious maniac, and might once have been jilted by a prostitute. Or, again, he might not.

Nobody, however, can turn their noses up at the evidence laid bare by his poetry, with "The Nightmare of the Witch Babies" the most frequently quoted of his nightmarish confessions.

Encountering a woman who takes his fancy, a "lusty knight . . . on a swart steed" pursues her, only to discover that she is "corrupted"—that is, pregnant out of wedlock. So he slices open her belly, intent on killing her child, only to discover that the woman is carrying twins.

> *And its paunch was rent*
> *Like a brasten drum;*
> *And the blubbered fat*
> *From its belly doth come*
> *It was a stream ran bloodily under the wall.*
> *O Stream, you cannot run too red!*
> *Under the wall.*
> *With a sickening ooze—Hell made it so!*
> *Two witch-babies, ho! ho! ho!*

Another of Thompson's writings, the essay "Bunyan in the Light of Modern Criticism," rather clumsily compared vainglorious newspaper critics to a proud surgeon who "will lay his subject on the table, nick out every nerve of thought, every vessel of emotion, every muscle of expression with light, cool, fastidious scalpel and then call on [the author] to admire the 'neat dissection'."

Whether one should truly condemn a writer as a criminal because he happens to have some surgical experience, and enjoys writing violent verse,

Even at the time, there was no shortage of possible suspects.

Puck *magazine cover/Wikimedia Commons*

is a matter for the reader and researcher's own conscience. Thompson's life and work were fascinating in their own unique right, and while it is ironic that it is his tangential links to the Whitechapel murders that have become the focus for their modern rediscovery, still that does not condemn him as a killer.

19

Après Moi, Le Debris

The Ripper Lives On

A sinister hump in the eiderdown gave an inkling of what lay beneath. There was an unnatural stillness about it. When the bed-clothes were pulled back, the nude dead body of Margaret Lowe was revealed. Round her neck was tightly knotted a much-darned silk stocking, but it was not these things which attracted my eye, so much as the vicious mutilations which has been wreaked upon the dead woman.

—*Chief Superintendent Fred Cherrill*, Cherrill of the Yard, *1954*

A nniversaries, in the vernacular of the Ripper's London, are rum buggers. The vast majority of them pass by nearly unnoticed, celebrated by the people directly involved with them, but otherwise all but forgotten.

Occasionally, a coincidence might pass into the pages of a "strange but true" column—family members whose deaths and birthdays fall on the same date; historical events from era that find a serendipitous echo years, or even centuries, later.

The Ripper killings were different. Deep into the first half of the twentieth century, long after the day-to-day horrors of the murderous rampage had passed into memory, the people who lived through those terrifying times would still suppress a shudder when they glanced at the calendar and realized that another of his killing days had come around again—three nights in August, two more in September, one in November, and more if you wanted them.

But with every passing year, the number of people who remembered those days was being whittled down, and by the time Great Britain went to war in 1939, even those for whom the Ripper was but a vague childhood memory would have been into their mid-fifties. Teens from that age were approaching retirement; adults were septuagenarians or more.

The streets still remembered, and the ghosts as well. But even they had changed radically across the past half century. And now they were about to change even more. On September 8, 1888, with the killing of Annie Chapman, the Whitechapel murderer took his first unequivocal step into legend, and with him grew up the popular image of the Ripper's happy hunting grounds.

Fifty-two years later, beginning on September 7, 1940, those grounds were blown to smithereens.

The first German bomb fell on Whitechapel that same afternoon. World War II was a little over a year old at that point, but beyond a brief raid on London the previous month, the conflict had thus far been fought at arm's length, across the English Channel in Europe.

That first Saturday evening of the month, however, saw the first phalanx of Luftwaffe bombers appear in the skies over London, and for hour after endless hour, explosive death and destruction rained down.

The bombers' target was ostensibly the docks, but so tightly packed was the area surrounding them, and so imprecise was the bomb-aiming equipment of the day, that civilian areas were impossible to miss. Homes and stores that had stood, however precariously, for a century or more were destroyed, tearing great gaps in the long brickwork terraces, while flames ripped through everything in their path.

Terror had returned to the East End.

Unlike the Ripper murders, however, or even the sporadic air raids that marked out the Great War, there would be no seemingly interminable wait for the next attack.

Night after night, the bombers returned, reducing streets . . . entire neighborhoods . . . to rubble, while the list of the dead and injured mounted higher every day.

By mid-November, after fifty-seven consecutive daily attacks, close to 20,000 Londoners had been killed by the bombs, and almost a million houses destroyed. Most of these were in the East End, many in Whitechapel. And few would be rebuilt or replaced for years to come.

Colin Wilson's *Ritual in the Dark* records its hero, Gerard Soame, returning to Whitechapel for the first time since the war. At the end of Buck's Row (or Durward Street as it was renamed in 1892), the "shell of a theatre" still stood, "with broken rafters and fire-blackened walls exposed."

Soame picked his way across the weed and rubble-strewn bomb site, "taking care to avoid treading on rusty barrel hoops," and headed toward another vacant lot, "bordered by empty houses and stumps of broken walls."

Peering through the windowless hole of another ruin, he saw rubble, rubbish and a torn pink brassiere, yet the house next door was still cheerfully occupied. He could smell sausages frying. By the early 1970s, however, even that would have gone, a victim of the wrecking ball, and that is how long it took for the authorities to clean up after the war. Until then, many of the slums the Ripper might have recognized still clung to the sidewalk, even if they had otherwise been destroyed.

Now, however, all trace has gone.

On Hanbury Street, an extension to Truman's Brewery obliterated the spot on which Annie Chapman met her end. On what had been Dorset Street and Miller's Court, a parking garage thoughtlessly buried Mary Jane Kelly's death house.

Streets have not simply changed beyond recognition—they have changed their names, as well. Buck's Row became Durward Street, Berner Street is now Henriques Street, George Yard is Gunthorpe Street.

And beyond the realms of morbid curiosity, so much else has been swept away, familiar old landmarks that might have been blasted to atoms in the course of one night, or else crudely dismantled over the course of years.

Almost every road the Ripper roamed, every alleyway and hidey-hole in which his victims conducted their business, all of them scratched out of existence.

When one considers their historical resonance, it is easy to mourn these losses. But in practical terms, the bombers of the war, and the developers since then, were merely continuing the clearance work the authorities had been undertaking since the 1890s, in much the same way as modern social historians credit the Whitechapel murderer with finally alerting the authorities to the sheer depths of depravity to which the neighborhood had sunk.

Of course there is a truth in that, just as there's truth in saying that by killing Annie Chapman quickly and relatively painlessly, he saved her from the lingering and certainly agonizing death her cancer-ridden body was already awaiting.

Besides, although living conditions, particularly regarding hygiene, overcrowding and crime, would improve vastly as the twentieth century rolled along; although the streets were now well lit, and the police more equipped to deal with all contingencies—still Whitechapel remained a grim environment.

Houses that were slums in the 1880s would, in many instances, remain slums, only now they had decades more in which to deteriorate.

Landlords remained usurious parasites who cared little for the well-being of their tenants, so long as the rent was paid on time, and lawlessness remained many occupants' chief pursuit.

Homelessness, too, remained rife, as it became painfully (if predictably) apparent that the vast majority of improvements imposed upon the area were for the benefit of commerce, not comfort.

The lodging houses on George Street, from whence Martha Tabram sallied forth, were demolished in 1891, together with the entire north side of Flower and Dean Street. Warehouses replaced them.

The mortuary to which so many of the Ripper's victims were carried was sacrificed in 1898, to make way for an extension to the Davenant School; and the Board School on Buck's Row was converted for storage,

Crossingham's lodging house and the Britannia pub were torn down in 1928, as the north side of Dorset Street was replaced by an extension to Spitalfields Market.

And that process has continued, of course, albeit for more up-to-date concerns. It is gentrification, not Germans, that today tears Whitechapel to shreds, but the historical record bears the scars all the same. The Frying Pan pub is now a balti restaurant. Half of Hanbury Street became a brewery in 1970, which in turn gave way to a Sunday market. Mr. Tenpenny's was lost around 1970. Commercial Street police station is today a luxury apartment block.

In some cases, the original fabric remains. It is difficult, however, to extract any tangible grasp of history from its presence.

The Blackout Ripper

Nevertheless, it was the blitz that contributed the most to this process, beginning on the night a bomb so badly damaged New Cottage—the closest home to where Mary Ann Nichols was found—that it had to be torn down. (It was eventually replaced by a garage.)

And it was the blitz that reawakened new fears, as London briefly, but memorably, became the stalking grounds of a new killer . . . a new Ripper.

The story of the Blackout Ripper is, in many ways, a testament to just how large a role plain luck plays in detective work, whether it be a chance identification of a wanted man or simple carelessness on the part of the felon. But it is also a reminder of just how reliant "modern" societies can become on the tools and toys that surround them.

London in the early 1940s was a far cry from the brightly lit, gaily bus-tling metropolis of the prewar years. A nightly blackout, imposed to deprive the enemy bombers of a vast illuminated bull's-eye at which to aim, had returned the streets to almost stygian darkness.

Thick, dark curtains prevented even the slightest chink of light from escaping the buildings that lined the streets, and even smoking a ciga-rette out of doors was frowned upon, lest an eagle-eyed air crew spot the telltale glow.

Once darkness fell, all but the most essential excursions out of doors were discouraged. The most familiar roads became a minefield of hidden obstacles to anybody making their way from one place to another, while any traffic that should be abroad—emergency vehicles for the most part, speeding through the silent streets—also did so in complete darkness.

Add to this the fogs that still rolled in to choke the streets, and the knowl-edge that the only people who would venture out in such conditions were those who had no alternative, and there could be no more perfect simula-tion of the world in which the Ripper was widely believed to have worked.

And so, it seemed, he returned.

At 8:30 in the morning of Sunday, February 9, 1942—a night that had passed with no air raids whatsoever—a worker passing by a bomb shelter on Montague Place, in the heart of London's West End, noticed something strange just inside the doorway.

Stepping closer, he saw it was the body of a woman, a forty-year-old pharmacist named Evelyn Hamilton. She had been gagged with her own silk scarf, strangled and robbed—Evelyn had been planning to travel to Grimsby that morning, and would have had some eighty pounds in her handbag.

It looked, the police were convinced, like a simple crime of opportunity, a mugging and a murder. The following morning, Monday, February 10, however, brought news of a second attack—a prostitute known as Nita Ward, found dead in her own apartment on Wardour Street.

She, too, had been strangled. But she had also been stripped naked, her throat had been cut and then, horrifyingly, she had been sexually mutilated with the can opener that still lay alongside her body.

Fingerprints were collected, and offhandedly, it was noted that, like Evelyn Hamilton, Nita had been murdered by a left-handed killer.

Forty-eight hours later, with the police still gathering information on both murders—which, aside from that one coincidence, bore no further similarities to one another—yet another murder was reported.

Again, the victim was a prostitute; again, she died in her own home. Doris Jouannet was discovered in the two-room apartment where she lived with her hotel manager husband, but from whence she frequently sallied forth to pick up servicemen in Leicester Square. She had been strangled with a scarf and sexually mutilated.

The media, which had paid little enough attention to the first two murders, now leapt to attention.

It's unclear who was the first enterprising journalist to christen the killer the "Blackout Ripper"—most likely, it was an act of osmosis, a spontaneous but unanimous movement on behalf of them all, animated by the media's now ingrained insistence upon adopting a pet name for every notable criminal (another quirk for which the original Jack could take credit). However the name was arrived at, though, it stuck.

Even more thrillingly, this Ripper did not waste time between killings. On Friday, February 13, at an apartment on Gosfield Street in Marylebone, the body of Margaret Florence Lowe was discovered in her own bed.

She, too, had first been strangled, this time with a silk stocking, and then her body was mutilated with, among other things, a knife, a candlestick and a razor blade. According to her husband, he had last seen her alive when he left for work the previous evening.

Assuming, as several in the police now were, that Evelyn Hamilton had been killed by the same man, the discovery of Lowe's body meant the murderer had taken four lives in five days. It was the press who reached another conclusion—two initial murders of increasing savagery, followed by a double event within hours of one another. Whether they admitted it or not, all braced themselves for a fifth attack.

It arrived, on schedule, on Valentine's Day. That evening, another prostitute, Greta Hayward, was attacked in a doorway in Piccadilly Circus. The difference was, she survived—a delivery boy was passing by at the time, and her attacker panicked and fled.

Hayward's statement left the detectives with next to nothing to do. Her attacker, who first made some sexual suggestions that she rejected outright, wore the uniform of a Royal Air Force cadet, confirming one of the theories that the police had been toying with, itself aroused by Doris Jouannet's alleged predilection for servicemen.

Her throat bore the evidence of his attempt to strangle her. After she rebuffed the man's advances, Greta said, he had leaned toward her and asked to at least be allowed to kiss her good night. She agreed, waiting as

The Ripper is reborn in this 1950s US comic book.

he lay his gas mask case on the ground, and then gasping as his hand closed over her throat.

She lost consciousness, and recalled nothing more until she became aware of the delivery boy helping her to her feet. It was he who led her to the police station, and while she made her statement, officers raced to the scene. There they found her handbag but, more importantly, they also found the gas mask case her assailant had left behind in his haste to escape. It bore its owner's service number.

The police had a name.

The killer, however, did not go to ground. Again echoing the behavior of his namesake when he was disturbed in the midst of an attack, he instead sought out another woman, Catherine Mulcahey. Together they caught a cab back to her apartment in Paddington.

But the Blackout Ripper's luck had finally run out. In the darkness of a sudden power failure, he grabbed Mulcahey's throat. But she kicked back with such ferocity that he lost his grip, and her screams of terror awakened the rest of the building.

Her attacker fled, this time leaving his belt behind. Just hours later, twenty-eight-year-old Gordon Frederick Cummins was traced to the Air Force cadet barracks where he was stationed, and placed in an identity parade. Without hesitation, both Greta Hayward and Catherine Mulcahey picked him out as the man who had attacked them.

By the end of April, Cummins was on trial for his life.

The police chose to charge him with just one murder, the first, knowing that if he should be found not guilty, they could then line up the other three. But their caution was unnecessary. After just two days in court, the jury needed no more than thirty-five minutes to deliver their verdict of guilty. Two months later, with a failed appeal behind him, Cummins was hanged.

From Hammersmith to Bradford

Gordon Cummins might have been the first man to rejoice in the guise of a modern-day Ripper, but he would not be the last. In 1964, west London was plagued by the so-called Hammersmith Ripper—or, as some of the more salacious tabloids preferred, Jack the *Stripper*. He was responsible for at least six, and possibly eight, murders, all of them prostitutes, and all found naked. The killer was never apprehended.

A decade later, the north of England was visited by the Yorkshire Ripper, whose five-year toll among the prostitutes of Leeds and Bradford more than doubled the official tally of either of his predecessors—thirteen women were killed, and seven more attacked, including several who were not in any way involved with that profession.

It required one of the most intensive manhunts in British legal history to finally track down lorry driver Peter Sutcliffe, by which time the police had spoken with some 30,000 men, including Sutcliffe himself. Indeed, he was interviewed on no fewer than *nine* occasions.

Yet it was not the investigation itself that trapped Sutcliffe. Rather, it was the fake registration plates on the car he was driving, after he was stopped by a routine police check.

Only after his description was matched (and not for the first time) to the statements of sundry witnesses and victims did the police truly focus their inquiries on him, beginning with a return to the spot where he was arrested.

There they discovered a knife, a hammer and a rope—hidden, it seems, after Sutcliffe asked the arresting officers to let him slip off to urinate: "I'm bursting for a pee." A second knife was then found in a toilet cistern at the police station, deposited when Sutcliffe took another bathroom break.

Again, echoes of the original Jack ran through both the killer's modus operandi and the investigation that pursued him—including the receipt of several letters from the alleged killer, taunting the police and signed, among other things, by "Jack the Ripper." And, as if to recall Victorian actor Richard Mansfield's brief moment beneath the spotlight of suspicion, rock singer John Miles was among the men being interviewed after police were alerted to a song on his *Zaragon* album, "Nice Man Jack."

Sutcliffe was sentenced to a minimum of thirty years' imprisonment in 1981; amid increasingly hysterical media speculation that he would thus be eligible for parole in 2011, the sentence was altered to a so-called "whole life tariff" in 2010.

In each of these instances, the introduction of the word "Ripper" to the investigation was the work of the media, an instantly recognizable tag that would convey the sheer horror of the killer's actions to the public and, hopefully, boost the paper's circulation.

In 2009, however, the British TV series *Whitechapel* asked what would become of a modern police force if the *real* Ripper ever returned. Would they, with all the forensics, profiling and technology with which they are now equipped, have any more luck catching him than their 1888 forebears?

Expertly drawn by writers Ben Court and Caroline Ip, and exquisitely cast as well, *Whitechapel's* Ripper does absolutely everything by the book, even down to recreating the original crimes in every possible detail.

If the original Ripper killed a woman with thirty-nine stab wounds (as he did to Martha Tabram), then his twenty-first-century counterpart would as well, and at exactly the same points of the body. If the original Ripper used a bayonet and suggested himself to be a soldier, so did his modern doppelgänger. And so on.

True, the '09 model drew the line at eating half a human kidney for breakfast, but he did drop the other half into the mail. He didn't leave a cryptic message daubed on a wall, either.

But there was one Ripper trick he did not miss. He left absolutely no usable trace of his identity on, or near, any of his victims, and the investigators—headed up by the wryly named Detective Inspector Joseph Chandler (Rupert Penry-Jones), Sergeant Ray Miles (Phil Davis) and Ripperologist Ed Buchan (Steve Pemberton)—were as much in the dark as their predecessors.

Fastidious in its attention to historical detail (the first doctor on the crime scene was even named Llewellyn!) and so atmospherically shot and designed, *Whitechapel* arrived on screens at a time when it sometimes felt as though you could wallpaper a house with new "true-life" Ripper documentaries. In terms of giving viewers a genuine sense not only of events as they unfolded back in 1888, but also of the sheer frustration and despair the police must have felt, *Whitechapel* ripped the rest to pieces.

And, just to add to the historical frisson, they didn't apprehend this one, either.

20

Murder Is Money

Cashing In on Crime

Enter three Editors:
Round about the cauldron go
In it slips of "copy" throw
Headlines of the largest size
Murderer's letters—all faked lies
And other spicy bits we've got
To simmer in our charm-ed pot
Bubble bubble! Crime and trouble
Made our circulation double.

—Fun Magazine, *October 1888*

T he victims of the Whitechapel murders may have been penniless, and sometimes even worse off than that. But there was money to be made from the Ripper, and a lot of people were doing so.

The newspapers, of course, could count upon a bumper payday whenever they placed his name in the headlines, even if there was no fresh news to report. But what about the pavement artist who made his way to Whitehall to sketch the killings in all their gory glory, in the brightest of blood-red chalks?

Or the International Working Men's Club owners, charging admission to their upstairs rooms, the ones with the best view of where Long Liz perished?

Or even the unnamed entrepreneur who was banging on landlord John McCarthy's door, offering a small fortune for the blood-soaked bed upon which Mary Jane Kelly was carved up? McCarthy, to his eternal credit, refused the offer and probably sent the purchaser off with some choice words ringing in his ears. But others were not so fickle.

Journalists roaming the streets of Whitechapel found no shortage of people willing to talk about their relationships with the dead women, even if (as one suspects was often the case) they had never heard of them before they died. If the price was right, their story would fit.

Even before he had ended his reign, Jack the Ripper was a media phenomenon. He still is. Counting back from the present day to the very dawning of his legend, it sometimes feels as though there have been more books, movies, television series, plays, radio shows, documentaries, magazines, songs and stories dedicated to Jack, his victims, his pursuers and his haunts than every other murderer in history combined.

So the industry got under way early, and it was already an international affair. Even before the Parisian debut of *Jack l'Eventreur*, an American author named Samuel E. Hudson published *Leather Apron; Or, the Horrors of Whitechapel, London,* an eighty-two-page booklet that left the presses less than a month after Mary Jane's murder. Other American efforts followed, but of course, the United States was not the only land to have become enraptured by the Ripper.

In 1889 in Sweden, the anonymously penned *Hwem är Jack uppskäraren? (Who is Jack the Ripper?)* updated the saga to include the murder of Alice McKenzie. From Portugal, there came the massive, five-volume *Jack, O Estripador: Grande Romance de Actualidade, Illustrado com Gravuras,* which combined detailed descriptions of the killings with full-length "biographies" of each of the victims; from Spain, another play, *El Destripador: Juguete Comico en un Acto y en Prosa*—a comedy!

Another Swedish author made the first-ever attempt at conjuring up the Ripper's diary, via a short story included in the anthology *Uppskäraren* (The Ripper) in 1892; while at home, the public's appetite for the Ripper—as voracious as it was vicarious—was to be salved, but never sated, by books that appeared even as the murders were under way.

John Francis Brewer's *The Curse Upon Mitre Square,* with the murder of Catherine Eddowes as its center piece, was published during the hiatus that divided the double event from the death of Mary Kelly; and the following year saw Margaret Harkness's *In Darkest London* pin the crimes on a non-Jewish slaughterhouse worker, who nevertheless hid out within the Jewish community.

The Police Answer Back

It was a German author who first pitted Jack the Ripper against Sherlock Holmes (and, inevitably, lose), in 1907, in an edition of the magazine *Aus den Geheimakten des Welt-Detektivs*—much to the chagrin of Sir Arthur Conan Doyle. Conan Doyle had purposefully avoided allowing Holmes to confront any nonfictional unsolved case, so as to avoid insulting, or prejudicing, the real-life forces of law and order. The prospect of his vengeful rage is said to have been sufficient to prevent any British publisher from translating the German work.

But those same real-life police were themselves now gearing up to defend their turf, with a succession of true-life memoirs of their days on the front line of the war against crime. Indeed, many of these memoirs are fascinating in themselves, even without the added fillip of the Ripper. But his presence certainly added to the excitement.

So many legends of British law enforcement committed their memories to print—Sir Robert Anderson, Sir Melville Macnaghten, Sir Henry Smith and Frederick Wensley among them—and all, in their own way, shed fresh light on both the investigations and the world within which those investigations took place.

From Wensley's *40 Years of Scotland Yard*, for example, we learn that the Whitechapel police were in the habit of nailing strips of rubber, "usually bits of old bicycle tires," to the soles of their "clumsy regulation boots," in the hope of deadening the sound of their footsteps.

From Macnaghten's *Days of My Years*, we discover that among the very first documents he read following his arrival at Scotland Yard was a piece of doggerel allegedly composed by the Whitechapel murderer, found among the myriad letters, theories, hoaxes and admonishments that every day's post piled higher:

> *I'm not a butcher, I'm not a Yid,*
> *Nor yet a foreign Skipper,*
> *But I'm your own light-hearted friend,*
> *Yours truly, Jack the Ripper.*

And so on. But Sir Robert Anderson won himself few fresh admirers, and probably lost a lot more, when he haughtily sniffed, in 1907's *Criminals and Crime*, "no amount of silly hysterics could alter the fact that these crimes were a cause of danger only to a particular section of a small and definite class of women, in a limited district of the East End; and that the inhabitants of the metropolis generally were just as secure during the weeks the fiend was on the prowl, as they were before the mania seized him, or after he had been safely caged in an asylum."

In an age when the empowerment of women, in the form of the suffragette movement, was among the most burning issues of the day, such a remark was swiftly seized upon as a blatant admission that the law did far less than it ought to in its attempts to rein in the Ripper. He was, after all, only slaughtering whores.

The Lodger

In pure literary terms, the Ripper industry reached its initial peak with the publication, in 1913, of Marie Belloc Lowndes's *The Lodger*, a novel that even earned the praise of Sir Melville Macnaghten, in his memoir the following year.

> Only last autumn I was very much interested in a book entitled The Lodger, which set forth in vivid colours what the Whitechapel murderer's life might have been while dwelling in London lodgings. The talented authoress portrayed him as a religious enthusiast, gone crazy over the belief that he was predestined to slaughter a certain number of unfortunate women, and that he had been confined in a criminal lunatic asylum and had escaped therefrom.

Born in 1868, the older sister of humorist Hilaire Belloc, Marie Belloc Lowndes was an astonishingly prolific author, both a brilliant crime and mystery novelist and a skilled biographer. Of all her forty-plus publications, however, *The Lodger* is unanimously regarded as her finest, if only because of its lingering afterlife—first made into a movie in 1927 by Alfred Hitchcock, the story has undergone periodic remakes ever since (the most recent by director David Ondaatje in 2009).

The story first appeared in 1911 in the pages of *McLure's Magazine*. A retired married couple, the Buntings, are renting out rooms in their home to lodgers, a common practice at that time. But it is not an especially successful enterprise, and they are on the point of giving up when a gentleman arrives, offering to take their upstairs rooms at a far higher rate than they could ever have hoped to attract.

They agree, however, that he is an unusual sort of chap, prone to reading his Bible aloud through the day, and then disappearing out at night and not returning until the early hours.

Even more suspiciously, they realize that his absences coincide exactly with a series of murders taking place at the same time, credited to a killer who calls himself the Avenger. His primary targets are prostitutes.

Inspired, Belloc Lowndes explained, by a real-life dinner conversation in which one of the guests claimed that his mother's former cook and butler had themselves rented rooms to Jack the Ripper, the story is only loosely based upon the real-life exploits of Saucy Jack.

Indeed, the Avenger himself is little more than bit player in the drama, the novella's true focus being the sheer terror that envelops the Buntings' life. Neither, according to Macnaghten, was the character of the Avenger at all similar to the man the Whitechapel police believed they were seeking. There was no religious mania present in the Ripper's psychological makeup, he insisted; neither had he ever been confined to an asylum or lived in lodgings.

Laird Cregar in the 1944 remake of Hitchcock's *The Lodger*—a portrait of anguish and madness.   *Photofest*

"I incline to the belief that the individual who held up London in terror resided with his own people ; that he absented himself from home at certain times, and that he committed suicide on or about the 10th of November 1888, after he had knocked out a Commissioner of Police and very nearly settled the hash of one of Her Majesty's principal Secretaries of State," Macnaghten wrote.

He speaks, of course, of Montague John Druitt.

Hitchcock's cinematic realization of Belloc Lowndes's tale shifts the focus back to the Ripper, but nevertheless borrows one of the author's own greatest contributions to the genre, the all-pervading fog that chokes every street scene.

In both book and novel, "on foggy nights, once the quiet household is plunged in sleep," the killer "creeps out of the house."

We see how the fog reduces the police's efforts to "a game of blind man's bluff," with the detective's eyes securely bandaged. And when the fog lifts, "rolling off in that sudden, mysterious way in which local fogs sometimes do . . . in London," the lodger sounds profoundly disappointed. There would be no killing that night.

The Lodger lost nothing in its translation to film. Hitchcock was still very much a rising star at that time—this latest effort would, in fact, be the movie that established him as the master of cinematic horror, as *The Bioscope* magazine instantly declared. "It is possible that this film is the finest British production ever made."

Shot in the north London neighborhood of Islington, and starring Ivor Novello and the singularly named June [Tripp], *The Lodger* either blueprints or predicts all of Hitchcock's later achievements, while effortlessly recapturing the claustrophobic terrors so intrinsic to the original novella.

Even as a silent film, *The Lodger* generates deafening suspense; and when Hitchcock retooled it five years later with sound, all the earlier plaudits were simply amplified even further. Remakes in 1944 (starring Merle Oberon and George Saunders), 1953 (as *Man in the Attic* with Jack Palance) and 2009 all have their moments. But this is one movie where the old adage of "The original remains the best" is indisputably true.

A Thoroughly Modern Ripper

Although the Ripper remained a reliable publishing standby throughout the pre–World War II era, it was in the postwar era that the modern interpretation of him truly came into being.

In many ways, it was birthed by Robert Bloch's "Yours Truly, Jack the Ripper," published in *Weird Tales* magazine in 1943, and allowing Jack, for the first time, to step out as both an entertainment (as opposed to all the other guises he has fulfilled) and as an alien, doomed to forever offer up human sacrifice in order to preserve his immortality.

It is in these two guises that the legend of the Ripper truly stepped out of the earthbound realities of Victorian Whitechapel and into a realm that is uniquely his own—a steampunk superhero created half a century before steampunk was born. And then, secure within that status, he returns to his own time to wreak further havoc, unassailable in the knowledge that he is forever uncatchable—even on those occasions when an author provides a solution to the mystery.

He becomes a time traveler, both in spirit and in person (and meets Doctor Who in Neil Penswick's novel *The Pit*). Like Dracula, himself a child of late Victorian England, the Ripper can be born and reborn throughout time and space.

Colin Wilson's *Ritual in the Dark* is by far the most successful of these ventures, effectively both having its cake and eating it, too, by making certain that *everybody* knows who the killer is, Scotland Yard included, and still having him evade justice. But another Robert Bloch short story, "Toys for Juliette," twists the knife even further by recasting the Ripper as the titular Juliette, and then causing her to commit her crimes throughout history. She, however, *will* be caught, after arriving in London in 1888, without any idea of that year's significance.

The Ripper has been blessed with children (the movie *Hands of the Ripper*, see below), accomplices, even a pet dog named Snuff (the narrator of Roger Zelazny's *A Night in the Lonesome October*). He has been a prince, a pauper, and a militant vegetarian (the 1937 French movie *Drôle de Drame*).

Paul Cornell's *The Severed Streets* (2014) sees him return as a murderous ghost, summoned by a rapacious media tycoon to ferment a popular uprising, the "Summer of Blood." And why did the tycoon select the Ripper? Because he was "the greatest outrage marketing brand of all time. The greatest aspirational cheerleader . . . encouraging people to copy him. The Ripper gets people furious and interested and aroused all at the same time."

Which does sum things up rather nicely.

He is a rock icon, inspiring songs by sixties showman Screaming Lord Sutch ("Jack the Ripper"), heavy metal icons Judas Priest ("The Ripper"), electro-punk pioneers Rikki and the Last Days of Earth ("Twilight Jack") and former Velvet Undergrounder John Cale—whose "Jack the Ripper in the Moulin Rouge" single was withheld from release in 1977, for fear of being seen to prey on the notoriety of the Yorkshire Ripper.

He is a comic-book hero. *Crime Must Pay the Penalty* issue eight (1949) paints him as "the crookedest croupier and dirtiest killer this side of Hades," a knifeman who slices his way across the Wild West eight years *before* his namesake began carving a swath through the Whitechapel streets.

In the debut issue of *Beyond*, in 1950, Jack was reborn as a murderous marionette, perishing only when his creator burned down the lodging house where they were both living. And, according to *Eerie* issue five (1952), it wasn't Jack who was actually the problem. It was his knife, a supernatural terror that chose both its victims *and* its user itself.

Soon fiction would even be taking on fiction, echoing the occasional attempts to pair the Ripper with Sherlock Holmes (Lyndsay Faye's *Dust and*

John Cale, whose "Jack the Ripper in the Moulin Rouge" single was cancelled at the height of the Yorkshire Ripper scare.

Screaming Lord Sutch, the iconic British rocker (and politician!), promoting his 1963 single "Jack the Ripper."   *Alamy*

Shadow: An Account of the Ripper Killings by Dr. John H. Watson is a prime recent example), by introducing other characters to the universe.

Echoing the fears of 1888, Edward Hyde, of *Dr. Jekyll and . . .* notoriety, became the Ripper in Ray Russell's *Sagittarius* (1962), and again in the movie *Dr. Jekyll and Sister Hyde* (1971); while Kim Newman's *Anno Dracula* (1992) sees Jack being pursued by a police department whose ultimate controller is the titular count—married now to Queen Victoria.

Equally outrageous is Anthony Boucher's *A Kind of Madness* (1972), which contemplates a fateful encounter between the Ripper and Michel Eyraud and Gabrielle Bompard, a French couple who rose to almost equal heights of notoriety in Paris in 1889, after they murdered civil servant Toussaint-Augustin Gouffé and left his remains in an oilskin bag by the side of a country road.

The body, which might have been stashed for anything up to five summertime weeks before its discovery, was unearthed only after a road worker was sent to investigate a foul stench on a certain stretch of the highway—by which time the killers had already fled to San Francisco.

But their relationship ended once they arrived there, and when Bompard returned to France in the new year, she was promptly arrested; the couple really had not covered their tracks particularly well. Eyraud, too, was soon picked up, by a French policeman in Cuba, and he was executed in February 1891. Bompard was spared the death sentence and released in 1905.

The idea that such a pair of amateurs could ever prove a match for the super slick and slippery Ripper should have doomed *A Kind of Madness* at the very moment of conception. It didn't, and the result is a peculiarly enjoyable (if still unlikely) read.

Where such efforts fall within the realms of serious Ripperology, of course, is a moot point. In earlier centuries, it was common for novelists to rescue, from the most obscure annals of criminology, one felon or another, and to breathe both new life, and a whole new existence, into his frame.

All that we are led to believe about the highwayman Dick Turpin, for example, was drawn from the almost wholly fictional biography penned by William Harrison Ainsworth in 1834's *Rookwood*.

A host of similar miscreants, murderers, highwaymen and housebreakers alike, were lionized in the pages of the so-called penny dreadfuls that proliferated later in that century, glorified not only beyond the recognition of their families, but beyond the scope of their true crimes as well.

Into the 1970s, the housebreaker Charlie Peace was a staple of the British comic *Buster*, having long since been transformed from an utterly distasteful little burglar, sneak thief and murderer into an astonishingly lovable scamp.

The Ripper falls into this same category, with one unavoidable caveat. Nobody who reads of Jack's "new" adventures does so without some awareness of the sheer ghastliness of his crimes. Thus he occupies a remarkable status in the echelon of modern cultural iconoclasts; the ultimate antihero he may be, but he has an heroic quality regardless, to the point where readers (and, when he graces the silver screen, viewers) all but encourage him to carry on killing, to continue confounding the blundering policemen, and to keep on drenching every page or frame with lashings of lovely ketchup.

The Shadow on the Screen

Away from the printed page, Jack the Ripper swiftly adapted to both stage and screen, with an early triumph emerging in the form of Frank Wedekind's 1904 stage play *Die Büchse der Pandora* (1904).

It is the story of Lulu, wild and immoral, the living personification of Lust, the most powerful of the Seven Deadly Sins—how appropriate, then, that she should perish at the hands of Jack the Ripper.

A success from the moment it opened, the play would subsequently be adapted for screen in 1929 (by Austrian director Georg Wilhelm Pabst) as *Pandora's Box*, with Louise Brooks spellbinding as Lulu. Indeed, arriving on the screen so swiftly after Hitchcock's adaptation of *The Lodger*, *Pandora's Box* likewise played exquisitely into that world of ever-darker decadence that characterized the (admittedly exclusive) worlds of Weimar Berlin, Prohibition-dodging America, and the Bright Young Things of Evelyn Waugh's England—a morality play delivered at a time when morality itself seemed in ever shorter supply.

Of course all three of these societies would soon be drawn to a screeching haunt, in the U.S. and Britain by the Great Depression, in Germany by the rise of Nazism.

Yet the notion of Jack as some kind of all-seeing killjoy is not seeded wholly in the minds of those people (Wedekind among them) who disapproved of the liberties that society takes with propriety.

Often lost within any survey of the last years of Britain's once legendary Hammer horror studio, 1971's *Hands of the Ripper* takes this attraction of opposites to the inevitable extreme, as the titular Jack's daughter Anna (portrayed with uncanny grace by Angharad Rees) finds herself incapable of receiving affection without repaying it with the ultimate violence.

Even the attentions of a well-meaning psychologist (Eric Porter) cannot break through her conditioning—which itself, we discover, was birthed by the childhood memory of her father murdering her mother. Indeed, soon the psychologist is himself complicit in Anna's murder spree, covering up her crimes for reasons the viewer alone can determine. Yet such a weighty subtext in no way disguises its maker's penchant for gore, as Anna sets about her victims with an imagination that would shame even her father.

A fake medium is impaled on a door with a poker. A prostitute is slaughtered with hatpins. A housemaid has her throat cut with a broken mirror, and the doctor, having already survived being run through with a sword, finally meets his end in St. Paul's Cathedral, as Anna leaps from the Whispering Gallery, 259 steps above him, and lands smack on top of him.

Louise Brooks as Lulu in Pabst's spellbinding 1929 movie *Pandora's Box.*   *Photofest*

Hammer was also responsible for *Room to Let* (1949), Margery Allingham's skillful reinterpretation of *The Lodger*, in which the insane Dr. Fell escapes from the asylum where he has spent the last sixteen years and simply picks up the life he left behind—as the Ripper. And doctors loom large, too, in 1959's *Jack the Ripper*, an adaptation of author Leonard Matters's notion of the killer being a physician avenging the death of his son; and in the German *The Monster of London City* (1954), in which the son is avenging his father.

Perhaps the most pervasive of all the cinematic solutions to the Ripper mystery, however, is that which insists one should look no further than that

Mummies, monsters, madmen . . . and, of course, Jack the Ripper: typical fare for the U. S. comic reader of the fifties.

most stubborn of all theories: that the royal household held the secret of who the guilty man might have been.

Murder by Decree (1979) again ropes Sherlock Holmes in to prove that the killer was a palace physician; *The Ripper* (1997) places Prince Eddy at the heart of the drama. The focus returns to a surgeon in 1999's *Love Lies Bleeding*; while 2001's *From Hell* sees Johnny Depp take the role of Inspector Abberline, unmasking Dr. William Gull, the Royal Physician, as the Ripper.

In truth, this last saga is infinitely better enjoyed (and employed) in author Alan Moore and artist Eddie Campbell's original graphic-novel form, while its apogee is most skillfully dissected in Iain Sinclair's debut novel *White Chappell, Scarlet Tracings* (1987). Gorgeously staged and skill-fully plotted though it is, the cinematic *From Hell* simultaneously suffers from such clunky dialogue and grotesque overacting that even the most understanding viewer will soon be pleading for a swift, sudden and bloody end—to the movie, at any rate.

Even without its own peculiar failings, however, *From Hell* was always destined to shortchange its ambition, a downfall that awaits almost every movie (and, indeed, documentary) that takes a well-argued (if not well-founded) solution to a genuine historical riddle, and then tries to cram it into a couple of hours.

That journey can only, successfully, be undertaken in book (or, nodding again to Moore and Campbell, graphic-novel) form, where the reader can be led, hand in hand, through the labyrinth of the author's ideas and evidence.

Moore, for example, has spoken at length about both his research for *From Hell* and its development. His biographer, Lance Parkin, quotes him thus:

> We start out with the murder of five people in London. A well-known murder that took place in the late 1880s . . . . Now from that we find there are threads of meaning that stretch back as far as, say, the Dionysiac architects of ancient Crete, that stretch into the architecture of London and London's history. That stretch into all these different areas of society and privilege that run all the way up to the twentieth century . . . . The whole system is connected and you can start at any point and from there you will find this radiant web of connections that sort of spans everything.

How do you even *begin* to condense all of that into what is, after all, being marketed as a couple of hours of escapist entertainment? You cannot, and attempting to do so can lead only to the distortion of some truths, the omission of others and, ultimately, the utter demolition of many of the elements that perhaps induced a half-interested viewer to sit down with the movie in the first place.

Even more so than in the realms of novel, successful Ripper cinema is that which tears the killer as far from his own normalcy as it does the reader from his or hers—which is why 1972's *The Ruling Class* finds a far more believable Jack in the delusions of the Fourteenth Earl of Gurney (Peter O'Toole) than any pseudo-shocking attempt to reveal that the Ripper was really Phil Collins. (Why not? In 2016, swaths of the American electorate purported to believe that onetime presidential candidate Ted Cruz was actually the Zodiac Killer.)

Likewise, 1994's *Deadly Advice* depicted the Ripper as a hairdresser (John Mills) who passes handy tips on to his serial-killer customer (Jane Horrocks), and if you believe 1987's *Amazon Women on the Moon*, the Ripper was actually the Loch Ness Monster in disguise.

None of these solutions holds any kind of historical water. But both make far more sense than another earnest effort to blame the Duke of Clarence.

21

A Very American Murderer

The Transatlantic Connection

I should have gone right to work in a commonsense way, and not believed in mere theories. With the great power of the London police I should have manufactured victims for the murderer. I would have taken 50 female habitues of Whitechapel and covered the ground with them. Even if one fell a victim, I should get the murderer. Men un-uniformed should be scattered over the district so nothing could escape them. The crimes are all of the same class, and I would have determined the class to which the murderer belonged. But – pshaw! What's the good of talking? The murderer would have been caught long ago.

—Inspector Thomas Byrnes, NYPD

The United States' love affair with Jack the Ripper started early and has never abated.

To begin with, it was a purely vicarious fascination—the chance to watch with horrified awe (and maybe a little smugness) as London, so secure in its self-imposed status as the capital of the world, cowered beneath the dripping blade of the man who could not be caught.

In time, however, other emotions appear to have crept into the relationship; a certain jealousy, perhaps, or at least disquiet, that the United Kingdom should once again be leading the world in something, even if it was something as grotesque as mass murder. Ripper envy had arrived, and the U.S. had it bad.

The killings were still under way when novelist Jacob Ringgold opened the door to a forest's worth of American Ripper fiction with the publication of *Lord Jacquelin Burkney: The Whitechapel Terror*, in which several then-current theories over the killer's identity came together in the form of a deranged surgeon.

Latching on to the growing belief that the only thing preventing the Metropolitan Police from apprehending the killer was their absolute lack of any detective skills, one A. Frank Pinkerton opportunistically followed through with *The Whitechapel Murders, or, an American Detective in London.*

The author himself appears to have had no connection whatsoever with the famed Pinkerton Agency, the Chicago-based detective organization so instrumental in bringing a host of Stateside felons to justice. But the very conflation of *that* name and *that* profession was surely sufficient to imbibe his book with, if not a vivid fission, then at least a wealth of possibilities.

Of course, it is very doubtful whether even Pinkerton's famed agents could have apprehended the real Ripper, for short of shadowing every woman on every street (a solution suggested to the Metropolitan Police on several occasions), how could anyone catch a killer who hunted in darkness and permitted not a sound to be heard?

They couldn't.

Nonfictional accounts, too, proliferated, with Richard K. Fox's forty-three-page *The History of the Whitechapel Murders: A Full and Authentic Narrative of the Above Murders, With Sketches,* serving as a well-wrought reminder of just how powerfully the saga had impacted the American imagination.

Within hours of Mary Ann Nichols's body being discovered on August 31, 1888, the *New York Times*'s "own correspondent" was reporting, "A strangely horrible murder took place at Whitechapel this morning.

> The victim was a woman who, at 3 o'clock, was knocked down by some man unknown and attacked with a knife. She attempted to escape and ran a hundred yards, her cries for help being heard by several persons in adjacent houses. No attention was paid to her cries, however, and when found at daybreak she was lying dead in another street, several hundred yards from the scene of the attack. Her head was nearly severed from her body, which was literally cut to pieces, one gash reaching from the pelvis to the breastbone.
>
> The strangest part of the affair is that this is the third murder of the kind which has been done lately. In the last one, two weeks ago, the victim was stabbed 39 times. In the case before it, some months ago, the victim was stabbed with a stick, which was forced through the body. All three victims have been women of the lowest class; all three murders have taken place in the same district, at about the same hour, and have been characterized by the same inhuman and ghoul-like brutality.
>
> The police have concluded that the same man did all three murders and that the most dangerous kind of a lunatic is at large. The excitement is intense over the matter, and the women in

Whitechapel are afraid to stir out of their doors unprotected after dark.

The coverage increased in tandem with the murders until, by the end of the year, the American public was probably as well informed, or at least as chillingly titillated, as its British counterpart.

Soon, too, came the first suggestions that the killer might either be an American or have escaped *to* America, where he could continue the slaughter under even greater anonymity than he had hitherto enjoyed.

At least one man, however, believed he would not be at liberty for long. At the height of the Ripper manhunt, Thomas Byrnes, chief inspector of the New York Police Department, let it be known very loudly that, were such a killer to be operating on *his* patch, the criminal would be caught within two or three days.

Byrnes's boast may or may not have been put to the test, however, just three years later. For, according to both the Macnaghten Memorandum and Inspector Abberline, the Ripper might well have both relocated to the United States once he had completed his London slaughter, and recommenced it smack on Thomas Byrnes's doorstep.

And when Scotland Yard heard that news, said the *Chicago Times*, "officials [were] exultant over the fact that Inspector Byrnes, whose sometime criticism of the London police still rankles in the bosom of those functionaries, ha[d] now the opportunity to exercise his powers in a direction which has baffled Londoners."

George Chapman

Severin Antoniovich Klosowski was born in Nargornak, Poland, in 1865, and studied as a surgeon throughout his late teens.

He arrived in London sometime around late 1887 or early 1888, and found work as a barber's assistant on the West India Dock Road, before opening his own shop at 126 Cable Street. In October 1889, he married Lucy Baderski, a woman he had met just five weeks previous, and so his life continued, unobtrusive, unnoticed, unremarkable.

Or so he thought. What he had failed to take into account was just how closely knit the Polish

A contemporary sketch of George Chapman.

community was, not only in London, but also with relatives back home. Because suddenly it was revealed that he had been married once before— and, in the eyes of both law and church, he still was.

His first wife, too, was outraged when she learned, presumably from someone in London, that her husband was a bigamist, and early in 1890, she arrived in London, determined to stake her claim on the man. Indeed, she even moved into the newlyweds' home, a state of affairs that lingered until the birth of Wladyslaw, Klosowski's first son by Baderski, in September, 1890. The original Mrs. Klosowski moved out; her husband and his new family moved on.

In March 1891 baby Wladyslaw died from "pneumonia asthenia," and that seems to have convinced the couple to make a fresh start. Later that same year, they migrated to the United States, where Klosowski resumed his career at a barber store in Jersey City, New Jersey.

He also resumed his career as a womanizer. Klosowski, it seems, was a natural-born cheat, and prone to violence as well. One day in Jersey City, he and Lucy had a violent row, in the course of which Klosowski threw her down on the bed, pressing his face against her mouth to prevent her from screaming.

In the midst of this, a customer arrived. Klosowski released his wife and went out into shop; Lucy, still struggling to catch her breath, turned over on the bed and noticed a wooden handle sticking out from beneath the pillow.

It was a very long, very sharp knife and, when she later confronted her husband on the subject, he was coolly methodical in his response. He had intended to decapitate her with it, and he had even selected where in the room he would bury her body. If any of the neighbors inquired after her, he explained, he'd just say she'd gone to New York.

Lucy left him soon after, returning to Whitechapel in February 1892, where the couple's second child, daughter Cecilia, was born. Klosowski, too, was back in London soon enough, and although they would attempt a reconciliation, it was clear that the marriage was over. The couple parted shortly after.

There is a sordid inevitability to the remainder of Klosowski's life.

In 1893, now living in the north London neighborhood of Tottenham, he met a woman named Annie Chapman (not, for obvious reasons, the Ripper victim) and they moved in together. She became pregnant, but Klosowski had now moved another woman into the house, and Chapman packed her bags. She sued for child support, but suddenly Klosowski vanished.

He had, in what was surely a final act of scorn for his spurned former mistress, changed his name—he was now George Chapman, working at a barber's in Leytonstone and living with an alcoholic named Mary Spink.

It was a well-starred move. Soon after they moved in together, Mary came into some money and the couple were able to open their own barber's in the coastal town of Hastings.

There, they prospered.

A skilled musician, Mary would play the piano while Chapman cut his customers' hair; their "musical shaves" became a local phenomenon, and soon the money was rolling in. Chapman even purchased a sailing boat.

But he remained a cruel man, with an eternal eye for other women. The relationship was pocked with violence, and Mary was frequently seen nursing the bruises and scars of another evening's beating. And as the novelty and earning power of the musical shaves wore off, Chapman began looking for another way out.

Giving up the barber's shop, he became manager of a local pub, the Prince of Wales. He also bought a one-ounce dose of tartar emetic, a slow-acting poison, from a chemist on High Street.

Mary's health declined. Stomach pains, cramps and nausea wracked her frame, and all who witnessed her suffering commented upon how devoted her husband was throughout the ordeal, seldom leaving her bedside except to open the pub. When she finally passed away on Christmas Day, her body reduced to skeletal proportions, Chapman's grief seemed inconsolable. The official cause of death was consumption.

But so, strangely, was that of his next lady friend, Bessie Taylor, who had been hired to take over some of Mary's duties in the pub, and soon found herself replacing the dead woman elsewhere in Chapman's life.

She, too, sickened slowly but suddenly; but lest tongues should wag at this uncanny coincidence, Chapman left the Prince of Wales and moved to Bishop's Stortford in Essex to manage a pub there. Then, with Bessie's health continuing to decline, he returned to London, to a pub in Borough, where his "wife" finally passed away. It was Valentine's Day, 1901.

Chapman remained outwardly calm, but he was clearly losing the plot. The pub, the Monument, was failing, and when he tried to burn it down, and at least collect the insurance money, he failed at arson as well.

So he soldiered on, taking another wife, Maud Marsh, and incredibly, repeating the cycle once again. Only this time, the onset of his wife's seemingly incurable, and unidentifiable, illness aroused suspicions, not only on the part of Marsh's mother, but also from Chapman's latest lover, Florence Rayner.

One day, Chapman suggested that he and Florence run away together to America. Rayner refused, saying, "No, you have your wife downstairs," to which Chapman simply snapped his fingers and replied, "Oh, I'd give her that, and she would be no more Mrs. Chapman."

When Maud finally died on October 22, 1902, the attending doctor refused to issue a death certificate. Instead, he ordered an autopsy, where the poor woman's body was found to be riddled with both antimony (the active poison in tartar emetic) and arsenic. Panicked by Mrs. Marsh's suspicions over her daughter's health, Chapman had thrown all of his past caution to the wind and administered his victim one final, massive dose of poison.

Three days later, he was arrested, and the confused web of his past was untangled. The two previous wives he had buried were exhumed, and Chapman discovered the one major disadvantage of antimony poisoning.

The poison itself might be near undetectable in terms of taste and color, but it has a remarkably powerful preservative effect. Both corpses were exquisitely preserved; both provided sufficient evidence to hang their murderer. The jury required just eleven minutes to arrive at their verdict, and on April 7, 1903, George Chapman was executed.

So what does any of this have to do with Jack the Ripper? One killer, after all, was a mutilator, the other was a poisoner. Very different methods and very different motives—the Ripper killed strangers, Chapman killed his wives. Surely the only thing they had in common was that both were in Whitechapel during that awful summer and fall of 1888, but even there, the similarities fade, for while one was cutting throats, the other was cutting hair.

Inspector Abberline, however, was drawing other conclusions, and so powerful were they that, when word of Chapman's conviction came through, he turned to the arresting officer, Inspector Godley, and said, "You've got Jack the Ripper at last!"

He detailed his reasoning for the *Pall Mall Gazette*:

> I have been so struck with the remarkable coincidences in the two series of murders that I have not been able to think of anything else for several days past—not, in fact, since the Attorney-General made his opening statement at the recent trial, and traced the antecedents of Chapman before he came to this country in 1888.

> Since then, the idea has taken full possession of me, and everything
> fits in and dovetails so well that I cannot help feeling that this is the
> man we struggled so hard to capture fifteen years ago . . .

He had never, he said, subscribed to those theories that insisted the Ripper had been caged for another crime, perhaps in an asylum, or those that insisted the killer had taken his own life. Abberline *knew* in his heart that the man was still out there somewhere, living a free and seemingly blameless life among the anonymous crowds of unremarkable citizens. Just as he *knew*, the moment he had acquainted himself with Chapman's background, that the barber was also a butcher.

There were, he said, "a score of things which make one believe that Chapman is the man."

> The fact that he studied medicine and surgery in Russia before he
> came over here is well established, and it is curious to note that the
> first series of murders was the work of an expert surgeon, while
> the recent poisoning cases were proved to be done by a man with
> more than an elementary knowledge of medicine. The story told
> by Chapman's wife of the attempt to murder her with a long knife
> while in America is not to be ignored.

It was true that Chapman fit none of the descriptions the police had received of the man believed to be the Ripper, but they scarcely tallied with one another either; and besides, most witnesses saw the killer only from behind. As for the change in murderous method, Abberline had no doubt. "A man who could watch his wives being slowly tortured to death by poison, as he did, was capable of anything."

Evidence of Chapman's voracious sexual appetite was produced, backed up by the belief that he regularly consorted with prostitutes, even while married. Friends from his Whitechapel days recalled Lucy complaining that he frequently stayed out late into the night, or even until morning. He could be secretive, and he was known to be violent.

There are problems with his identification as Jack the Ripper, however. For instance, we simply do not know if Chapman, or Klosowski as he then was, learned English while he was in Poland—but if he did, he would certainly have spoken with an accent. The Ripper, from all accounts, was credited with a cultured, educated voice, and no trace of a foreign accent was ever mentioned.

Abberline overlooked that issue. For he had one more damning coincidence up his sleeve.

Not only did Chapman's arrival in England coincide with the beginning of the series of murders in Whitechapel, his departure for the United States also matched their cessation, particularly if one accepts that Frances Coles really was a victim of the Ripper. And most fascinatingly of all, though London was now free of the fiend, no sooner had Chapman arrived in America than "similar murders began to be perpetrated . . . there."

This declaration, sensational at the time, is merely puzzling today. In fact, decades of rummaging through the newspaper archives of the time, by scores of researchers and students, have unearthed just one "similar" killing in the New Jersey / New York area during Chapman's stay in the States, a savagely mutilated prostitute named Carrie Brown, discovered in a New York City boardinghouse, the East River Hotel, on April 24, 1891.

It certainly sounds like a textbook Ripper killing. According to news reports, "the dead body of the old woman was found lying on the bed. It was shockingly cut and mutilated. The body was completely naked.

"A deep gash extended from the lower part of the abdomen upward to the breast, which disembowelled it completely. The entrails had apparently been torn from the body and were scattered over the bed. There were also two deep cuts crossing each other on the back in the form of an exact cross. It is believed the murderer strangled his victim first and then proceeded' to his horrible butchery."

Of course the local media was swift to pick up on the similarities between Carrie Brown's death and the Whitechapel murders; indeed, one reporter asked the head of the investigation, Inspector Byrnes, outright: "Was the cutting such as would have been done by a surgeon as the cutting done by Jack the Ripper of London, is said to be?"

Byrnes retort dripped with scorn. "If it was done by a surgeon he was a butcher. It was horrible hacking."

The reporter pressed on. "Would you suppose this murder was committed by the London Jack the Ripper?"

Byrnes did not take the bait: "I am not advancing theories. I cannot say." And when an arrest was announced, the *Brooklyn Daily Eagle* sighed, "the detectives [have] not arrested Jack the Ripper."

In fact, Carrie Brown's true killer would never be captured. An Algerian Arab, Ameer ben Ali (known locally as Frenchy), was charged and convicted, but few people were satisfied with either the investigation or the trial. Ali would eventually be pardoned; and Byrnes, for all of his boasts about catching a serial killer in just two or three days, had proven unable to solve even one single murder.

And the *Brooklyn Daily Eagle* was correct. The killer was not Jack the Ripper, and he probably wasn't Klosowski / George Chapman, either.

The description provided by the hotel's assistant housekeeper, Mary Miniter, only vaguely matched George Chapman—five-foot-eight, slim, with a fair mustache and a long, sharp nose. He wore a dark brown cutaway coat and black trousers, an old and dented black derby hat, and Ms. Miniter thought, from his accent, that he was German. (Byrnes, incidentally, wholly discounted Miniter's testimony, declaring that the woman was "an opium fiend, and has associated with Chinamen.")

What was ironic was that another of the NYPD's initial suspects, a Moroccan sailor named Arbie La Bruckman (aka John Stephens) *was* arrested in London in December 1889 and held as a suspect in the Whitechapel murders. He was held for a month before being released.

It is unclear whether or not the New York police knew of this when they began investigating him, or whether he dodged a major bullet when the law decided to devote its full attention to Ali, at the expense of any other leads.

Neither is there any certainty that Chapman himself was even in New Jersey at the time of the murder. He and Lucy were certainly still in London on April 5, for they appear on the census that was prepared that day.

A modern plaque immortalizes George Chapman's claim to Ripper fame.   *Alamy*

The voyage across the Atlantic took a little over a week at that time—the record, set by the steamship *Etruria* in 1888, was just shy of six days and two hours, but that vessel was deliberately racing against the clock. The average passenger liner would have been somewhat more leisurely. But still, if the couple did leave England within days of the census, and had already booked their passage and packed their possessions, they could possibly have at least started to settle in their new home sometime before Carrie Brown met her end.

So, no less than in Whitechapel, maybe Chapman did it, and maybe he didn't. Because, just as one could point to the rash of gruesome murders committed in Singapore, allegedly by secret societies, around the same time as Sir Charles Warren was appointed garrison commander in 1889, the mere presence of an individual in a particular place barely qualifies even as circumstantial evidence, let alone a damning indictment.

The Tale of Mr. Tumblety

If the Ripper was abroad in the United States, however, there is certainly no paucity of other possible suspects, including an American quack doctor named Francis Tumblety, who arrived in London in the mid-1860s with a handful of deaths (but no convictions) allegedly already behind him.

A dyed-in-the-wool Southerner, Tumblety (such a delightful name for such an apparently odious character) was originally arrested in connection with a gruesome plot to spread yellow fever through the American North with infected blankets.

He was, in fact, innocent of the charge. With supreme bad luck, however, Tumblety had been recently operating under the pseudonym of Dr. J. H. Blackburn at the same time the feds were seeking a Dr. L. P. Blackburn. It was sheer misfortune that saw Tumblety arrested, but while he was quickly cleared of one charge, news of his capture was conflated with the ongoing investigation into the assassination of President Lincoln, and now rumor insisted he was a part of that conspiracy.

He did the only thing any sensible person would do. He fled.

Tumblety spent the next decade or so traveling around Europe and America, but in Liverpool in November 1888, he was arrested first on charges of gross indecency—a euphemism for homosexual activities—and then on suspicion of the Whitechapel murders.

It was not the most well-founded charge, and may well have been based more upon his flamboyance and his alleged sexual deviance (another euphemism, albeit a less gentle one) than any cast-iron suspicion he was the killer.

If nothing else, after all, his appearance stood against him. Far from some sinister black-clad shadow, Tumblety dressed in the most dramatic fashions he could find, with his short, roly-poly frame topped by so extravagant a mustache that there would be no mistaking him, even on the darkest night.

Of course, if a suspicion had been raised, then a suspicion needed to be investigated. Tumblety, however, was not playing ball. Again he fled, first to France and then back to New York, from whence Scotland Yard not only tried to extradite him, they even dispatched officers across the Atlantic to affect his capture.

Unfortunately, the American authorities were not about to surrender a citizen on the unproven whim of the British. The New York police knew exactly where Tumblety was hiding out and had placed him under surveillance of their own. But, as an official statement put it, "there is no proof of his complicity in the Whitechapel murders, and the crime for which he was under bond in London is not extraditable."

Neither did a word of this appear in the British press; although the American media kept almost as close a watch on Tumblety as the New York Police Department felt it prudent to do, Scotland Yard was adamant that the so-simple escape of any suspect should not become a matter for public debate. And so Tumblety lived free until his death in 1903, his suspected guilt recorded in just one document—the so-called "Littlejohn letter," penned by Chief Inspector John Littlechild to journalist G. R. Sims in 1913.

This in turn remained unpublished until 1993, when its contents were revealed by authors Stewart Evans and Paul Gainey in their book *Jack the Ripper: First American Serial Killer.* And while Tumblety's guilt of course remains a subject for speculation and inference only, still the appearance of a hitherto unpublished element of the original investigation might well be regarded among the most crucial steps forward in the case in over a century.

Lizzie Halliday

And then there is Lizzy Halliday, an Irish émigré who not only confessed to the Whitechapel murders, but has also been depicted as possessing the necessary temperament, too.

Born around 1859 in County Antrim, Ireland, the erstwhile Eliza Margaret McNally was still a child when her family moved to the United States.

She was twenty when she married her first husband, a Philadelphia gent differing accounts name as either Ketspool Brown or Charles Hopkins; uncertainty, too, attends the suggestion that they had a son who ended his days in an institution.

Whatever his name, Lizzie's first husband was not long for this world. He died in 1881, and within a year or so, she had buried a second spouse, an elderly man named Artemus Brewer. A third husband, war veteran Hiram Parkinson, walked out on the marriage within twelve months of the ceremony, while her bigamous fourth, George Smith (who had served alongside Parkinson) was himself deserted—but not before Lizzie laced his tea with arsenic and then looted the house before escaping to Bellow Falls in Vermont.

Smith survived, and Lizzie's fifth husband, Charles Playstel, might also be said to have enjoyed a lucky escape. Lizzie ran out on the marriage after just two weeks.

By early 1888, Lizzie was back in Philadelphia, staying with some old friends at the saloon they ran on North Front Street. She was now calling herself Maggie Hopkins, and under this name, she went into business for herself, opening a store, and then burning it down.

The insurance company was immediately suspicious, and investigations proved that they were right to be. On March 17, Lizzie was convicted of fraud and sentenced to two years in Eastern State Penitentiary. She served no more than half her term, however, before being released, and in 1889, "Lizzie Brown" met a twice-widowed farmer, seventy-year-old Paul Halliday.

Apparently he, too, hailed from County Antrim, and it was the shared heritage that first drew them together. According to Halliday's son Robert, "He first met her in an intelligence office in Newburg, where he secured her services as a housekeeper. None of the family liked the woman. Her appearance was against her. She did not conduct herself as a wife should. My father, however, was infatuated with her. She held a peculiar influence over him which nothing could shake."

MRS. HALLIDAY IN HANDCUFFS.

Lizzie Halliday, one of America's most notorious female serial killers.
Public Domain/Wikimedia Commons

They married the following May and went to live with Halliday's two sons, Robert and the mentally handicapped John, at his farm in Burlingham, New York.

Barely had she settled in, however, than Halliday was excusing his wife's increasingly bizarre behavior by telling people that she was subject to spells of temporary insanity. Utterly unpredictable, prone to horrific changes of mood and manner, Lizzie was also growing increasingly dangerous.

On May 6, a suspicious fire destroyed the Halliday farmhouse. Twenty days later, another destroyed one of the barns. Certainly Lizzie was suspected, but no legal action appears to have been taken until Lizzie blatantly rode her husband's horse and buggy to market in Newburgh, where she sold it. She was charged, but soon acquitted on the none-too-surprising grounds of insanity.

Back at the farm, Lizzie's fire-raising continued, but this time with fatal consequences. In May 1893, her younger stepson, John, died in yet another dubious blaze.

Again she was arrested, and this time, she did not get off. Not at first, anyway. But doctors at Middletown asylums soon declared her cured, and by August, Lizzie was back living on the Halliday farm. Which meant, when her husband suddenly vanished that same month, she was there to reassure the neighbors that he had simply gone to a nearby town to undertake some masonry work.

Oddly, the neighbors did not believe her.

On September 4, a warrant was produced and the authorities commenced searching the farm. Of old Mr. Halliday, however, there was no trace—not yet, anyway. But two bodies were discovered, shot dead and then hidden beneath some hay in the barn. Even more damningly, both were (or had been) friends of Lizzie's: Sarah and Margaret McQuillan, relatives of her saloon-owning friends in Philadelphia.

Lizzie was arrested and the search went on until finally, few days later, Paul Halliday's body was discovered beneath the floorboards of the marital home.

It was apparent, however, that neither prosecution or defense were going to get anywhere with Lizzie. Although doctor after doctor insisted that she was faking her condition, she remained absolutely incoherent, tearing at her clothes while babbling nonsense. She stopped eating, set her bed on fire and attacked Sullivan County Sheriff Harrison Beecher's wife.

She also made at least two suicide attempts, first trying to hang herself, and then slashing her throat with broken glass. Asked why, she simply explained, "I wanted to see if I would bleed."

By the time her court appearance came up, Lizzie was spending most of her days and nights chained to the floor of her cell. But chains could not still her tongue, and so she continued reeling off her inchoate delusions. Or were they confessions?

Charged with what were surely the most sensational crimes in the recent history of Sullivan County, Lizzie became an immediate media star. She was proclaimed a former gypsy queen and feted with a fascination normally attendant only upon the most superlative celebrities.

The legendary Nelly Bly, a pioneering journalist who did so much to better the lot of New York's criminally insane, took an interest in her case and secured the interview that filled in most of what we today know about Lizzie's life.

In fact, the two women met twice, once at Bly's instigation and once at Lizzie's.

The first interview saw Lizzie expertly playing her insanity card.

"Did you or did you not kill those people?"

She looked up. There was real alarm in her face. "I have been crazy; I was drugged," she ejaculated, defiantly.

... "Tell me," I urged, "you did it yourself?"

"What shall I say, dear?" she said, turning to the sheriff.

"Are you guilty or innocent? Tell me now. I may be able to help you. Anyway, I am going away and you will never see me again," I said to her at last when it was drawing close to the hour of midnight.

"Some other time. My head feels bad now. Some other time," was her answer.

It was the second interview that saw Lizzie open up, not only about her life (and her defense—at one point, she claimed the murders were committed by a gang of men who first drugged her, and forced her to witness the killings), but also about yet another killing in which she could, at the very least, be implicated: a peddler murdered some twelve miles from her home, some months earlier. No trace of this crime was ever found, but the mere possibility that her story was true added much to Lizzie's allure.

New York World reporter Edwin Atwell was certainly employing a degree of hyperbole when he described her life as "unprecedented and almost without parallel in the annals of crime." Again, we have only Lizzie's word for a lot of what she did and didn't do, and that word changed like the weather.

Nevertheless, there appeared to be mounting reason to believe that the three corpses found on the farm in September were only the most recent murders for which Lizzie could be accused. Add the peddler, John Halliday, and two mysteriously deceased husbands to the tally, and already she had seven deaths on her (admittedly, decidedly unconcerned) conscience.

Her claims to have killed another spouse while she still lived in Ireland constituted an eighth, and the attempted poisoning of her third Stateside husband came close to making it nine. And those were only the killings that people knew (or could guess) about. Lizzie might still have been a long way behind the awful tally that condemned Englishwoman Mary Ann Cotton, but as careers in homicide went, she was certainly racking them up.

It was Sheriff Beecher who suggested that the world did indeed know a lot less about Lizzie Halliday's murderous spree than it believed; that she was also involved—if not as the actual killer, then at least as an accomplice—in the Whitechapel murders.

It's an unlikely claim, but the press had a field day, regardless. According to Beecher, "It has been proved that she was in Europe at the time [and] she frequently refers to the subject both when she is in possession of her mental faculties and when she is raving." In fact, no such proof has ever been forthcoming, but why let something that mundane stand in the way of a great story?

On one occasion, in fact, Beecher told Lizzie that she was to be accused of the Whitechapel murders, and asked her outright, "Are you guilty?"

"Do they think I am an elephant?" she replied. "That was done by a man."

The case for John Merrick, the London Hospital's most famous nineteenth-century resident, begins here.

On June 27, 1894, Lizzie was found guilty of the murders of the McQuillans and sentenced to death, the first woman ever to be condemned to the electric chair.

She responded to the judge's words by biting Sheriff Beecher on the hand, and doing so with such strength ("tigress ferocity," said the *New York Tribune*) that she not only cut through his glove with her teeth, she also left him a wound so serious that the inflammation spread as far as his elbow, and there were fears he might even lose his arm.

She did not take that final journey. With a medical commission reporting that Lizzie was indeed insane, New York Governor Roswell P. Flower had her sentence commuted to life in an institution, and she was dispatched to the Matteawan State Hospital for the Criminally Insane.

There she would live out the remainder of her life, until her death on June 18, 1918. Her career as a killer was not ended by her sentencing, however. Within a year of arriving at the asylum, Lizzie tried to strangle one of her attendants, Catherine Ward; and in 1906, she assaulted another, nurse Nellie Wicks, armed with a pair of scissors snatched from the woman's own belt.

No fewer than two hundred stab wounds later, the nurse was dead.

The *Logansport Pharos* newspaper told the tale:

> For ten years this strange and diabolical woman, once a gypsy queen, led a career of murder, theft, and arson, but of all her crimes this was perhaps the most fiendish.
>
> Miss Wicks, a graceful and pretty young woman, had been in the asylum is nurse a little more than a year. Mrs. Halliday manifested for her a peculiar fondness. The girl, touched by the woman's apparent affection, did all in her power for the unfortunate creature.
>
> Lizzie Halliday had no object, so far as could ever be learned, for the previous murders she had committed. For this one she had a reason. Miss Wicks was going away from the asylum. She had arranged to take a course at the New York hospital to fit her as a trained nurse, and Mrs. Halliday, in her insane affection, had determined that the girl should not go . . .

They Seek Him Here . . .

The notion that the Ripper could have somehow shifted his base of operations from the UK to the United States is not a recent one, then, no matter how arresting fresh variations on that theme can seem.

In the 1979 movie *Time After Time* (itself based on a novel by Karl Alexander), we saw the Ripper obtain a time machine and arrive in present-day San Francisco, with the writer H. G. Wells (author of the classic 1895 novel *The Time Machine*) in hot pursuit.

A few years later, in 1985's *Terror at London Bridge,* we learn that the Ripper's spirit arrived in Lake Havasu City, Arizona, trapped inside one of the stones from which the bridge's new owner would be reconstructing his purchase. (Built in the 1830s, the London Bridge was indeed saved from demolition when it was purchased in 1967 by Arizona businessman Robert P. McCulloch, who re-erected it on the Colorado River.)

In 1989's *Gotham by Gaslight* graphic novel, no less an American icon that Batman returned to his hometown Gotham City from a recent tour of Europe, to learn not only that Jack the Ripper was at large on the streets, but that he was also framing Batman's civilian alter ego, millionaire Bruce Wayne, for his murders. The tale is still regarded among Batman aficionados as one of their hero's finest-ever adventures.

And in 2017, *Time After Time* came up for a revival, with a new primetime television series pursuing Jack (Josh Bowman) and Wells (Freddie Stroma) around modern-day Manhattan.

In truth, it is unlikely that Jack the Ripper either moved to America or hailed from there in the first place. No less than among the home-based suspects, there is much to admire in every attempt to prove that he might have, and much to disdain as well. But one thing is certain: imitation remains the sincerest form of flattery.

22

Jack's Journal

The Killer Kept a Diary

> Begin with the rings, one ring, two rings bitch, it took a while before I could wrench them off. Should have stuffed them down the whores throat. I wish to God I could have taken the head.
>
> —The Diary of Jack the Ripper

F ake diaries are nothing new. Both Benito Mussolini, wartime leader of Fascist Italy, and Adolf Hitler, his Nazi German counterpart, had their so-called innermost thoughts revealed first for public scrutiny, and then for public ridicule, in the late 1950s and early 1980s, respectively. And in 1992, Jack the Ripper may (or may not) have joined this same select band.

That was the year a former Liverpool scrap dealer, Michael Barrett, went public with a diary he said he'd acquired the previous year from a friend, Tony Devereux, and which was very swiftly determined to be the secret musings of Jack the Ripper.

The story begins in Whitechapel, of course, but not the London one. There is a similarly named quarter of Liverpool, and it was there that the diary's anonymous author saw his American-born wife, Florence—whom he henceforth refers to as either "the bitch" or "the whore"—in the company of an unnamed lover.

Enraged, the writer made his way to London, to that city's own Whitechapel district, and proceeded to murder and mutilate five prostitutes—whose deaths and dismemberments he then spelled out in stupendously gruesome detail, across the pages of a typical scrapbook of the era—albeit one with the first twenty pages torn out.

> The pleasure was far better than I expected. The whore was only too willing to do her business. I recall all and it thrills me, There was no scream when I cut. I was more than vexed when the head would not come off. I believe I will need more strength next time. I struck deep into her. I regret I never had the cane, it would have been a

delight to have rammed it hard into her. The bitch opened like a ripe peach. I have decided next time I will rip all out.

The entries are undated, but both the accounts of the murders and the response of the law ("they remind me of chickens with their heads cut off running fools with no heads, ha ha") follow the established chronology of the killings.

Sometimes the diarist writes in straightforward (if appallingly punctuated) prose; other times he lapses into verse, or whimsical limerick—this piece, for instance, recalling the murder of Elizabeth Stride:

> With a rose to match the red
> I tried to cut off the head
> Damn it, I cried
> The horse went and shied
> But I could still smell her sweet scented breath.

Or, following Mary Jane Kelly's dismembering,

> I had a key
> and with it, I did flee
> The hat I did burn
> For light I did yearn
> And I thought of the whoring mother.

He was clearly proud of his poetical prowess, too. "I wonder if next time," he muses a little further down the page, "I can carve my funny little rhyme in the whores flesh? I believe I will give it a try."

And so on and so forth, until the diary comes to an end with a flourish that suggests this was never intended to be a private journal after all. "I give my name that all know of me, so history do tell, what love can do to a gentle man born. Yours truly, Jack the Ripper."

Rapidly, the book's innermost secrets were untangled. The writer, it appeared, was James Maybrick, a Liverpool cotton merchant whose own serial infidelities were an open secret both in his hometown and in the United States, where he regularly traveled for business—he had, in fact, met the then seventeen-year-old Florence as he returned from one such trip, in the first-class tearoom of the White Star liner *Baltic*. Maybrick was forty at the time.

The couple married in July 1880 and their first son, James Chandler (no relation to the Whitechapel police officer of the same name, of course), was born in March 1881.

Life was divided between Liverpool and Norfolk, North Virginia—where Maybrick had already secreted one mistress. His philanderings notwithstanding, however, Maybrick appears to have led a reasonably blameless life. So did Florence, at least by her husband's standards of decency, for she, too, had a lover: Alfred Brierley, one of Maybrick's cotton-broking colleagues.

But the couple fought constantly, usually over Maybrick's affairs, but also over his particularly unpleasant habit of sprinkling everything he ate with arsenic—a deadly poison, of course, but if used in the correct amounts, claimed Maybrick, a remarkable fortifier.

His doctor discouraged him from this strange dietary aid, and his family pleaded with him, too. But Maybrick paid them no heed; flew, in fact, into an incandescent fury every time the subject was broached.

His temper was growing worse in other ways, too. One night in March 1889, Florence came downstairs from their bedroom in tears, her face white, her dress in shreds, and with every servant in the house second-guessing what Maybrick could have been referring to, a few moments

Mr. and Mrs. John Maybrick—a potential Ripper and the woman who murdered him.
Wikimedia Commons

earlier, when he bellowed, "Such a scandal will be all over town tomorrow! Florrie, I never thought you would come to this."

But the fact that she had just spent three days in London with Brierley, followed up by a very visible trip to the Grand National horse race, was probably close to the truth.

Florence was on the verge of leaving Maybrick that night, only for him to dissuade her, but the arguments continued the following day, until finally, she collapsed. A doctor was called, and Florence spent the rest of the week in bed. Then, the moment she recovered, she went out to visit Brierley.

This is where things get confused. Many cosmetics of the Victorian era contained arsenic—it was said to improve the complexion. Flypapers, for catching bugs, were likewise impregnated with the stuff.

So when James Maybrick first sickened, at the end of April, and then died on May 11, from what was instantly determined to be arsenic poisoning, Florence's purchases of such common products should have aroused far less suspicion than the fact that her husband was devouring the poison like candy.

But a spiteful nurse with the oddly appropriate name of Alice Yapp, and the whispered innuendo of Maybrick's own friends, turned the police's attentions in the opposite direction entirely.

On May 14, Florence was arrested, and at the end of July, she became the first American woman ever to be tried for murder in the United Kingdom.

Of course her defense hinged upon her husband's addiction, and most likely it would have been accepted in any other court in the country. But the presiding magistrate, Justice Stephens, appeared to have taken an intense dislike to her.

Details of her relationship with Brierley spooled out before a shocked courtroom. Letters she had written to him were produced. Witnesses to her adultery were encouraged to let their imaginations run free, and all the while, a prim and proper jury sat with mouths wide open and faces blanched at the sight and sound of the harlot who stood accused in the dock.

Long before the prosecution induced Florence to admit that yes, she had occasionally prepared her husband's favorite delicacy for him, but only at his insistence, jury and judge had made up their mind.

She should swing, but it is not hard to surmise that she was condemned to death not for the murder of James Maybrick, but for so blatantly challenging one of the unspoken rules of Victorian life—that husbands were free to do what they wanted, but a wife's place was in *his* bed alone.

Florence was not, in the end, executed. So many questions were asked about the conduct of her trial that her sentence was commuted to one of life imprisonment, and when the affair was reexamined in 1904, she was released. She died in October 1941.

Already, then, James Maybrick was at the center of a major, headline-devouring murder case, albeit as the victim rather than the perpetrator. Could he really have reversed those same roles just six months before he died?

Expert after expert poured their opinions out on the contents of the diary, both before and after its publication, in 1993, as *The Diary of Jack the Ripper*.

To some, the journal unquestionably dated back to the late Victorian age; to others, it was clearly a latter-day fake. Forensic studies proved equally muddleheaded, and the whole affair ought to have ground to a standstill when Michael Barrett admitted he had created the diary himself and then dictated it to his ex-wife, Ann.

Except it didn't, because he then retracted his confession (before later retracting the retraction), around the same time that Ann apparently demolished any lingering suspicions regarding the diary's provenance by insisting it had been in her family's possession since 1950, when her father had received it among a pile of old books.

She had owned the book since 1968, and it was she who handed it to Tony Devereux to pass on, knowing that Barrett would be interested, but not wanting him to know where it came from. Relations between Barrett and her family were not in the best of health, after all.

Barely was that story being circulated, however, than another appeared—that the diary was originally discovered by workmen carrying out repairs at the old Maybrick home, Battlecrease House on Riverdale Road, in Aigburth, one of Liverpool's more affluent suburbs.

Where the diary truly originated remained in doubt, of course, but suspicions that it was a modern-day concoction were at least dampened down.

There were still innumerable difficulties to negotiate, however, before the diary could be proclaimed genuine. Attempts to match the killings with Maybrick's own known movements were, of course, futile—no such records existed, if they ever had, and he had not kept the train tickets or any relevant receipts either. Which in itself was a point in the diary's favor—any competent forger would surely have added a period document or two for validation?

The handwriting did not really match Maybrick's, what little of it remained, and it did not match the Ripper's either, or at least any of the communiqués he was purported to have sent. But again, those were not insurmountable hurdles, particularly given the uncertainties that had forever clung to Jack's mailbag.

What was damning was that the facts as laid out in the diary didn't tell researchers anything that they didn't already know.

The details of the author's "own" movements and motives, of course, were laid out in all of their glory, and were littered with both personal and private information. But when he came to describe the murders themselves, and the information that had been so painstakingly documented by doctors and detectives alike, nothing the writer included could not have been gleaned from either the period newspapers or, even more damagingly, the misconceptions and errors that had turned up in sundry subsequent writings on the subject.

The question on everyone's lips. And walls.   *Alamy*

He does add some gloriously gratuitous details, of course—that, having sliced off Mary Jane Kelly's breasts, he then spent some time kissing them before carefully arranging them on her bedside table.

The first claim might have been true. But the second most certainly wasn't—there were no breasts found on the table, and no evidence they had ever been placed there. One lay under Mary Jane's head, the other was placed by her right foot.

Neither was his description of her entrails being festooned around the room like Christmas decorations anything more than the kind of vicarious fabrication a tabloid journalist might have invented, in order to convey the sheer horror of the room. They were, in fact, found on the bed.

Such details surely pointed to the diary being an entertaining, but ultimately fraudulent hoax. However, the drama still had one more act to play out.

In 1993, at the height of the diary's infamy, a Mr. Albert Johnson purchased an antique gold watch, made by the famed watchmakers William Verity around 1848.

Inspecting it closely once he returned to his home, Johnson discovered that somebody had gone to the trouble not only of inscribing the initials MN, MK, AC, ES, and CE (presumably standing for Mary Nichols, Mary Kelly, Annie Chapman, Elizabeth Stride and Catherine Eddowes) on the watch, but also the signature J. Maybrick; and, finally, the words "I am Jack."

Like the diary, the watch was examined; as with the diary, the results were contrary. The inscriptions could very likely have been made in the late 1880s, but they could just as easily have not.

But was it not just a little too convenient that, within a year of a whole new suspect arising out of obscurity to claim the Ripper's throne, a second piece of evidence should miraculously manifest itself?

Yes, it probably was, and for all its claims to be the real McCoy, the diary of Jack the Ripper, and the name of James Maybrick, are now given no more, or less, credence than any of the many alternate suspects.

The question that remains, then, is simple.

If the Whitechapel murderer was not James Maybrick . . . if it wasn't Montague John Druitt . . . if it wasn't Kłosowski or Kosminski, Ostrog or Pizer, James Thomas Sadler or Francis Tumblety, William Henry Bury, Thomas Neill Cream, Thomas Hayne Cutbush, Frederick Bailey Deeming, Carl Feigenbaum, a mad midwife, Arbie La Bruckman, Robert Donston Stephenson, Joseph Barnett, Lewis Carroll, David Cohen, William Withey Gull, George Hutchinson, Hyam Hyams, James Kelly, Charles Allen

Lechmere, Lizzie Halliday, Jacob Levy, Alexander Pedachenko, Walter Sickert, Joseph Silver, James Kenneth Stephen, the Duke of Clarence and Avondale, Sir John Williams or Sir Charles Warren, or any of the others that have been accused of the crimes . . .

. . . then who in blazes was it?

Epilogue

Every time there's a stabbing in Whitechapel, they come crawling out of the woodwork. I hate Ripperologists.

—*Ray Miles*, Whitechapel *(UK TV, 2009)*

Frances Coles was laid to rest, and the Whitechapel murderer never returned. *A* Whitechapel murderer, however, would—and in one of the most evocative locations imaginable.

Eighteen years had passed since Coles's murder, and twenty-one since the slaughters of the so-called Autumn of Fear; and Whitechapel was changing. In 1894, the newly formed London County Council took over supervision of the metropolis, and one of its very first actions was to look into the lamentable state of the city's lodging houses, not only laying out a series of required reforms and improvem ts (that was old news), but vigorously enforcing them, as well.

Lodging houses were to be officially registered on an annual basis. Water closets were to be provided on a ratio of one for every twenty people. Clean towels were to be made available to every occupant.

Walls were to be lime-whited and cleaned every six months. Bunkbeds and oilskin mattresses were to be replaced with proper beds and fresh, clean bedding. Double (or greater) occupancy of beds was outlawed, and men and women could no longer be lodged in the same rooms.

The more resilient landlords went along with the changes, however unwillingly, and seized the opportunity to buy up the properties of those who weren't willing to move with the times. By the time the dust settled, John McCarthy and William Crossingham between them now owned more or less the whole of Dorset Street, and numerous properties beyond.

The new regulations perhaps improved the lot of the people who slept in the boardinghouses. But Whitechapel as a whole continued to decline. Vicious street gangs were even more in evidence than before—eastern Europeans and Greeks with names like the Bessarabians and the Odessians.

Local shops were little more than fences for stolen goods, and when the social reformer Charles Booth sent one of his researchers out into the neighborhood, the agent found even the precepts of Christ Church,

Nicholas Hawksmoor's most beautiful creation, were littered with prostitutes, its funereal monuments doubling as bathrooms, its benches as beds, and its denizens so riddled with vermin that the churchyard itself was now known as Itchy Park. Few music fans listening to the Small Faces' 1967 hit "Itchycoo Park"—so evocative as it is of pastoral peace and psychedelic whimsy—would ever imagine it referred to the same place!

But it did.

Unsolved murders continued to dog the area, and of course, every time the bloodied body of another prostitute turned up on the streets, the local media would at least muse upon, if not rage about, its similarities to the darkest days of old. Particularly if the murderer was never brought to justice.

And especially when Dorset Street, the axis around which so many of the Ripper killings seemed to revolve, was at the center of events.

On May 25, 1901, a prostitute named Mary Ann Austin turned up at William Crossingham's boardinghouse at 35 Dorset Street—the same establishment that Annie Chapman had left on the night of her murder in 1888—with a man in tow.

The deputy, a Mr. Moore, refused them entry; the house was a women's-only establishment now. But when Mary Ann's companion produced the staggering sum of one shilling and sixpence—at least three times the going rate for a single bed—the deputy relented. He gave them bed number fifteen, up on the third floor of the building, and thought no more about it.

That was at 10:30 p.m. The following morning, around 8:30, another of the lodgers burst into Moore's office with the news that Mary Ann had been attacked. Moore's wife, Mary, rushed up the stairs to find Mary Ann still alive, but clearly bleeding to death from a number of stab wounds.

Of course Mrs. Moore called for a doctor. But she also knew that if her husband's bending of the rules ever came to light, the consequences would be terrible, not only for him, but possibly for the boardinghouse itself, as well. So she also called for his brother-in-law, Daniel Sullivan, who lived on nearby Whites Road, and together they hatched a plan.

First, the dying woman was stripped naked and redressed in clothing belonging to another lodger—Mary Ann's own outfit was burned. She was then moved to a bed two floors down, while the murder site itself was vigorously scrubbed clean. By the time the doctor arrived, every trace of the attack had been removed, with the exception of the victim.

Mary Ann was swiftly taken to the hospital, but it was too late. She died from her injuries the following day, and the police had a manhunt on their hands.

They knew perfectly well what had happened. They even had the man who had joined Mary Ann at number 35, a stoker who claimed to be the dead woman's husband, William. He probably wasn't, of course, but he also claimed to be innocent of the murder—explaining that he had left earlier in the night, and that the killer must have entered the room sometime after that.

The police, and the inquest, turned to the other witnesses. None could keep their stories straight, all tripped over their own fabrications. Try as the authorities might, not a shred of genuine evidence was forthcoming, and, by the time the baffled jury delivered its seemingly traditional indictment of "Willful Murder against some person or persons unknown," both police and coroner were so confused that they didn't even argue.

Mary Ann's killer was never apprehended, at least by the authorities. But Whitechapel was not wholly lawless. A form of mob rule, or at least mob justice, was in place, a belief—patently engendered by the fruitless search for the Ripper—that the law was next-to-useless, and that retribution should be handled locally, by the community that had suffered from the crime.

More than one voice murmured that, had Scotland Yard only turned the Ripper investigation over to the people—had interfering coppers not rescued more than one suspect from the hands of the lynch mob—then the devil would have been apprehended long before he wound up his killing spree himself.

The police were powerless to resist. Dorset Street itself was effectively a no-go area for law enforcement, just as the rookeries of almost a century before had been, and while the London County Council was a dab hand at cosmetic improvements, it turned out to have very few practical solutions.

When an admittedly sensationalist newspaper article claimed Dorset Street suffered "an attempt at murder on an average of once a month, of a murder in every house and, in one house at least, a murder in every room," few people outside of the street itself even thought to contradict it. Not even the police, for whom such grim statistics might well have been true. The fact is, they didn't know.

In 1905, in a particularly asinine attempt to clean up the area's reputation, the London County Council decreed that Dorset Street should henceforth be known as Duval Street, the reasoning being that the road's reputation contributed as much to its present state as its residents.

Of course it didn't work, and besides, the courts and alleyways that led off the main thoroughfare were left unaltered, and so it was that sometime early in the summer of 1909, a twenty-something prostitute named

Little Kitty Ronan, together with her boyfriend, newspaper vendor Henry Benstead, paid the deposit and moved into the recently vacated upstairs room behind 26 Duval Street—number 12, Miller's Court.

Both were young; too young to remember the days of the Ripper, and too young, too, to associate the grim little archway and the darkened cobbled courtyard with any past notoriety. Otherwise, they may have realized that their room, their bed, lay directly above that in which Mary Jane Kelly had been so gruesomely butchered.

It would probably not have made a difference, of course. A home was a home, no matter what its history, and proof of that can be found in a Canadian news article published in 1892.

Toronto Mail journalist Kathleen Blake Watkins had taken it upon herself to visit Whitechapel, and in the course of her trip introduced herself to Elizabeth Prater, the upstairs neighbor whose slumbers were disturbed on the night of Mary Jane Kelly's death by a faint cry of "Murder!"

Prater still lived at number 12, and the downstairs room was now occupied by one Lottie Owen, who happily showed Miller the bloodstains that *still* blackened the wall beside the bed. Four years on from that dreadful November night, landlord McCarthy had not once thought to redecorate number 13.

Lottie had known Mary Jane, the article noted.

> "I was her friend" [she] said, speaking with difficulty because of a broken and battered nose given to her by a kick from her husband's heavy boot. "I was living further up the court then. [Mary] says 'I'm afraid to go out alone at night because of a dream I had that a man was murdering me. Maybe I'll be next. They say Jack's been busy in this quarter.'
>
> "She said it with such a laugh ma'am that it just made me creep. And been sure enough ma'am she was the next to go. I heard her through the night singin'—she had a nice voice—'The violets grow on your mothers grave'—but that's all we 'urd'."

Soon, the room had filled with other local women, shocking the Canadian as they gathered "like birds of prey . . . and [growing] voluble over the hideous details . . . . They had hard faces with an evil look on them—the demands for money, for beer, the curses, the profane language, jests about the awful fiend who did his deadly work here, the miserable shrewd faced children listening eagerly: it was horrible beyond expression."

The bloodstains might still have been there in 1909, but Kitty and Benstead did not think to ask. Instead, they settled down to make the best of their rude little room and, though Benstead's earnings were scarcely sufficient to cover the rent, Kitty was soon making enough on the streets to keep the now sixty-year-old John McCarthy off their backs.

It was in the early hours of July 2 that Benstead, returning home from an evening's drinking, noticed the front door to the cottage, leading onto the dark, narrow stairway up to his apartment, was open. So, at the top of the stairs, was his own door.

The room itself was in darkness, so he lit a lamp—and leapt back in horror as he saw Little Kitty lying on the bed, her mouth stuffed with a handkerchief, her throat cut open and blood oozing out of the gaping wound to soak the bedclothes.

Benstead ran back downstairs and into McCarthy's shop, his cries of "Someone has cut Kitty's throat!" bringing the rest of the neighborhood out to see.

By the time Benstead and McCarthy had pushed their way through the crowds that clogged the stairway, the room was already packed with onlookers—including one, downstairs neighbor John Callaghan, who had found a blunt but bloodstained penknife on the floor.

The police were called, and any veterans on the force must surely have suppressed a shudder as they passed again through that cursed archway.

Weary déjà vu would have afflicted them in other ways, too, as neighbors and possible witnesses were interviewed, and all claimed not to have heard a sound.

A couple of vague sightings were reported. Andrew Stevens, a seventeen-year-old market porter, told the *Illustrated Police News*,

> I was standing out in the street opposite the court about five minutes to twelve last night and I saw Kitty come down the street with a strange man, pass up the court and enter her house. About 12.20 I saw him come down the court again. He looked round sharply once or twice and the walked briskly up to Commercial Street. From what I remember of him he struck me as being a man of military appearance or perhaps a sailor; but he was well set up . . . he had a moustache and was wearing a dark suit and a dark cloth cap.

And that was it so far as usable evidence was concerned.

A conviction would be secured later in the month, a lonely destitute named Harold Hall who walked into a police station in Bristol, 120 miles west of London, and confessed to having killed Little Kitty after he caught her going through his pockets.

But even after he was found guilty, so many doubts remained that the death sentence was never carried out and Hall vanished from the record. Officially, Little Kitty's killing had been solved; unofficially, it remained as great a mystery as the rippings that preceded it.

Few people at the time, or in the years since, truly believed Kitty Ronan was killed by the same man who may have murdered so many women twenty-one years before. It was just a creepy coincidence, both in terms of street address and methodology. Even the media's inevitable speculation acknowledged that much: "Jack the Ripper crimes recalled!" was the headline in the *East End News*, and that's all they were. Recalled.

But ghosts are not so easy to lay, regardless of how much common sense might be thrown into their exorcism.

It does not matter how ruthlessly the passing decades have wrought their own form of merciless carnage across the face of the Ripper's Whitechapel; how wounding it is for the modern researcher to learn that just one of the historical sites, Mitre Square, even exists amid the vainglorious clutter and brightly lit tat of the modern city; how absurdly overdramatic are the guides who lead their walking tours through what remains of the streets the Ripper once haunted. Behind all the facades and fakery of twenty-first-century

The London Dungeon, a tourist-trap repository for so many of the city's grisliest secrets and darkest deeds. *Daniel Gale/Shutterstock*

Whitechapel, the malignant miasma of merciless murder still shifts in the shadows and drifts in the darkness.

It laughs behind the library shelves that groan beneath the weight of Ripper whodunits. It stands over your shoulder as you watch late-night showings of classic movies and daft documentaries.

It is a part of the very fabric of London, past, present and future; as tangible as the giants Gog and Magog, the traditional guardians of the city; as vibrant as the tales of resilience and courage that lived through the blitz of World War II; and as choking as the fogs that once shrouded those same streets in a gloom as dark as the Ripper's own cloak.

He is Boudicca burning the Roman citadel. He is the Great Plague decimating the city's population, and the Great Fire purging the streets of the disease. He is the Kaiser's zeppelins and the IRA's bombs. He is Sherlock Holmes and Dick Whittington's cat.

He lurks in the London Dungeon and in Madame Tussauds waxworks. He grins from the exhibits in his Cable Street Museum, and, decades after his own body must have returned to dust, he lives as loudly and luridly as any of London's modern inhabitants. Because, like it or not, he is part of what we know *as* London.

The city will never shake off the shadow of the Ripper—not because it values the tourists who flock to walk in his footsteps, nor because his story is too good to lie untold.

It will never shake him off because it can't. For how can you shake off a nightmare that you awaken to discover is still under way?

The Whitechapel murderer was real. Jack the Ripper is the immortal terror that he unleashed upon the world.

Appendix One
The Autopsy Reports

Annie Millwood

It appears the deceased was admitted to the Whitechapel Infirmary suffering from numerous stabs in the legs and lower part of the body.

She stated that she had been attacked by a man who she did not know, and who stabbed her with a clasp knife which he took from his pocket. No one appears to have seen the attack, and as far as at present ascertained there is only the woman's statement to bear out the allegations of an attack, though that she had been stabbed cannot be denied . . . .

Her death was attributed to 'sudden effusion into the pericardium from the rupture of the left pulmonary artery through ulceration.' The death was from natural causes, unrelated to her vicious attack over a month before.

Eastern Post, April 7, 1888

Emma Smith

Mr. George Haslip, house surgeon, stated [to the inquest] that when the deceased was admitted to the hospital she had been drinking but was not intoxicated. She was bleeding from the head and ear, and had other injuries of a revolting nature. Witness found that she was suffering from rupture of the peritoneum, which had been perforated by some blunt instrument used with great force.

The Times, April 9, 1888

Martha Tabram

Dr. T. R. Killeen, of 68, Brick-lane, said [at the inquest] that he was called to the deceased, and found her dead. She had 39 stabs on the body. She had been dead some three hours. Her age was about 36, and the body was very well nourished.

Witness had since made a post-mortem examination of the body. The left lung was penetrated in five places, and the right lung was penetrated in two places. The heart, which was rather fatty, was penetrated in one place, and that would be sufficient to cause death. The liver was healthy, but was penetrated in five places, the spleen was penetrated in two places, and the stomach, which was perfectly healthy, was penetrated in six places.

The witness did not think all the wounds were inflicted with the same instrument. The wounds generally might have been inflicted by a knife, but such an instrument could not have inflicted one of the wounds, which went through the chest-bone. His opinion was that one of the wounds was inflicted by some kind of dagger, and that all of them were caused during life.

The Times, August 9, 1888

Mary Ann Nichols

Henry Llewellyn, surgeon, said [at the inquest]:

On Friday morning I was called to Buck's-row about four o'clock. The constable told me what I was wanted for. On reaching Buck's-row I found the deceased woman lying flat on her back in the pathway, her legs extended. I found she was dead, and that she had severe injuries to her throat.

Her hands and wrists were cold, but the body and lower extremities were warm. I examined her chest and felt the heart. It was dark at the time. I believe she had not been dead more than half-an-hour. I am quite certain that the injuries to her neck were not self-inflicted. There was very little blood round the neck. There were no marks of any struggle or of blood, as if the body had been dragged.

I told the police to take her to the mortuary, and I would make another examination. About an hour later I was sent for by the Inspector to see the injuries he had discovered on the body. I went, and saw that the abdomen was cut very extensively.

I have this morning made a post-mortem examination of the body. I found it to be that of a female about forty or forty-five years. Five of the teeth are missing, and there is a slight laceration of the tongue.

On the right side of the face there is a bruise running along the lower part of the jaw. It might have been caused by a blow with the fist or pressure by the thumb. On the left side of the face there was a circular bruise, which also might have been done by the pressure of the fingers.

On the left side of the neck, about an inch below the jaw, there was an incision about four inches long and running from a point immediately below the ear.

An inch below on the same side, and commencing about an inch in front of it, was a circular incision terminating at a point about three inches below the right jaw. This incision completely severs all the tissues down to the vertebrae.

The large vessels of the neck on both sides were severed. The incision is about eight inches long. These cuts must have been caused with a long-bladed knife, moderately sharp, and used with great violence. No blood at all was found on the breast either of the body or clothes.

There were no injuries about the body till just about the lower part of the abdomen. Two or three inches from the left side was a wound running in a jagged manner. It was a very deep wound, and the tissues were cut through. There were several incisions running across the abdomen. On the right side there were also three or four similar cuts running downwards. All these had been caused by a knife, which had been used violently and been used downwards.

The wounds were from left to right, and might have been done by a left-handed person. All the injuries had been done by the same instrument.

Daily Telegraph, September 1, 1888

Annie Chapman

Mr. George Baxter Phillips, divisional-surgeon of police, said:

On Saturday last I was called by the police at 6.20 a.m. to 29, Hanbury-street, and arrived at half-past six. I found the body of the deceased lying in the yard on her back, on the left hand of the steps that lead from the passage.

The head was about 6in in front of the level of the bottom step, and the feet were towards a shed at the end of the yard. The left arm was across the left breast, and the legs were drawn up, the feet resting on the ground, and the knees turned outwards.

The face was swollen and turned on the right side, and the tongue protruded between the front teeth, but not beyond the lips; it was much swollen. The small intestines and other portions were lying on the right side of the body on the ground above the right shoulder, but attached.

There was a large quantity of blood, with a part of the stomach above the left shoulder. I searched the yard and found a small piece of coarse muslin, a small-tooth comb, and a pocket-comb, in a paper case, near the railing. They had apparently been arranged there.

I also discovered various other articles, which I handed to the police. The body was cold, except that there was a certain remaining heat, under the intestines, in the body. Stiffness of the limbs was not marked, but it was commencing.

The throat was disseevered deeply. I noticed that the incision of the skin was jagged, and reached right round the neck. On the back wall of the house, between the steps and the palings, on the left side, about 18in from the ground, there were about six patches of blood, varying in size from a sixpenny piece to a small point, and on the wooden fence there were smears of blood, corresponding to where the head of the deceased laid, and immediately above the part where the blood had mainly flowed from the neck, which was well clotted.

Having received instructions soon after two o'clock on Saturday afternoon, I went to the labour- yard of the Whitechapel Union for the purpose of further examining the body and making the usual post-mortem investigation. I was surprised to find that the body had been stripped and was laying ready on the table. It was under great disadvantage I made my examination. As on many occasions I have met with the same difficulty, I now raise my protest, as I have before, that members of my profession should be called upon to perform their duties under these inadequate circumstances.

The Coroner: The mortuary is not fitted for a post-mortem examination. It is only a shed. There is no adequate convenience, and nothing fit, and at certain seasons of the year it is dangerous to the operator.

The Foreman: I think we can all endorse the doctor's view of it.

The Coroner: As a matter of fact there is no public mortuary from the City of London up to Bow. There is one at Mile-end, but it belongs to the workhouse, and is not used for general purposes.

Examination resumed: The body had been attended to since its removal to the mortuary, and probably partially washed. I noticed a bruise over the right temple. There was a bruise under the clavicle, and there were two distinct bruises, each the size of a man's thumb, on the fore part of the chest. The stiffness of the limbs was then well-marked. The finger nails were turgid. There was an old scar of long standing on the left of the frontal bone. On the left side the stiffness was more noticeable, and especially in the fingers, which were partly closed. There was an abrasion over the bend of the first joint of the ring finger, and there were distinct markings of a ring or rings—probably the latter. There were small sores on the fingers.

The head being opened showed that the membranes of the brain were opaque and the veins loaded with blood of a dark character. There was a large quantity of fluid between the membranes and the substance of the brain. The brain substance was unusually firm, and its cavities also contained a large amount of fluid.

The throat had been severed. The incisions of the skin indicated that they had been made from the left side of the neck on a line with the angle of the jaw, carried entirely round and again in front of the neck, and ending at a point about midway between the jaw and the sternum or breast bone on the right hand.

There were two distinct clean cuts on the body of the vertebrae on the left side of the spine. They were parallel to each other, and separated by about half an inch. The muscular structures between the side processes of bone of the vertebrae had an appearance as if an attempt had been made to separate the bones of the neck.

There are various other mutilations of the body, but I am of opinion that they occurred subsequently to the death of the woman and to the large escape of blood from the neck. The witness, pausing, said: I am entirely in your hands, sir, but is it necessary that I should describe the further mutilations. From what I have said I can state the cause of death.

The Coroner: The object of the inquiry is not only to ascertain the cause of death, but the means by which it occurred. Any mutilation which took place afterwards may suggest the character of the man who did it. Possibly you can give us the conclusions to which you have come respecting the instrument used.

The Witness: You don't wish for details. I think if it is possible to escape the details it would be advisable. The cause of death is visible from injuries I have described.

The Coroner: You have kept a record of them?

Witness: I have.

The Coroner: Supposing any one is charged with the offence, they would have to come out then, and it might be a matter of comment that the same evidence was not given at the inquest.

Witness: I am entirely in your hands.

The Coroner: We will postpone that for the present. You can give your opinion as to how the death was caused.

Witness: From these appearances I am of opinion that the breathing was interfered with previous to death, and that death arose from syncope, or failure of the heart's action, in consequence of the loss of blood caused by the severance of the throat.

The Coroner: Was the instrument used at the throat the same as that used at the abdomen?

Witness: Very probably. It must have been a very sharp knife, probably with a thin, narrow blade, and at least six to eight inches in length, and perhaps longer.

The Coroner: Is it possible that any instrument used by a military man, such as a bayonet, would have done it?

Witness: No; it would not be a bayonet.

The Coroner: Would it have been such an instrument as a medical man uses for post-mortem examinations?

Witness: The ordinary post-mortem case perhaps does not contain such a weapon.

The Coroner: Would any instrument that slaughterers employ have caused the injuries?

Witness: Yes; well ground down.

The Coroner: Would the knife of a cobbler or of any person in the leather trades have done? -

Witness: I think the knife used in those trades would not be long enough in the blade.

The Coroner: Was there any anatomical knowledge displayed?

Witness: I think there was. There were indications of it. My own impression is that that anatomical knowledge was only less displayed or indicated in consequence of haste. The person evidently was hindered from making a more complete dissection in consequence of the haste.

The Coroner: Was the whole of the body there? -

Witness: No; the absent portions being from the abdomen.

The Coroner: Are those portions such as would require anatomical knowledge to extract?

Witness: I think the mode in which they were extracted did show some anatomical knowledge.

The Coroner: You do not think they could have been lost accidentally in the transit of the body to the mortuary?

Witness: I was not present at the transit. I carefully closed up the clothes of the woman. Some portions had been excised.

The Coroner: How long had the deceased been dead when you saw her?

Witness: I should say at least two hours, and probably more; but it is right to say that it was a fairly cold morning, and that the body would be more apt to cool rapidly from its having lost the greater portion of its blood.

The Coroner: Was there any evidence of any struggle?

Witness: No; not about the body of the woman. You do not forget the smearing of blood about the palings.

The Coroner: In your opinion did she enter the yard alive?

Witness: I am positive of it. I made a thorough search of the passage, and I saw no trace of blood, which must have been visible had she been taken into the yard.

The Coroner: You were shown the apron?

Witness: I saw it myself. There was no blood upon it. It had the appearance of not having been unfolded recently.

The Coroner: You were shown some staining on the wall of No. 25, Hanbury-street?

Witness: Yes; that was yesterday morning. To the eye of a novice I have no doubt it looks like blood. I have not been able to trace any signs of it. I have not been able to finish my investigation. I am almost convinced I shall not find any blood. We have not had any result of your examination of the internal organs.

The Coroner: Was there any disease?

Witness: Yes. It was not important as regards the cause of death. Disease of the lungs was of long standing, and there was disease of the membranes of the brain. The stomach contained a little food.

The Coroner: Was there any appearance of the deceased having taken much alcohol?

Witness: No. There were probably signs of great privation. I am convinced she had not taken any strong alcohol for some hours before her death.

The Coroner: Were any of these injuries self-inflicted?

Witness: The injuries which were the immediate cause of death were not self-inflicted.

The Coroner: Was the bruising you mentioned recent?

Witness: The marks on the face were recent, especially about the chin and sides of the jaw. The bruise upon the temple and the bruises in front of the chest were of longer standing, probably of days. I am of opinion that the person who cut the deceased's throat took hold of her by the chin, and then commenced the incision from left to right.

The Coroner: Could that be done so instantaneously that a person could not cry out?

Witness: By pressure on the throat no doubt it would be possible.

The Forman: There would probably be suffocation.

The Coroner: The thickening of the tongue would be one of the signs of suffocation?

Witness: Yes. My impression is that she was partially strangled. Witness added that the handkerchief produced was, when found amongst the clothing, saturated with blood. A similar article was round the throat of the deceased when he saw her early in the morning at Hanbury-street.

The Coroner: It had not the appearance of having been tied on afterwards?

Witness: No. Sarah Simonds, a resident nurse at the Whitechapel Infirmary, stated that, in company of the senior nurse, she went to the mortuary on Saturday, and found the body of the deceased on the ambulance in the yard. It was afterwards taken into the shed, and placed on the table. She was directed by Inspector Chandler to undress it, and she placed the clothes in a corner. She left the handkerchief round the neck. She was sure of this. They washed stains of blood from the body. It seemed to have run down from the throat. She found the pocket tied round the waist. The strings were not torn. There were no tears or cuts in the clothes.

Daily Telegraph, September 13, 1888

Elizabeth Stride

Mr. George Baxter Phillips:

I live at No. 2, Spital-square, and am surgeon of the H Division of police. I was called on Sunday morning last at twenty past one to Leman-street Police-station, and was sent on to Berner-street, to a yard at the side of what proved to be a club-house.

I found Inspector Pinhorn and Acting-Superintendent West in possession of a body, which had already been seen by Dr. Blackwell, who had arrived some time before me. The body was lying on its left side, the face being turned towards the wall, the head towards the yard, and the feet toward the street. The left arm was extended from elbow, and a packet of cachous was in the hand. Similar ones were in the gutter. I took them from the hand and gave them to Dr. Blackwell.

The right arm was lying over the body, and the back of the hand and wrist had on them clotted blood. The legs were drawn up, feet close to wall, body still warm, face warm, hands cold, legs quite warm, silk handkerchief round throat, slightly torn (so is my note, but I since find it is cut). I produce the handkerchief. This corresponded to the right angle of the jaw. The throat was deeply gashed, and there was an abrasion of the skin, about an inch and a quarter in diameter, under the right clavicle.

On Oct. 1, at three p.m., at St. George's Mortuary, present Dr. Blackwell and for part of the time Dr. Reigate and Dr. Blackwell's assistant; temperature being about 55 degrees, Dr. Blackwell and I made a post-mortem examination, Dr. Blackwell kindly consenting to make the dissection, and I took the following note: "Rigor mortis still firmly marked. Mud on face and left side of the head. Matted on the hair and left side.

"We removed the clothes. We found the body fairly nourished. Over both shoulders, especially the right, from the front aspect under colar bones and in front of chest there is a bluish discolouration which I have watched and seen on two occasions since.

"On neck, from left to right, there is a clean cut incision six inches in length; incision commencing two and a half inches in a straight line below the angle of the jaw. Three-quarters of an inch over undivided muscle, then becoming deeper, about an inch dividing sheath and the vessels, ascending a little, and then grazing the muscle outside the cartilages on the left side of the neck.

"The carotid artery on the left side and the other vessels contained in the sheath were all cut through, save the posterior portion of the carotid, to a line about one-twelfth of an inch in extent, which prevented the separation of the upper and lower portion of the artery.

"The cut through the tissues on the right side of the cartilages is more superficial, and tails off to about two inches below the right angle of the jaw. It is evident that the haemorrhage which produced death was caused through the partial severance of the left carotid artery.

"There is a deformity in the lower fifth of the bones of the right leg, which are not straight, but bow forward; there is a thickening above the left ankle. The bones are here straighter. No recent external injury save to neck.

"The lower lobe of the ear was torn, as if by the forcible removing or wearing through of an earring, but it was thoroughly healed. The right ear was pierced for an earring, but had not been so injured, and the earring was wanting.

"On removing the scalp there was no sign of bruising or extravasation of blood between it and the skull-cap. The skull was about one-sixth of an inch in thickness, and dense in texture. The brain was fairly normal. Both lungs were unusually pale.

"The heart was small; left ventricle firmly contracted, right less so. Right ventricle full of dark clot; left absolutely empty. Partly digested food, apparently consisting of cheese, potato, and farinaceous edibles. Teeth on left lower jaw absent."

On Tuesday, at the mortuary, I found the total circumference of the neck 12 inches. I found in the pocket of the underskirt of the deceased a key, as of a padlock, a small piece of lead pencil, a comb, a broken piece of comb, a metal spoon, half a dozen large and one small button, a hook, as if off a dress, a piece of muslin, and one or two small pieces of paper. Examining her jacket I found that although there was a slight amount of mud on the right side, the left was well plastered with mud.

A Juror: You have not mentioned anything about the roof of the mouth. One witness said part of the roof of the mouth was gone.

Witness: That was not noticed.

The Coroner: What was the cause of death?

Witness: Undoubtedly the loss of blood from the left carotid artery and the division of the windpipe.

The Coroner: Did you examine the blood at Berner-street carefully, as to its direction and so forth?

Witness: Yes.

The Coroner: The blood near to the neck and a few inches to the left side was well clotted, and it had run down the waterway to within a few inches of the side entrance to the club-house. Were there any spots of blood anywhere else?

Witness: I could trace none except that which I considered had been transplanted—if I may use the term—from the original flow from the neck. Roughly estimating it, I should say there was an unusual flow of blood, considering the stature and the nourishment of the body.

By a Juror: I did notice a black mark on one of the legs of the deceased, but could not say that it was due to an adder bite. (*Daily Telegraph* October 3, 1888)

I was requested to make a re-examination of the body of the deceased, especially with regard to the palate, and I have since done so at the mortuary, along with Dr. Blackwell and Dr. Gordon Brown.

I did not find any injury to, or absence of, any part of either the hard or the soft palate. The Coroner also desired me to examine the two handkerchiefs which were found on the deceased. I did not discover any blood on them, and I believe that the stains on the larger handkerchief are those of fruit.

Neither on the hands nor about the body of the deceased did I find grapes, or connection with them. I am convinced that the deceased had not swallowed either the skin or seed of a grape within many hours of her death.

I have stated that the neckerchief which she had on was not torn, but cut. The abrasion which I spoke of on the right side of the neck was only apparently an abrasion, for on washing it it was removed, and the skin found to be uninjured. The knife produced on the last occasion was delivered to me, properly secured, by a constable, and on examination I found it to be such a knife as is used in a chandler's shop, and is called a slicing knife. It has blood upon it, which has characteristics similar to the blood of a human being. It has been recently blunted, and its edge apparently turned by rubbing on a stone such as a kerbstone. It evidently was before a very sharp knife.

The Coroner: Is it such as knife as could have caused the injuries which were inflicted upon the deceased?

Witness: Such a knife could have produced the incision and injuries to the neck, but it is not such a weapon as I should have fixed upon as having caused the injuries in this case; and if my opinion as regards the position of the body is correct, the knife in question would become an improbable instrument as having caused the incision.

The Coroner: What is your idea as to the position the body was in when the crime was committed?

Witness: I have come to a conclusion as to the position of both the murderer and the victim, and I opine that the latter was seized by the shoulders and placed on the ground, and that the murderer was on her right side when he inflicted the cut. I am of opinion that the cut was made from the left to the right side of the deceased, and taking into account the position of the incision it is unlikely that such a long knife inflicted the wound in the neck.

The Coroner: The knife produced on the last occasion was not sharp pointed, was it?

Witness: No, it was rounded at the tip, which was about an inch across. The blade was wider at the base.

The Coroner: Was there anything to indicate that the cut on the neck of the deceased was made with a pointed knife?

Witness: Nothing.

The Coroner: Have you formed any opinion as to the manner in which the deceased's right hand became stained with blood?

Witness: It is a mystery. There were small oblong clots on the back of the hand. I may say that I am taking it as a fact that after death the hand always remained in the position in which I found it—across the body.

The Coroner: How long had the woman been dead when you arrived at the scene of the murder, do you think?

Witness: Within an hour she had been alive.

The Coroner: Would the injury take long to inflict?

Witness: Only a few seconds—it might be done in two seconds.

The Coroner: Does the presence of the cachous in the left hand indicate that the murder was committed very suddenly and without any struggle?

Witness: Some of the cachous were scattered about the yard.

The Foreman: Do you not think that the woman would have dropped the packet of cachous altogether if she had been thrown to the ground before the injuries were inflicted?

Witness: That is an inference which the jury would be perfectly entitled to draw.

The Coroner: I assume that the injuries were not self-inflicted?

Witness: I have seen several self-inflicted wounds more extensive than this one, but then they have not usually involved the carotid artery. In this case, as in some others, there seems to have been some knowledge where to cut the throat to cause a fatal result.

The Coroner: Is there any similarity between this case and Annie Chapman's case?

Witness: There is very great dissimilarity between the two. In Chapman's case the neck was severed all round down to the vertebral column, the vertebral bones being marked with two sharp cuts, and there had been an evident attempt to separate the bones.

The Coroner: From the position you assume the perpetrator to have been in, would he have been likely to get bloodstained?

Witness: Not necessarily, for the commencement of the wound and the injury to the vessels would be away from him, and the stream of blood—for stream it was—would be directed away from him, and towards the gutter in the yard.

The Coroner: Was there any appearance of an opiate or any smell of chloroform?

Witness: There was no perceptible trace of any anaesthetic or narcotic. The absence of noise is a difficult question under the circumstances of this case to account for, but it must not be taken for granted that there was not any noise. If there was an absence of noise I cannot account for it.

The Foreman: That means that the woman might cry out after the cut?

Witness: Not after the cut.

The Coroner: But why did she not cry out while she was being put on the ground?

Witness: She was in a yard, and in a locality where she might cry out very loudly and no notice be taken of her. It was possible for the woman to draw up her legs after the wound, but she could not have turned over. The wound was inflicted by drawing the knife across the throat. A short knife, such as a shoemaker's well-ground knife, would do the same thing. My reason for believing that deceased was injured when on the ground was partly on account of the absence of blood anywhere on the left side of the body and between it and the wall.

A Juror: Was there any trace of malt liquor in the stomach?

Witness: There was no trace.

Dr. Blackwell [recalled] (who assisted in making the post-mortem examination) said: I can confirm Dr. Phillips as to the appearances at the mortuary.

I may add that I removed the cachous from the left hand of the deceased, which was nearly open. The packet was lodged between the thumb and the first finger, and was partially hidden from view. It was I who spilt them in removing them from the hand.

My impression is that the hand gradually relaxed while the woman was dying, she dying in a fainting condition from the loss of blood. I do not think that I made myself quite clear as to whether it was possible for this to have been a case of suicide.

What I meant to say was that, taking all the facts into consideration, more especially the absence of any instrument in the hand, it was impossible to have been a suicide. I have myself seen many equally severe wounds self-inflicted.

With respect to the knife which was found, I should like to say that I concur with Dr. Phillips in his opinion that, although it might possibly have inflicted the injury, it is an extremely unlikely instrument to have been used. It appears to me that a murderer, in using a round-pointed instrument, would seriously handicap himself, as he would be only able to use it in one particular way. I am told that slaughterers always use a sharp-pointed instrument.

The Coroner: No one has suggested that this crime was committed by a slaughterer.

Witness: I simply intended to point out the inconvenience that might arise from using a blunt-pointed weapon.

The Foreman: Did you notice any marks or bruises about the shoulders?

Witness: They were what we call pressure marks. At first they were very obscure, but subsequently they became very evident. They were not what are ordinarily called bruises; neither is there any abrasion. Each shoulder was about equally marked.

A Juror: How recently might the marks have been caused?

Witness: That is rather difficult to say.

Daily Telegraph, October 5, 1888

Catherine Eddowes

Dr. Frederick Gordon Brown was then called, and deposed:

I am surgeon to the City of London Police. I was called shortly after two o'clock on Sunday morning, and reached the place of the murder about twenty minutes past two.

My attention was directed to the body of the deceased. It was lying in the position described by Watkins, on its back, the head turned to the left shoulder, the arms by the side of the body, as if they had fallen there. Both palms were upwards, the fingers slightly bent. A thimble was lying near. The clothes were thrown up. The bonnet was at the back of the head.

There was great disfigurement of the face. The throat was cut across. Below the cut was a neckerchief. The upper part of the dress had been torn open. The body had been mutilated, and was quite warm—no rigor mortis. The crime must have been committed within half an hour, or certainly within forty minutes from the time when I saw the body. There were no stains of blood on the bricks or pavement around.

By Mr. Crawford: There was no blood on the front of the clothes. There was not a speck of blood on the front of the jacket.

By the Coroner: Before we removed the body Dr. Phillips was sent for, as I wished him to see the wounds, he having been engaged in a case of a similar kind previously. He saw the body at the mortuary. The clothes were removed from the deceased carefully. I made a post-mortem examination on Sunday afternoon. There was a bruise on the back of the left hand, and one on the right shin, but this had nothing to do with the crime. There were no bruises on the elbows or the back of the head. The face was very much mutilated, the eyelids, the nose, the jaw, the cheeks, the lips, and the mouth all bore cuts. There were abrasions under the left ear. The throat was cut across to the extent of six or seven inches.

The Coroner: Can you tell us what was the cause of death?

Witness: The cause of death was haemorrhage from the throat. Death must have been immediate.

The Coroner: There were other wounds on the lower part of the body?

Witness: Yes; deep wounds, which were inflicted after death.

(Witness here described in detail the terrible mutilation of the deceased's body.)

Mr. Crawford: I understand that you found certain portions of the body removed?

Witness: Yes. The uterus was cut away with the exception of a small portion, and the left kidney was also cut out. Both these organs were absent, and have not been found.

The Coroner: Have you any opinion as to what position the woman was in when the wounds were inflicted?

Witness: In my opinion the woman must have been lying down. The way in which the kidney was cut out showed that it was done by somebody who knew what he was about.

The Coroner: Does the nature of the wounds lead you to any conclusion as to the instrument that was used?

Witness: It must have been a sharp-pointed knife, and I should say at least 6 in. long.

The Coroner: Would you consider that the person who inflicted the wounds possessed anatomical skill?

Witness: He must have had a good deal of knowledge as to the position of the abdominal organs, and the way to remove them.

The Coroner: Would the parts removed be of any use for professional purposes?

Witness: None whatever.

The Coroner: Would the removal of the kidney, for example, require special knowledge?

Witness: It would require a good deal of knowledge as to its position, because it is apt to be overlooked, being covered by a membrane.

The Coroner: Would such a knowledge be likely to be possessed by some one accustomed to cutting up animals?

Witness: Yes.

The Coroner: Have you been able to form any opinion as to whether the perpetrator of this act was disturbed?

Witness: I think he had sufficient time, but it was in all probability done in a hurry.

The Coroner: How long would it take to make the wounds?

Witness: It might be done in five minutes. It might take him longer; but that is the least time it could be done in.

The Coroner: Can you, as a professional man, ascribe any reason for the taking away of the parts you have mentioned?

Witness: I cannot give any reason whatever.

The Coroner: Have you any doubt in your own mind whether there was a struggle?

Witness: I feel sure there was no struggle. I see no reason to doubt that it was the work of one man.

The Coroner: Would any noise be heard, do you think?

Witness: I presume the throat was instantly severed, in which case there would not be time to emit any sound.

The Coroner: Does it surprise you that no sound was heard?

Witness: No.

The Coroner: Would you expect to find much blood on the person inflicting these wounds?

Witness: No, I should not. I should say that the abdominal wounds were inflicted by a person kneeling at the right side of the body. The wounds could not possibly have been self-inflicted.

The Coroner: Was your attention called to the portion of the apron that was found in Goulston-street?

Witness: Yes. I fitted that portion which was spotted with blood to the remaining portion, which was still attached by the strings to the body.

The Coroner: Have you formed any opinion as to the motive for the mutilation of the face?

Witness: It was to disfigure the corpse, I should imagine.

A Juror: Was there any evidence of a drug having been used?

Witness: I have not examined the stomach as to that. The contents of the stomach have been preserved for analysis. (*Daily Telegraph*, October 10, 1888)

Mr. William Sedgwick Saunders, medical officer of health for the City, said: I received the stomach of the deceased from Dr. Gordon Brown, carefully sealed, and I made an analysis of the contents, which had not been interfered with in any way. I looked more particularly for poisons of the narcotic class, but with negative results, there being not the faintest trace of any of those or any other poisons.

Daily Telegraph, October 11, 1888

"The Whitehall Mystery"

On October 2nd, shortly before four, I was called to the new police buildings, and there shown the decomposed trunk of a woman. It was then lying in the basement and partially unwrapped. I visited the vault where it was found, and saw that the wall against which it had lain was stained black. I should imagine the parcel must have been in the vault more than three days.

At the mortuary I superintended the placing of the remains in spirits. On the following morning I made an examination, assisted by Dr. Hibberd. The sixth cervical vertebra had been sawn through in removing the head from the trunk. The lower limbs and pelvis had been removed, and the four lumbar vertebrae had been sawn through by a series of long, sweeping cuts. The length of the trunk was 17 inches, and the circumference of the chest 35½ inches. The circumference of the waist was 28½ inches. The trunk was very much decomposed.

I examined the skin thoroughly, but did not detect any marks of wounds. In the neighbourhood of the cut surfaces decomposition was especially advanced. The skin was light. Both arms had been removed at the shoulder joints by several incisions. The cuts had apparently been made obliquely from above downwards, and then round the arms. Disarticulation had been effected straight through the joints.

Over the body were clearly-defined marks, where the strings had been tied. The body appeared to have been wrapped up in a very skilful manner. The neck had been divided by several jagged incisions at the bottom of the larynx, which had been sawn through.

On opening the chest we found that the left lung was healthy, but that the right lung was firmly adherent to the chest wall of the diaphragm, showing that at some time the woman had suffered from severe pleurisy.

The rib cartilages were not ossified. In connection with the heart there were indications that convinced me that the woman did not die of suffocation or drowning. The liver was normal, and the stomach contained about an ounce of partly digested food. Portions of the body were missing.

Appearances of the collar-bones indicated that the woman was of mature development, undoubtedly over 24 or 25 years of age. It appeared that she was full fleshed, well nourished, with a fair skin and dark hair.

The appearances went to prove that deceased had never borne, or at any rate had never suckled, a child. The date of death as far as could be judged, was from six weeks to two months before the examination.

The body had not been in the water. I examined an arm that was brought to the mortuary, and I found that it accurately fitted the trunk. The hand was long and appeared to be very well shaped. Apparently it was the hand of a person not used to manual labour.

All the cuts on the trunk seemed to have been made after death. There was nothing to indicate the cause of death, though as the inside of the heart was pale and free from clots, it probably arose from haemorrhage or fainting.

From a series of measurements we took we came to the conclusion that the woman was about 5ft. 8in.in height.

Daily News, October 9, 1888

Mary Jane Kelly

Position of Body

The body was lying naked in the middle of the bed, the shoulders flat, but the axis of the body inclined to the left side of the bed. The head was turned on the left cheek. The left arm was close to the body with the forearm flexed at a right angle & lying across the abdomen. the right arm was slightly abducted from the body & rested on the mattress, the elbow bent & the forearm supine with the fingers clenched.

The legs were wide apart, the left thigh at right angles to the trunk & the right forming an obtuse angle with the pubes.

The whole of the surface of the abdomen & thighs was removed & the abdominal Cavity emptied of its viscera. The breasts were cut off, the arms mutilated by several jagged wounds & the face hacked beyond recognition of the features. The tissues of the neck were severed all round down to the bone.

The viscera were found in various parts viz: the uterus & Kidneys with one breast under the head, the other breast by the Rt foot, the Liver between the feet, the intestines by the right side & the s pleen by the left side of the body. The flaps removed from the abdomen and thighs were on a table.

The bed clothing at the right corner was saturated with blood, & on the floor beneath was a pool of blood covering about 2 feet square. The wall by the right side of the bed & in a line with the neck was marked by blood which had struck it in a number of spearate splashes.

Postmortem Examination

The face was gashed in all directions the nose cheeks, eyebrows and ears being partly removed. The lips were blanched & cut by several incisions running obliquely down to the chin. There were also numerous cuts extending irregularly across all the features.

The neck was cut through the skin & other tissues right down to the vertebrae the 5th & 6th being deeply notched. The skin cuts in the front of the neck showed distinct ecchymosis.

The air passage was cut at the lower part of the larynx through the cricoid cartilage.

Both breasts were removed by more or less circular incisions, the muscles down to the ribs being attached to the breasts. The intercostals between the 4th, 5th & 6th ribs were cut through & the contents of the thorax visible through the openings.

The skin & tissues of the abdomen from the costal arch to the pubes were removed in three large flaps. The right thigh was denuded in front to the bone, the flap of skin, including the external organs of generation

& part of the right buttock. The left thigh was stripped of skin, fascia & muscles as far as the knee.

The left calf showed a long gash through skin & tissues to the deep muscles & reaching from the knee to 5 ins above the ankle.

Both arms & forearms had extensive & jagged wounds.

The right thumb showed a small superficial incision about 1 in long, with extravasation of blood in the skin & there were several abrasions on the back of the hand moreover showing the same condition.

On opening the thorax it was found that the right lung was minimally adherent by old firm adhesions. The lower part of the lung was broken & torn away.

The left lung was intact: it was adherent at the apex & there were a few adhesions over the side. In the substaces of the lung were several nodules of consolidation.

The Pericardium was open below & the Heart absent.

In the abdominal cavity was some partially digested food of fish & potatoes & similar food was found in the remains of the stomach attached to the intestines.

(This is the original post-mortem report as written by Dr. Thomas Bond. Having been presumed lost for almost a century, the report was returned anonymously to Scotland Yard in 1887.)

Rose Mylett

Mr. Matthew Brownfield, divisional surgeon of police, deposed to making a post-mortem examination. He found the body to be that of a woman about 30 years of age, complexion fair, hazel eyes, and well nourished.

Blood was oozing from the nostrils, and on the right side was a slight abrasion. On the right cheek was a scar apparently of old standing. The mark on the nose might have been caused by any slight violence.

On the neck he found a mark which had evidently been caused by a cord drawn tightly round from the spine of the back of the lobe of the left ear. He had since found that the mark could be produced by a piece of four-fold lay cord. Beside the mark, the impression of the thumbs, and middle and index fingers, were plainly visible on each side of the neck. There were no injuries to the arms or legs.

On opening the brain he found the vessels engorged with almost black fluid blood. The stomach was full of food, recently eaten, and there was no smell or sign of poison.

The cause of death, in his opinion, was suffocation, by strangulation. There were no signs of a struggle except the mark on the cheek.

In reply to the coroner, witness said he did not think the woman could have done it herself, as in that case he should have expected to find the cord round the neck, but it was not, nor had any cord been found near the spot. He ascribed the finger marks to the woman's efforts to pull off the cord.

He thought the murderer must have stood at the left rear of the woman and having the ends of the string wrapped round his hands, thrown the cord round her throat and crossing his hands so strangled her.

Where the hands crossed would be just where the marks and the cords were absent. The cords being tight would prevent the woman from crying out for help. Having studied the questions as to the position of the man and the force used, he thought it quite possible that the cord was run through two holes or rings and then twisted by a turn of the wrist until death ensued.

East London Advertiser, December 29, 1888

Alice McKenzie

Dr. G. Bagster Phillips, divisional surgeon, gave additional evidence. He said that there were five marks on the abdomen not dealt with on the last occasion, and with the exception of one they were immediately over the middle line.

The largest was the lowest, the smallest being the exceptional one mentioned, and was typical of a finger-nail mark. In his opinion they were caused by the nails of a hand. The important cut would prevent the victim from crying out. There was no mark suggestive of pressure against the windpipe.

He detected in the injuries a knowledge of how effectually to deprive a person of life, and that speedily. The injuries to the abdomen were not similar to those he had seen in the other cases, neither were the injuries to the throat. It was probable the woman's assailant was on the right side of the body. The instrument used was a sharp one—with a sharp blade, and pointed.

East London Advertiser, August 17, 1889

The Pinchin Street Torso

Mr. J. Clarke, surgeon, said:

I am assistant to the divisional surgeon. A little before 6 a.m. on the 10th inst. I was called by the police to Pinchin-street.

Under a railway arch there, about 8 ft. from the road and about 1 ft. from the right wall of the arch, I saw the trunk of a woman, minus the head and legs. It was lying on its anterior surface, with the right arm doubled under the abdomen. The left arm was lying under the left side. The arms were not severed from the body. There was no pool of blood, and there were no signs of any struggle having taken place there.

On moving the body I found that there was a little blood underneath where the neck had lain. It was small in quantity and not clotted. The blood had oozed from the cut surface of the neck.

Over the surface of the neck and the right shoulder were the remnants of what had been a chemise. It was of common length and such a size as would be worn by a woman of similar build to the trunk found.

It had been torn down the front, and had been cut from the front of the armholes on each side. The cuts had apparently been made with a knife. The chemise was bloodstained nearly all over, from being wrapped over the back surface of the neck. There was no clotted blood on it.

I could find no distinguishing mark on the chemise. Rigor mortis was not present. Decomposition was just commencing.

The body was lifted, in my presence, on to the ambulance and taken to the St. George's mortuary by constables. On re-examining it there I found the body appeared to be that of a woman of stoutish build, dark complexion, about 5ft. 3in. in height, and between 30 and 40 years of age.

I should think the body had been dead at least 24 hours. Besides the wounds caused by the severance of the head and legs, there was a wound 15ins. long through the external coat of the abdomen. The body was not bloodstained, except where the chemise had rested upon it.

The body had not the appearance of having been recently washed. On the back there were four bruises, all caused before death. There was one over the spine, on a level with the lower part of the shoulder blade. It was about the size of a shilling. An inch lower down there was a similar bruise, about the middle of the back, also on the spine, and that was a bruise about the size of a half-a-crown. On the level of the top of the hip bone was a bruise 2½ins. in diameter. It was such a bruise as would be caused by a fall or a kick. None of the bruises were of old standing.

Round the waist was a pale mark and indentation, such as would be caused by clothing during life. On the right arm there were eight distinct bruises and seven on the left, all of them caused before death and of recent date. The back of both forearms and hands were much bruised.

On the outer side of the left forearm, about 3in. above the wrist, was a cut about 2in. in length, and half an inch lower down was another cut. These were caused after death. The bruises on the right arm were such as would be caused by the arms having been tightly grasped. The hands and nails were pallid. The hands did not exhibit any particular kind of work.

Dr. George Bagster Phillips said:

I live at 2, Spital-square, and am divisional surgeon. I first examined the body at 6 o'clock on the day the remains were found. I confirm, so far as I have observed, the evidence given by my colleague, Mr. Clarke, who was present when I first examined the body.

The next morning at 10 o'clock, in the presence of Dr. Gordon Brown and Mr. Hibberd, I further examined the body. Having described the nature of the cuts by which the head and limbs had been separated, witness continued: The marks on the fingers had fairly healed, and had evidently been in a process of healing for some time previous to death.

The pallor of the hands and nails is an important element in enabling me to draw a conclusion as to the cause of death. I agree with the remarks of Mr. Clarke as regards the marks on the arms. I found the length of the trunk to be 2ft. 2in., and the measurement round the nipple 34in., and below the breast 31¾in. The length of hand was 6½in.

The weight of the body, taken with a balance which was not exactly accurate, was 67lb. There was throughout the body an absence of blood in the vessels. The right lung was adherent, except at the base; the left lung free, and, taking them both together, fairly competent. All the other organs, except the spleen and the liver, were fairly healthy. The live weighed 50oz. In my opinion it was diseased and fatty before death.

The Coroner: Did the stomach show any irritation?

Witness: It did not strike one with any particular disease, or the presence of any poison. I believe that death arose from loss of blood. I believe the mutilation to have been subsequent to death, that the mutilations were effected by some one accustomed to cut up animals or to see them cut up, and that the incisions were effected by a strong knife 8in. or more long.

The Coroner: Is there anything to show where the loss of blood occurred?

Witness: Not in the remains; but the supposition that presents itself to my mind is that there was a former incision of the neck, which had disappeared with the subsequent separation of the head.

The Coroner: The loss of blood could not have come from either the lungs or the stomach?

Witness: Certainly not the stomach, and I could not trace any sign of its coming from the lungs. I have a strong opinion that it did not.

The Coroner: The woman did not die of phthisis?

Witness: There was no tubercle, but the top part of the lung was diseased. The draining of the blood from the body was such that it must have been a main artery that was severed?—Undoubtedly; and was almost as thorough as it could be although not so great as I have seen in some cases of cut throats.

By the jury.—What I found in the stomach was fresh plums. I have no reason for thinking that the person who cut up the body had any anatomical knowledge.

The Times, September 12, 1889

Frances Cole

George Bagster Phillips, M.R.C.S., divisional surgeon, also described the condition of the body when found, and said:

On Saturday morning I made a minute examination of the incision in the throat.

There was an external wound, the edges of the skin being not exactly cut through, there being a portion of about an inch long undivided. In my opinion, there were three distinct passings of the knife across the throat—one from left to right, one from right to left, and the third from left to right.

Below the wound there was an abrasion, as if caused by a finger nail. Above the wound there were four abrasions, possibly caused by finger nails. From the position of these marks I opine that the left hand was used.

There were some contused wounds on the back of the head, which I am of opinion were caused by the head coming into violent contact with paving stones.

I came to the conclusion that death had been almost instantaneous, occasioned by the severance of the carotid arteries and other vessels on the left side. In my opinion, the deceased was on the ground when her throat was cut.

I think that her assailant used his right hand in making the incisions in the throat, and that he had used his left hand to hold her head back by the chin; that he was on the right side of the body when he made the cuts. The tilting of the body to the left was to prevent the perpetrator from being stained with blood.

There was a complete absence of any struggle or even any movement from pain, but it may have arisen from the fact that the woman was insensible from concussion. The knife produced would be capable of inflicting all the wounds found on the neck. It was not a very sharp knife that caused the wounds.

On Monday, the 16th, I examined the sailor's cap produced. It was saturated with blood. The left and right cuffs of a shirt were stained with blood. The coat had two spots of blood on the right breast and two drops on the right sleeve. There was also a deposit of blood inside the right sleeve. The boots had no blood on them.

On Monday, the 16th, I examined Sadler at Arbour-square police-station. I found two wounds on the scalp, and the appearances of the blood on the clothes were consistent with its having come from either of these wounds.

The Times, February 24, 1891

Appendix Two
Jack on Film:
A Selected Filmography

Waxworks (1924)
Germany—Dir: Paul Leni / Leo Birinsky

The Lodger (1927)
UK—Dir: Alfred Hitchcock

Pandora's Box (1929)
Germany—Dir: Georg Wilhelm Pabst

The Phantom Fiend (1932)
UK—Dir: Maurice Elvey

Bizarre, Bizarre (1937)
France—Dir: Marcel Carné

The Lodger (1944)
USA—Dir: John Brahm

Room to Let (1950)
UK—Dir: Godfrey Grayson

Man in the Attic (1953)
USA—Dir: Hugo Fregonese

Jack the Ripper (1959)
UK—Dir: Robert S. Baker / Monty Berman

Lulu (1962)
West Germany—Dir: Rolf Thiele

Das Ungeheuer von London-City (1964)
West Germany—Dir: Edwin Zbonek

A Study in Terror (1965)
UK—Dir: James Hill

Dr. Jekyll & Sister Hyde (1971)
UK—Dir: Roy Ward Baker

Blade of the Ripper (1971)
Italy—Dir: Sergio Martino

Hands of the Ripper (1971)
UK—Dir: Peter Sasdy

Seven Murders for Scotland Yard (1972)
Spain—Dir: José Luis Madrid

The Ruling Class (1972)
UK—Dir: Peter Medak

Terror in the Wax Museum (1973)
USA—Dir: Georg Fenady

Jack the Ripper (TV miniseries—1973)
UK

A Man with a Maid (1975)
USA—Dir: Vernon P Becker

The Groove Room (1975)
Sweden/USA—Dir: Vernon P. Becker

Jack the Ripper (1976)
Switzerland/West Germany—Dir: Jess Franco

Assault! Jack the Ripper (1976)
Japan—Dir: Yasuharu Hasebe

Murder by Decree (1979)
Canada/UK—Dir: Bob Clark

Time After Time (1979)
USA—Dir: Nicholas Meyer

Lulu (1980)
France/Italy/Germany—Dir: Walerian Borowczyk

The New York Ripper (1982)
USA—Dir: Lucio Fulci

Terror at London Bridge (1985)
USA—Dir: E. W. Swackhamer

Amazon Women on the Moon (1987)
USA—Dir: Joe Dante, Carl Gottlieb

Jack's Back (1988)
USA—Dir: Rowdy Herrington

Jack the Ripper (TV miniseries 1988)
UK/USA—Dir: David Wickes

Edge of Sanity (1989)
UK/USA/France/Hungary—Dir: Gérard Kikoïne

The Ripper (TV movie 1997)
USA/Australia—Dir: Janet Meyers

Love Lies Bleeding (1999)
USA/Australia—Dir: William Tannen

Jill Rips (2000)
USA—Dir: Anthony Hickox

Ripper (2001)
USA—Dir: John E. Eyres

From Hell (2001)
USA—Dir: Albert Hughes / Allen Hughes

Bad Karma (2002)
USA—Dir: John Hough

Hell's Gate (2002)
USA—Dir: John Hough

Jack, the Last Victim (2005)
UK—Dir: Phil Peel

The Legend of Bloody Jack (2007)
USA—Dir: Todd Portugal

Whitechapel (TV series—2008)
UK

The Lodger (2009)
USA—Dir: David Ondaatje

A Rogue in Londinium (2010)
USA—Dir: Whitney Hamilton

Bibliography

Any attempt to compile a comprehensive bibliography of Ripper-related books and publications is doomed to failure. The following notes only the books either consulted for, or referenced in, this work.

Nonfiction

Adam, H. L. *The Trial of George Chapman*. William Hodge, London. 1930.

Alexander, Antonia. *The Fifth Victim: Mary Kelly Was Murdered by Jack the Ripper. Now Her Great Great Granddaughter Reveals the True Story of What Really Happened*. John Blake Publishing, London. 2013.

Anderson, Sir Robert. *Criminals and Crime*. James Nisbet, London. 1907.

Anderson, Sir Robert. *The Lighter Side of My Official Life*. Hodder & Stoughton, London. 1910.

Ball, Pamela. *Jack the Ripper: A Psychic Investigation*. Arcturus, London. 1998.

Barnard, Allen (editor). *The Harlot Killer Jack the Ripper*. Dodd, Mead & Co., New York. 1953.

Begg, Paul. *Jack the Ripper: The Facts* Robson Books, London. 2004.

Begg, Paul. *Jack the Ripper: The Definitive History*. Pearson Education, London. 2005.

Begg, Paul; Fido, Martin and Skinner, Keith. *The Jack the Ripper A to Z*. Headline Book Publishing, London. 1991.

Begg, Paul and Bennett, John. *Jack the Ripper: The Forgotten Victims*. Yale University Press, New Haven. 2013.

Begg, Paul (editor). *Ripperology: The Best of Ripperologist Magazine, Jack the Ripper and the Victorian East End*. Barnes & Noble, New York. 2000.

Bermant, Chaim. *Point of Arrival: A Study of London's East End*. MacMillan Pub Co., New York. 1975.

Bondesen, Jan. *Murder Houses of London*. Amberley Publishing, Stroud, UK. 2014.

Brewer, J. *The Curse Upon Mitre Square*. London, 1888.

Burn, Gordon. *Somebody's Husband, Somebody's Son: The Story of the Yorkshire Ripper*. Pan Books Ltd, London. 1985.

Clack, Robert and Hutchinson, Philip. *The London of Jack the Ripper Then and Now*. Breedon Books, Derby, UK. 2007.

Cornwell, Patricia. *Portrait of a Killer: Jack the Ripper, Case Closed*. Time Warner, New York. 2002.

Corton, Christine L. *London Fog: The Biography*. The Belknap Press of Harvard University Press, Cambridge, MA. 2015.

Covell, Mike. *Annie Chapman: Wife, Mother, Victim. The Life and Death of a Victim of Jack the Ripper*. CreateSpace Independent Publishing Platform, USA. 2014.

Cullen, Tom. *Autumn of Terror: Jack the Ripper, His Crimes and Times* Bodley Head, London. 1966.

Dew, Walter. *I Caught Crippen*. Blackie, London. 1938.

Eddlestone, John J. *Jack the Ripper: An Encyclopedia*. Metro Books, London. 2002.

Edwards, Ivor. *Jack the Ripper's Black Magic Rituals: Satanism, the Occult, Murder . . . the Sinister Truth of the Doctor Who Was Jack the Ripper*. John Blake Publishing Ltd, London. 2003.

Evans, Stewart and Gainey, Paul. *Jack the Ripper: First American Serial Killer*. Kodansha International, New York. 1996

Evans, Stewart and Rumbelow, Donald. *Jack the Ripper: Scotland Yard Investigates*. Sutton Books, Stroud, UK. 2001.

Evans, Stewart P. and Skinner, Keith. *Jack the Ripper: Letters from Hell*. Sutton Publishing Ltd, Stroud, UK. 2001.

Fairclough, Melvyn. *The Ripper and the Royals*. Duckworth Press, London. 1991.

Farson, Daniel. *Jack the Ripper*. Michael Joseph Ltd, London. 1972.

Feldman, Paul H. *Jack the Ripper: The Final Chapter*. Virgin Books, London. 1997.

Fido, Martin. *The Crimes, Detection and Death of Jack the Ripper*. Weidenfeld and Nicolson, London. 1987.

Flanders, Judith. *The Invention of Murder: How the Victorians Revelled in Death and Detection and Created Modern Crime*. Thomas Dunne Books, New York. 2011.

Hainsworth, J. J. *Jack the Ripper: Case Solved 1891*. McFarland. Jefferson, NC. 2013.

Harris, Melvin. *Jack the Ripper: The Bloody Truth*. Columbus Books, London. 1987.

Harrison, Michael. *Clarence—Was He Jack the Ripper?* WH Allen, London. 1972.

Harrison, Paul. *Jack the Ripper: The Mystery Solved.* Robert Hale, London. 1991.

Harrison, Shirley. *The Diary of Jack the Ripper: The Discovery, the Investigation, the Debate.* Hyperion, New York. 1993.

Howells, Martin and Skinner, Keith. *The Ripper Legacy.* Sidgwick and Jackson, London. 1987.

Hughes, M. V. *A London Girl of the 1880s.* Oxford University Press, Oxford. 1946.

Jackson, Lee. *Dirty Old London: The Victorian Fight Against Filth.* Yale University Press, New York. 2015.

Jones, Richard. *Uncovering Jack the Ripper's London.* Barnes & Noble, New York. 2007.

Kelly, Alexander. *Jack the Ripper: A Bibliography and Review of the Literature.* Association of Assistant Librarians, London. 1973.

Klinger, Leslie. *The New Annotated Sherlock Holmes.* W.W. Norton, New York. 2005.

Knight, Stephen. *Jack the Ripper: The Final Solution.* Grafton Books, London. 1977.

Le Queux, William. *Things I Know About Kings, Celebrities and Crooks.* Eveleigh, Nash & Grayson Ltd, London. 1923.

Leighton, D. J. *Ripper Suspect: The Secret Lives of Montague Druitt.* Sutton Books, Stroud, UK. 2006.

Lilly, Marjorie. *Sickert, The Painter and His Circle.* Elek Books Ltd, London. 1971

Linder, Seth; Morris, Caroline and Skinner, Keith. *Ripper Diary—the Inside Story.* Sutton Books, Stroud, UK. 2003.

Matthews, Rupert. *Jack the Ripper's Streets of Terror. Life During the Reign of London's Most Brutal Killer.* Arcturus Publishing Ltd, London. 2013.

Matters, Leonard. *The Mystery of Jack the Ripper.* WH Allen, London. 1929.

McCormick, Donald. *The Identity of Jack the Ripper.* Jarrolds, London. 1959.

Macnaghten, Sir Melville. *Days of My Years.* Edward Arnold, London. 1915.

Meikle, Dennis. *Jack the Ripper: The Murders and the Movies.* Reynolds and Hearne, London. 2002.

Middleton, Jacob. *Spirits in an Industrial Age: Ghost Impersonation, Spring-heeled Jack and Victorian Society.* CreateSpace Independent Publishing Platform, USA. 2014.

Monaghan, David and Cawthorne, Nigel. *Jack the Ripper's Secret Confession: The Hidden Testimony of Britain's First Serial Killer.* Constable & Robinson, London. 2010.

Moore, Alan, and Campbell, Eddie. *From Hell and Its Companion.* Top Shelf Productions, Marietta, GA. 2006.

Odell, Robin. *Jack the Ripper in Fact and Fiction.* Harper & Co., London. 1965.

Parkin, Lance. *Magic Words: The Extraordinary Life of Alan Moore.* Aurum Press, London. 2013.

Ramsey, Winston G. *The East End Then and Now.* After the Battle, London. 1997.

Ramsey, Winston G. *Scenes of Murder, Then and Now.* After the Battle, London. 2011.

Rule, Fiona. *The Worst Street in London.* Ian Allen Publishing, Hersham, UK. 2008.

Rumbelow, Donald. *Jack the Ripper: The Complete Casebook.* Contemporary Books, Chicago. 1988..

Smith, Lieut. Col. Sir Henry. *From Constable to Commissioner.* Chatto & Windus, London. 1910.

Spiering, Frank. *Prince Jack.* Doubleday, New York. 1978.

Stewart, William. *Jack the Ripper: A New Theory.* Quality Press, 1939.

Stubley, Peter. *1888: London Murders in the Year of the Ripper.* The History Press, London. 2012.

Sugden, Philip. *The Complete History of Jack the Ripper.* Carroll & Graf Publishers Inc, New York. 1995.

Thurgood, Peter. Abberline: *The Man Who Hunted Jack the Ripper.* The History Press, 2013.

Trow, M. J. *Jack the Ripper: Quest for a Killer.* Wharncliffe True Crime, Barnsley, UK. 2009.

Underwood, Peter. *Jack the Ripper: One Hundred Years of Mystery.* Javelin Books, London. 1988.

Wallace, Richard. *Jack the Ripper: "Light-hearted Friend."* Gemini Press, Melrose, MA. 1996.

Weller, Philip. *The Life and Times of Sherlock Holmes.* Bracken Books, Simsbury (1993)

Wensley, Frederick Porter. *Forty Years of Scotland Yard: A Record of a Lifetime's Service in the Criminal Investigation Department.* Doubleday, Doran & Co. Inc., New York. 1933.

Wescott, Tom. *The Bank Holiday Murders: The True Story of the First Whitechapel Murders.* Crime Confidential Press. 2013.

Weston-Davies, Wynne. *The Real Mary Kelly: Jack the Ripper's Fifth Victim and the Identity of the Man That Killed Her.* Blink Publishing, London. 2016.

Whittington-Egan, Richard. *A Casebook on Jack the Ripper.* Wildy & Sons Ltd, London. 1975.

Wilkes, Roger (editor). *The Giant Book of Murder: Real Life Cases Cracked by Forensic Science.* Constable & Robinson, London. 2005.

Williams, Tony and Price, Humphrey. *Uncle Jack.* Orion Books, London. 2005.

Williams, Watkin W. *The Life of General Sir Charles Warren.* Basil Blackwell, Oxford, UK. 194.

Wilson, Colin and Odell, Robin. *Jack the Ripper: Summing Up and Verdict* Corgi Books, London. 1988.

Winslow, L. Forbes. *Recollections of 40 Years.* John Ouseley Ltd., London. 1910

Fiction

Barrett, David V. *Tales from the Vatican Vaults.* Constable & Robinson, London, 2016.

Bentley, Chrissie. *The Adventures of Ambrose Horne.* Xcite Books, London. 2012.

Chaplin, Patrice. *By Flower and Dean Street.* Gerald Duckworth & Co, London. 1976.

Cohen, Paula Marantz. *What Alice Knew: A Most Curious Tale of Henry James & Jack the Ripper.* Sourcebooks Landmark, Naperville IL. 2010.

Cornell, Paul. *The Severed Streets.* Tor Books, New York. 2014.

Lowndes, Marie Belloc. *The Lodger.* Reader's Library, London. 1927.

Sinclair, Iain. *White Chappell, Scarlet Tracings – International Edition.* Penguin Books, London. 2004.

West, Paul. *The Women of Whitechapel and Jack the Ripper: A Novel.* Random House, New York. 1991.

Williams, Kate. *The Pleasures of Men: A Novel.* Voice Hyperion, New York, 2012.

Wilson, Colin. *Ritual in the Dark.* Victor Gollancz, London. 1960.

Index

THE FAQ SERIES

Johnny Cash FAQ
by C. Eric Banister
Backbeat Books
9781480385405................. $24.99

KISS FAQ
by Dale Sherman
Backbeat Books
9781617130915................. $24.99

Led Zeppelin FAQ
by George Case
Backbeat Books
9781617130250................. $22.99

Lucille Ball FAQ
by James Sheridan
and Barry Monush
Applause Books
9781617740824................. $19.99

M.A.S.H. FAQ
by Dale Sherman
Applause Books
9781480355897................. $19.99

Michael Jackson FAQ
by Kit O'Toole
Backbeat Books
9781480371064................. $19.99

Modern Sci-Fi Films FAQ
by Tom DeMichael
Applause Books
9781480350618................. $24.99

Monty Python FAQ
by Chris Barsanti, Brian Cogan,
and Jeff Massey
Applause Books
9781495049439................. $19.99

Morrissey FAQ
by D. McKinney
Backbeat Books
9781480394483................. $24.99

Neil Young FAQ
by Glen Boyd
Backbeat Books
9781617130373................. $19.99

Nirvana FAQ
by John D. Luerssen
Backbeat Books
9781617134500................. $24.99

Pearl Jam FAQ
by Bernard M. Corbett and
Thomas Edward Harkins
Backbeat Books
9781617136122................. $19.99

Pink Floyd FAQ
by Stuart Shea
Backbeat Books
9780879309503................. $19.99

Pro Wrestling FAQ
by Brian Solomon
Backbeat Books
9781617135996................. $29.99

Prog Rock FAQ
by Will Romano
Backbeat Books
9781617135873................. $24.99

Quentin Tarantino FAQ
by Dale Sherman
Applause Books
9781480355880................. $24.99

Robin Hood FAQ
by Dave Thompson
Applause Books
9781495048227................. $19.99

**The Rocky Horror
Picture Show FAQ**
by Dave Thompson
Applause Books
9781495007477................. $19.99

Rush FAQ
by Max Mobley
Backbeat Books
9781617134517................. $19.99

Saturday Night Live FAQ
by Stephen Tropiano
Applause Books
9781557839510................. $24.99

Seinfeld FAQ
by Nicholas Nigro
Applause Books
9781557838575................. $24.99

Sherlock Holmes FAQ
by Dave Thompson
Applause Books
9781480331495................. $24.99

The Smiths FAQ
by John D. Luerssen
Backbeat Books
9781480394490................. $24.99

Soccer FAQ
by Dave Thompson
Backbeat Books
9781617135989................. $24.99

The Sound of Music FAQ
by Barry Monush
Applause Books
9781480360433................. $27.99

South Park FAQ
by Dave Thompson
Applause Books
9781480350649................. $24.99

Star Trek FAQ
(Unofficial and Unauthorized)
by Mark Clark
Applause Books
9781557837929................. $19.99

Star Trek FAQ 2.0
(Unofficial and Unauthorized)
by Mark Clark
Applause Books
9781557837936................. $22.99

Star Wars FAQ
by Mark Clark
Applause Books
9781480360181................. $24.99

Steely Dan FAQ
by Anthony Robustelli
Backbeat Books
9781495025129................. $19.99

Stephen King Films FAQ
by Scott Von Doviak
Applause Books
9781480355514................. $24.99

Three Stooges FAQ
by David J. Hogan
Applause Books
9781557837882................. $22.99

TV Finales FAQ
by Stephen Tropiano and
Holly Van Buren
Applause Books
9781480391444................. $19.99

The Twilight Zone FAQ
by Dave Thompson
Applause Books
9781480396180................. $19.99

Twin Peaks FAQ
by David Bushman and
Arthur Smith
Applause Books
9781495015861................. $19.99

UFO FAQ
by David J. Hogan
Backbeat Books
9781480393851................. $19.99

Video Games FAQ
by Mark J.P. Wolf
Backbeat Books
9781617136306................. $19.99

The Who FAQ
by Mike Segretto
Backbeat Books
9781480361034................. $24.99

The Wizard of Oz FAQ
by David J. Hogan
Applause Books
9781480350625................. $24.99

The X-Files FAQ
by John Kenneth Muir
Applause Books
9781480369740................. $24.99

HAL•LEONARD®
PERFORMING ARTS
PUBLISHING GROUP

FAQ.halleonardbooks.com

0117